WITHDRAWN

# IMAGES of the PROPHET
# JOSEPH SMITH

No portion of this book may be reprinted or reproduced in any form without written permission from the publisher, Aspen Books, 6208 S. 380 W. Salt Lake City, Utah 84107.


Library of Congress Cataloging-in-Publication Data

Bitton, Davis, 1930—
    Images of the prophet Joseph Smith / by Davis Bitton.
        p.  cm.
    Includes bibliographical references and index.
    ISBN 1-56236-223-2 (pbk.)
    1. Smith, Joseph, 1805-1844.  2. Mormons—United States—Biography.  3. Church of Jesus Christ of Latter-Day Saints—Presidents—Biography.  4. Mormon Church—Presidents—Biography.
    I. Title.
    BX8695.S6B46   1996
    289.3'092—dc20
    [B]
                                                                          96-6416
                                                                          CIP


5 4 3 2 1

# IMAGES of the PROPHET
# JOSEPH SMITH

**DAVIS BITTON**

A S P E N
B O O K S

*For JoAn, eternal friend and companion,*
*a convert, first to Jesus Christ,*
*then to his modern prophet*

# Contents

# Introduction

This is not a conventional biography of Joseph Smith, but its intended purpose should not be hard to grasp. That purpose is to trace how Joseph Smith has appeared from different points of view. It is the *image* of Joseph Smith rather than the man himself that I seek to delineate. Other works have done the same thing for other subjects, as, for example, Merrill Peterson on Jefferson and John William Ward on Andrew Jackson. A similar study of a single event in Joseph Smith's life is my *The Martyrdom Remembered: A One-hundred-fifty-year Perspective on the Assassination of Joseph Smith* (Aspen Books, 1994), which considers how the Carthage murders were perceived from different angles of vision.

This book, in other words, is an examination of different perspectives. Some of these were contemporary with the life of Smith; others have been perpetuated by his followers in the generations after his death. A bibliography lists the available published primary sources by Joseph Smith and some of the scholarly books and articles written about him—an ongoing flood that shows no signs of abating.

I should explain the chapter entitled "Overview of an Incredible Life." Much in the manner of an encyclopedia article, this chapter lays out the basic biographical sequence of events. Its purpose is to orient the reader who approaches the subject for the first time or with insufficient factual information. Of course I run the risk here of being misunderstood, of being thought to claim that this is the one true or objective life sketch. I know better than that but have tried to sketch out an outline on which all would agree: when and where he was born, where he lived, his geographical peregrinations, his challenges or frustrations, and the circumstances of his early death. Readers already familiar with the subject may wish to skip the "Overview."

That I do not here claim to give any kind of definitive evaluation, if such were even possible, should be obvious from the remaining chapters of this book. They are all perspectival, showing different points of view. I remember as a graduate student reading Wallace K. Ferguson's *The Renaissance in Historical Thought* (1948), which examines different understandings of that period, generation by generation, from the Renaissance itself to the mid-twentieth century. "So much for the idea of historical objectivity," I commented to a fellow student. Books on the image of Washington and Lincoln, Jefferson and Jackson, Joan of Arc, and even Jesus have similarly shattered claims to definitiveness.

This does not mean that all evaluations are equal. They are not equally fair, equally informed, or equally substantiated. Even when we have cut through the rumor and misinformation that surround the life of all public figures, arriving at agreement on many details, differences of interpretation remain—not merely on incidentals but on the basic motivation and "meaning" of a life. St. Augustine may have been the first but was not the last to discover that understanding even of oneself is deficient, inconsistent, shifting, and ultimately imperfect. How flawed, then, must be any effort to write the life of another person! But we humans keep trying.

Chapters 4 and 5 deal with facets of Joseph Smith's self-understanding. Other expressions of what he saw as his role, expressed in diaries and letters, would form part of a full-scale biography, which this does not pretend to be. For what it is worth, though, I will state that I find Fawn Brodie's view—that Joseph Smith started by deliberate prevarication and then convinced himself that he was telling the truth—to be simplistic and unpersuasive. On the other hand, like all humans, he changed; his self-understanding grew, shaping and being shaped by the experiences he passed through.

In the final analysis, the truth of any human life is determined by the judgment of God. (Those who live in a flat, godless world need not cast this book aside, as I nowhere claim to read the divine mind.) In the meantime, we see through a glass darkly. When challenged by religious claims, we either dismiss them or, alternatively, make leaps of faith. Joseph Smith accepted that essential fact of life. He had no other choice. Some would believe him, while others—the great majority—would not. He did hope to induce as many as possible into trying an "experiment" upon his words, and many of those who did ended up with their own strong image—they called it a witness or testimony—of the reality of Smith's prophetic status.

Some of the chapters of the book were presented in preliminary form at meetings of the Mormon History Association. I thank the editors of *Restoration Studies* for permission to reprint with modifications an article first published by them.

# Overview of an Incredible Life

1

"I don't blame any one for not believing my history. If I had not experienced what I have, I could not have believed it myself."

—Joseph Smith

Some familiarity with the surface events is required before we can profitably consider different images. For orientation, therefore, let us pass in review, in the form of a brief life sketch, what Joseph Smith did. The series of facts here narrated are recognized by all writers on Joseph, I believe, whatever these authors might then wish to say by way of interpretation.

Joseph Smith was born on 23 December 1805 in Sharon, Windsor County, Vermont. He died violently on 27 June 1844 in Carthage, Illinois. He was almost exactly 38 1/2 years of age.

During that relatively brief life, he did not stay in one place. Before his birth, his parents had lived at Tunbridge, Vermont, where three older siblings—Alvin, Hyrum, and Sophronia—were born. The family moved to Sharon but soon after Joseph's birth moved back to Tunbridge. Then somewhere between 1808 and 1810 they moved to Royalton and in 1811 to Lebanon, New Hampshire.

Young Joseph experienced a major trauma in 1813, when he was seven years old. Recovering from typhoid fever, he found his leg to be seriously infected. Amputation was suggested, but finally Dr. Nathan Smith performed a successful operation. There were no anesthetics, and, as recounted by his mother, the lad refused to take alcohol and thus suffered the pain of the operation without any relief. After many months of recuperation, Joseph was left with a slight limp for the rest of his life. Such bare events are easily recited, but the trauma was doubtless severe and profoundly affected Joseph's psychic development.

In 1814 the family moved to Norwich, Vermont, but their farming there was unsuccessful for three successive years. In 1816 they moved to upstate New York, settling near Palmyra in the Finger Lakes region. Through hard work they finally began to enjoy some improvement, but their means of livelihood was not stable. They moved to a farm in Manchester, south of Palmyra, in 1818. In 1825, they were unable to make the final payment on a mortgage, which, despite their pleas for an extension, was promptly foreclosed. The owner did allow them to remain in the house for a period of time.

The Smiths were not paupers, at least not at first. When the parents married, Lucy Mack Smith brought a dowry that provided some backing. She had brothers who had money. But her husband, Joseph Smith, Sr., experienced crushing economic reverses early in their married life, one in merchandising, the other in a speculation in ginseng, for which he was never paid. From that time on, they lived close to the survival level. In the New York location, in addition to whatever crops they could grow, they cleared land and supplemented the family income by selling oilcloth and small items. As the children grew, they hired out in order to provide additional income. It was a family living close to the edge.

The ten years of Joseph Smith's life from about 1820 to 1830—from age 14 to age 24—present unusual challenges to the historian. These were years in which some of his great revelatory experiences occurred. At the start of the decade, he was an adolescent; at the end, he was married and stood at the head of a new religion.

The vision of 1820, known as the First Vision, has been criticized on two grounds. First, the documentary evidence is not exactly what the historian would prefer in terms of contemporaneousness and consistency. It was not written down for quite a few years after the event. The critics who level this charge imply, of course, that Smith made it up later when it served his purpose. When he did record it, starting in 1832, he did so in more than one version. The suspicion is raised that he felt free to invent or, at the very least, that his memory was faulty.

The other basis of criticism is the supposed absence of a religious revival at Palmyra in 1820. When the Reverend Wesley P. Walters, a zealous anti-Mormon, first reported the absence of conversions in the Palmyra church records for that year, some concluded, as he obviously intended them to, that Joseph Smith's story simply did not hold up. However, it took no more than a little research by historian Milton V. Backman and others to demonstrate that camp meetings and revivals were plentiful enough within a twenty-five mile radius, within "that region of country," which is all that Smith had claimed.

I wish to advance another modest argument in favor of Joseph's account of the 1820 experience. If you are making up something, you never choose details that are easily falsifiable. The Smith of the critics, obviously no honest man, was erecting a scaffolding on which to hang his claim to lead God's church, this in the 1830s when the details of the First Vision were first recorded—placed in written form on paper. But he had absolutely no need to insist on the year 1820 as the time of the vision when he could just as easily have left it in a more general time frame. Why, in the name of common sense, would he insist on including details about imaginary revivals when there were many people still around—some of them in his own family, others in the Church, but many outside of it—who could easily have blown the whistle? Of all the bitter opponents, who, pray tell, was the first to say, "Oh, no. That could not be. There were no such revivals at that time"?

Even if we somehow "accept" the First Vision of 1820, what are we doing? We could mean simply that, yes, he did *say* that these things happened; or that we can readily enough accept that indeed *something* happened; or that the *something* that occurred was simply subjective on Smith's part, but nonetheless real to him; or that the description later given of the event is indeed a factual recital. When dealing with any event and with any supposed eyewitness, the historian becomes entangled in epistemological complexities. These are compounded when the event is supernatural. Whatever happened in 1820, Joseph Smith at first made little of it in a public way or even in his family, which helps to explain some of the later confusion.

The death of Smith's oldest brother, Alvin, in 1823 is a verifiable event that, beyond the normal grief, impacted profoundly on Joseph and the entire family. As for the work that Joseph engaged in throughout his late teens and early twenties, this included clearing fields of trees and various other kinds of farm work. For a period of time he was paid to dig for buried treasure. His history written in 1838 tells of being employed by Josiah Stowell to dig for an abandoned Spanish silver mine and after a month, having had no success, convincing his employer to stop the project: "Hence arose the very prevalent story of my having been a money-digger." Some historians have sought to make money-digging and "magic" loom large in young Joseph Smith's life. But none, I think, has argued that it could have provided his or his family's livelihood. And whatever he may or may not have been doing by temporarily participating in the folk practices of his area, it does not explain the origin of the Book of Mormon, the organization of the Church in 1830, or the revelations that followed.

While working for Stowell, who lived in Chenango County, New York, Joseph had to find a place to stay. He was accepted as a boarder at the home of Isaac Hale. The Hales had a comely daughter named Emma. During the fall of 1825, then, one of the by-products of Joseph's employment was a friendship-growing-into-romance.

In March 1826 he was brought before a justice of the peace and charged with the misdemeanor of being a "disorderly person." Thanks to a thorough study by lawyer Gordon A. Madsen, we can say that there was no conviction for the excellent reason that Stowell, the presumed victim, testified in Joseph's favor.[1]

On 18 January 1827, twenty-one-year-old Joseph Smith married twenty-two-year-old Emma Hale. The young couple eloped. Looking back at the time of his death in 1844, Emma must have seen their marriage as the beginning of a roller coaster existence. At no point did they have financial security; often even physical safety seemed to elude them; settling down to a normal pattern with stability was a dream, a hope, but never a reality.

At first, they lived with Joseph's parents, whose farm he worked on. But soon began the period of the production of the Book of Mormon. The appearances of the angel Moroni, the miraculous deliverances, the supernatural process of translation—all this lies in the realm of faith. What the historian can comfortably present is what Smith *said* happened; his testimony is itself part of the historical record.

On 15 June 1828, a baby was born to Emma but lived only a few hours. During this year and the next, while working on the handwritten manuscript that became the Book of Mormon, Joseph Smith began to receive revelations from God on specific subjects, with instructions to Joseph himself, to his family and associates, and to the world in general. In August 1829, having obtained financial backing from Martin Harris, Joseph entered into a printing contract with E. B. Grandin, a publisher-printer-editor of Palmyra, New York.

Then came 1830, in many respects an *annus mirabilis*. Even in the political history of Western Europe, remembering especially the revolution that set up the July Monarchy in France, 1830 has more than usual significance. For Latter-day Saints it was above all the year of (a) the publication of the Book of Mormon, (b) the organization of the Church, and (c) the receipt of an outpouring of divine revelation. Whatever we make of the Book of Mormon, no one disputes that it was first published in the spring of 1830. Although there are scholarly discussions regarding details of place and personnel, the organization of the Church on 6 April is also an accepted fact. And although the worldly cynic might not wish to concede that they were "revelations" from God, again it is beyond dispute that a series of documents was issued by Joseph Smith and accepted by his followers as divine revelations.

It is a wonder that he had time for anything else. Yet during these same months we find Joseph Smith working on his "translation" (or inspired revision) of the Bible. On 28 June he was arrested and tried in South Bainbridge. The charge: disorderly preaching. When his former employer, Josiah Stowell, again testified on his behalf, Joseph was released. Rearrested and with questionable legality recharged, Joseph was again acquitted. Such contretemps did not stop him from presiding over important conferences at Fayette in September and January. The New York period, the initial phase of the new religion, however, was coming to an end.

On 1 February 1831, Joseph and Emma arrived in Kirtland, Ohio, having traveled by sleigh from New York. On 30 April, Emma gave birth to twins, a boy and a girl, but they died within hours. Within a few days twin infants whose mother had died were adopted by the Smiths.

But it was scarcely a time for settling down. Other members of the new Church from New York were following Joseph Smith's directive by moving into the Kirtland area, and they would be followed by converts from all sides. In part, what Joseph had to do now was organizational. Mechanisms had to be established that would provide for material needs. Reading through the revelations he issued at this time, we detect his preoccupation with practical matters, sending out missionaries and mustering resources.

As if this were not enough, there was also Missouri. For about eight years, from 1831 to 1839, the history of Mormonism and that of Joseph Smith moved along two parallel tracks: Ohio and Missouri. At the end of 1830 he had sent four missionaries to the western border of the United States to find the Zion that would be the great gathering place of the Saints (Doctrine and Covenants 32). Stopping in Ohio on their journey, they had met and converted Sidney Rigdon along with many of his congregation. Before long, there were two gathering places. Although Independence, Missouri, was declared to be Zion and the location of a great temple, many Latter-day Saints moved to Kirtland, Ohio, and its environs.

So Joseph's concerns were not only for the Mormons in Ohio but also for those, many of them poverty stricken, who moved into western Missouri. He set up leaders there, carried on correspondence, and then made the taxing journey to check on things. With seven traveling companions he left Kirtland on 19 June 1831. After a journey of three or four weeks—by stage, canal boat, and on foot—they arrived in Independence.

A sense of excitement accompanied Joseph as he met the Mormons already there, greeted others as they arrived, delivered sermons, issued additional revelations, and dedicated a site for the future temple. On 9 August, after a stay of less than four weeks, he and several companions left Independence in a canoe. They arrived back in Kirtland, Ohio, on 27 August.

That the twenty-five-year-old prophet had an abundance of physical energy is apparent. He was also prolific and creative on the spiritual plane, as evidenced by the revelations that issued from his mouth one after another. Written down by scribes, published later in periodicals and then compiled into a published volume, these revelations ranged across the wide expanse of eternity. Smith might be telling X that he should go on a preaching mission, warning Y that he should beware of pride, or instructing his people to move or buy a printing establishment. God was in his heaven and through his prophet trying to make things right in the world.

Predictably, there was opposition. Sometimes it became violent. After a mobbing by a dozen men, who stopped short of killing him (recounted in chapter 3), Joseph Smith and three traveling companions set out for Missouri. Grieving for one of the twin babies who had contracted measles and died, Emma stayed at the store operated by Newel K. Whitney, but when that didn't work out, she moved in with other friends.

The journey to Missouri took about three weeks. Once there, Joseph held a conference of the Church members, which recognized him as president of the High Priesthood. Decisions were made as to the connection between the mercantile business at Independence and the one at Kirtland. Another decision was made to publish 3,000 copies of his revelations under the title *Book of Commandments*. After encouraging the Missouri Mormons, he returned to Ohio.

The fecundity of Joseph's mind was incredible. Revelation after revelation dealt with questions ranging from organization, to missionary calls, to the practical health code known as the Word of Wisdom, to lofty doctrines regarding eternal judgment. For his followers, of course, these were not the production of a human mind, however brilliant, but communications of God to his prophet.

One of his teachings was the gathering. Those who joined the Church were to gather to a designated place. Kirtland, Ohio, was one such place, and the several hundred Mormons there looked forward to the construction of a temple. But those in Missouri were at the definitive gathering place, for Independence, Missouri, had been designated Zion, the New Jerusalem, and the site for the great temple.

By the summer of 1833 some 1,200 Mormons had flocked into Jackson County, Missouri.

In July, they began to be the victims of mob violence. The old Missourians viewed the influx of Mormons with alarm. A large group drew up a statement of grievances and demanded that the Mormons leave the county. The charges included that the Mormons were poor ("the dregs of society"), believed in a blasphemous religion, encouraged sedition among slaves, invited free Negroes to come to Missouri, and claimed that God had given them the state. A few days later several hundred excited mobsters tore down a house and printing shop. Two Mormon leaders were tarred and feathered.

By the fall, when the Missouri Mormons refused to move, having the governor's assurance of protection through the courts, violence broke out again. Houses were burned, people beaten, whipped, and driven from their homes. By early November about 1,200 refugees were huddled along the Missouri River.

How would Joseph Smith, far away in Ohio, respond? The news took about three weeks to reach him. Not claiming that the fault was all on the other side, he chastised the Missouri Mormons for their contention, for going there without adequate funds, and for making intemperate, provocative claims. They were not to sell the property they owned in Jackson County but were to work through the courts and the governor to achieve reinstatement.

He also began to think of mustering military support for his beleaguered people. In early 1834 he moved ahead with these plans by summoning a group of men to go to the rescue of the Missouri Saints. (A revelation, the key document initiating this process, is found in Doctrine and Covenants, section 103). After recruiters had scoured the different regions of the country, this little army, known as Zion's Camp, reached a total of 205 men. Getting them together, providing supplies, gaining some minimal skills in handling weapons, and traveling across the country without provoking opposition— these were the challenges. Outbreaks of internal dissension and finally cholera added to the difficulties. Although the contingent reached Missouri, it was enervated by disease and low in morale.

When Missouri's Governor Daniel Dunklin showed no willingness to support the return of the dispossessed Mormons to their properties in Jackson County, Joseph Smith dissolved the camp.

He returned to Kirtland, withstood charges against him by malcontents, and went to work with renewed vigor on the construction of a temple there. Outside opposition continued to intensify, including, for example, the publication of Eber D. Howe's *Mormonism Unvailed* (1834). But the work of construction went on, not just on the structure known as the temple, but on the Church itself. A Council of Twelve Apostles and a quorum of Seventies were formed. Veterans from Zion's Camp, who had demonstrated both stamina and loyalty, provided the backbone of this leadership.

By early 1836 the Kirtland Temple was completed and ready for dedication. Considering that the total number of Latter-day Saints cannot have exceeded a few thousand, most of them poor, this was an impressive achievement. At the dedication services, many in the congregation witnessed impressive spiritual manifestations. A school was now helping to train missionaries. As proselytizing expanded, converts continued to enter the fold.

Joseph Smith demonstrated an extraordinary capacity to rebound from disappointment and apparent failure. But he was not to have the luxury of relaxing. The Kirtland Temple had cost somewhere between $40,000 and $60,000. To help meet this obligation and to stimulate economic development in other ways, Church leaders in Ohio attempted to found a bank. When the state legislature denied them a charter as a bank, they changed the name to the Kirtland Safety Anti-Banking Company and began issuing banknotes. Soon there was a run on the bank, and its notes became almost worthless. By no means was this business failure unique, for in the Panic of 1837 hundreds of banks throughout the country suspended payments. In addition to exacerbating the already severe financial problems of the Church, this whole fiasco of the Kirtland banking venture led to rebellion in the ranks among those Mormons who lost money.

In the midst of these trials, Joseph Smith called Heber C. Kimball to go as a missionary to England, and he himself departed on a month-long mission to Canada. In his absence the discontent among those burned in the bank venture continued to simmer. Upon his return, he managed to hold things together. In the fall he left again, this time on a trip to Missouri. Returning after about five weeks, he found that the opposition group was virtually in control. Threatened by lawsuits, Joseph fled from Ohio with his family in early January 1838.

Arriving in Missouri in March, he was ready to make the best of the situation. The Latter-day Saints there had moved into Clay and Caldwell counties, where they were at first welcome. The main center was Far West, with a population of about 5,000. There, too, Joseph Smith found it necessary to impose discipline by cutting several local leaders off from the Church.

Fearing collusion between the dissenters and the old settlers, some Mormons, such as Sidney Rigdon, made angry, provocative declarations that they would defend themselves if necessary. With a continuing influx of converts and one large group from Kirtland, the Mormon population could not be confined to Caldwell County but spilled over into adjacent counties. Again, the Mormon-haters circulated rumors, complained, and among themselves talked of mob action.

On 6 August in Gallatin, Missouri, when a group of Mormons tried to vote, they were attacked. Two days later Joseph and several associates called upon Justice of the Peace Adam Black, asking him to sign a statement that he had not been involved in the Gallatin incident. This angered him. He immediately claimed duress. Soon Joseph Smith was a fugitive from justice, charged with unlawful violence. This whole scene, stretching over many days, is a spectacle of tit for tat, of attributing the worst to the others, of a breakdown of communication. Intemperate words were uttered on both sides. It is also a case study of escalation. Governor Lilburn W. Boggs, no friend of the Mormons, arranged to call up four hundred of the militia. In reaction, advised by lawyer Alexander Doniphan, Joseph organized "armies of Israel" among his followers. Led by officers of the state militia, they saw themselves as engaged in self-defense against mobs.

The situation rapidly deteriorated. Charges were made against Joseph and others in the courts. Accused of threatening the life of Adam Black, Joseph was fined, even with no confirming evidence. Groups of mobsters began to gather weapons. Mormon refugees from the surrounding area fled for security into Far West and organized militia units for self-defense.

It was not a small-scale confrontation. At Richmond, a mob of some 2,000 gathered. Not surprisingly, casualties started to occur. At a skirmish known as the Battle of Crooked River, Apostle David Patten was mortally wounded. A few days later, at Haun's Mill, where about 40 Mormons had sought refuge, 18 or 19 were killed and 15 wounded. About the same time, Governor Boggs issued his infamous extermination order: "The Mormons must be treated as enemies and *must be exterminated* or driven from the state, if necessary for the public good."[2]

Those fighting against the Mormons, of course, saw themselves as defending "the public good." They had their grievances, including actions by Mormon defenders, but especially fears of being overrun by those they considered beyond the limits of civilization. Prejudice and stereotyping were doing their ugly work and leading to the vigilantism that repeatedly raised its head in nineteenth-century America. With Boggs as governor, the anti-Mormons had the support of the state.

By the end of October, Far West was surrounded by some thirty-five hundred troops. Outnumbered and running short of supplies, the Mormons wished to avoid a bloodbath. When Joseph Smith and several colleagues raised a flag of truce and walked out to negotiate with their opponents, they were promptly taken prisoner and paraded in front of shouting, jeering soldiers. The next day, one general ordered that the prisoners be shot, to which Alexander Doniphan, in a display of courageous disobedience, replied, "It is cold-blooded murder. I will not obey your order. . . . If you execute these men, I will hold you responsible before an earthly tribunal, so help me God."

The prisoners were taken under guard to Richmond and placed in chains in an unroofed courthouse, the rain sometimes falling on them. The prisoners had every reason to fear execution. After a mock trial, most of the prisoners were released, but several, including Joseph Smith, were retained and sent to the jail at Liberty. There in a small room he would live for about six months, eating polluted food, and being jeered at by guards and curiosity-seekers.

Thus at the end of 1838 we find Joseph Smith at the bottom of the abyss. Kirtland appeared to be a lost cause. His people had been defeated in Missouri and were being driven from their homes. He himself was languishing in jail with no release in sight.

What he did was to delegate to Brigham Young the responsibility of organizing the evacuation of several thousand Mormons from Missouri. When it was determined that Illinois would receive them, the destitute refugees—individually, in families, some in larger groups—made their way eastward and across the icy, sometimes frozen Mississippi River. With four small children, Emma Smith carried some of Joseph's precious papers as she made the trip.

From Liberty Jail Joseph continued to show an alert interest in his people, giving encouragement and guidance. Long letters contained not only advice for the immediate extremity but sublime religious teaching (Doctrine and Covenants 121, 122, 123).

Finally, in April 1839, through collusion with the guards, who conveniently got drunk, Joseph and his fellow prisoners escaped. After an excruciating journey he reached Illinois and rejoined his family. How much physical and emotional trauma are compressed in these few words! Quickly he reasserted his leadership role, choosing Commerce (rechristened Nauvoo) as the gathering place for the scattered Mormons.

Incredibly, he had landed on his feet. Once again Joseph Smith was faced with the challenge of gathering the Mormons, building a city, and continuing the consolidation and development of organization and doctrine. Although he may not have known it, he had only five years to live.

The Nauvoo period in Mormon history was far from placid. Far from devitalized, Joseph exerted his prophetic leadership in ways that provided assurance and excitement, or discomfort and dismay, depending on how one reacted to the continuing struggle and the revelatory development of doctrine. The scriptural basis of Mormonism from its beginning in 1830 had included the Bible and the Book of Mormon. Modern revelations were soon given the same canonical status and published. With such an open-ended basis for the exposition of religious truth, the Church was seen by its devoted members as both true and living—growing and open to progressive revelation.

The developments of doctrine and ordinances at Nauvoo included baptism for the dead, endowment ceremonies, and eternal marriage—all of these to be consummated in the temple when it was completed there. Closely tied to these beliefs was the notion that God himself had progressed to achieve his present status and that humans could, if they were faithful to all the prerequisites, achieve a form of godhood in the eternities ahead. Most challenging to faithful Mormons, who after all had been instructed in a traditional monogamous morality since childhood, was the private introduction of polygamy among a few of the leaders. Organizational developments included the establishment of wards as the equivalent of a parish unit and giving increased responsibility to the Twelve Apostles, who, under Brigham Young, had proved their mettle in difficult circumstances.

It did not take long for resistance to mount, some external, some internal. The external opposition seems to have been motivated by a combination of revulsion against Joseph's religious claims and apprehension about the economic and political threat posed by Mormon Nauvoo. Clergymen had been among the leaders of the mob in Missouri, and they were not silent in Illinois. Other influences intensified opposition by the anti-Mormon party: complaints by Illinois Masons that the new Mormon Masonic lodges were growing too fast and would take over, rumors of polygamy that made Mormonism seem even more intolerable, and the decision of Joseph Smith in early 1844 to campaign for the presidency of the United States.

The opponents now raised the ante, demanding that something be done or else. The "or else" was a threat to use violence—powder and ball—to rid themselves of the Mormon juggernaut in Nauvoo. A meeting of anti-Mormons in neighboring Warsaw adopted the following resolution: "We hold ourselves at all times in readiness to cooperate with our fellow citizens in this state, Missouri, and Iowa, to exterminate, utterly exterminate, the wicked and abominable Mormon leaders, the authors of our troubles."[3] Although they were anti-Mormons—that is, opposed to the whole system—Joseph Smith was the focus of their resentment. If they could get rid of him, they thought, Mormonism would dissipate.

The internal opposition was equally relentless. From the beginning Joseph Smith had had to deal with dissenters and apostates. In Ohio and Missouri, embittered Church members or former Church members grieved him, threatened the unity among his followers, and sometimes worked actively with enemies on the outside to bring him down. The same pattern now repeated itself in Nauvoo. In 1842, when former close associate John C. Bennett turned on him, taking the lecture circuit and writing a defamatory book, the fires of hatred were fanned. Others in Nauvoo nursed grievances over some of Joseph's economic and business decisions. The practice of polygamy, carried on privately among an inner circle, could not be kept entirely secret. Tongues wagged. Rumors abounded. Correct information could not be readily differentiated from wild exaggeration. Some Mormons were offended to the point of immediate rejection of Joseph Smith's leadership. Others who already had their reasons for grumbling now used this as an excuse—it was the last straw.

In June 1844 a newspaper, *Nauvoo Expositor*, appeared. The word *expositor* of course suggests that it would be an exposé, not merely a one-shot book or pamphlet but, if allowed to continue, an ongoing opposition organ that would seek to bring down Joseph Smith. The issue was only four pages in length, but each page contained six columns of newsprint loaded with specific denunciations. Claiming to be true to the Bible, Book of Mormon, and the Doctrine and Covenants, the editors—William and Wilson Law, Robert and Charles Foster, Francis and Chauncey Higbee, and Charles Ivins—charged Joseph with polygamy, other doctrinal innovations, political ambition, and with denying their right to due process by summarily excommunicating them. Joseph Smith was "the Plebian, Patrician, or self-constituted Monarch." These critics called for the abolition of the Nauvoo Charter and implicitly welcomed a mob if necessary to enforce the law.[4]

This was too much for Joseph Smith and the other Mormon leaders. Meeting hastily, they voted that this newspaper was a public nuisance and, citing their charter authority to abate nuisances, sent police to destroy the press and scatter the type.

On 12 June, Thomas Sharp, editor of the *Warsaw Signal*, expressed his outrage at the destruction of the press. "Can you stand by and suffer such Infernal Devils! to rob men of their property and rights, without avenging them? We have no time to comment: every man will make his own. *Let it be made with powder and ball!!!*"

When efforts were made to arrest him, Joseph took out a writ of habeas corpus and was released by the court in Nauvoo. He wrote to the governor, explaining his position and expressing willingness to report at Springfield before a legal tribunal. Meanwhile, hearing rumors of mobs gathering all around Nauvoo, he declared martial law and ordered the Nauvoo Legion to make preparations to defend the city.

Hurriedly, Governor Thomas Ford traveled to Carthage, where his ears were filled with the grievances of the anti-Mormons and the *Expositor* group. He wrote a letter to Joseph Smith demanding that he come to Carthage and guaranteed the safety "of all such persons as may thus be brought to this place from Nauvoo either for trial or as witnesses for the accused." After a brief effort to escape across the river to the West, Joseph and his brother Hyrum Smith gave in to the entreaties of family and friends and returned. Stating several times that he knew he was going to his death, Joseph then traveled with Hyrum and others to Carthage, where they were arrested and charged with riot.

After paying bail and being freed, the defendants were committed to prison again on a different charge, treason—this for having declared martial law in Nauvoo. Claiming that he had no authority in a civil judicial process, the governor refused to countermand the illegal mittimus. Joseph and Hyrum Smith were then incarcerated in a room on the second floor of the jail at Carthage along with John Taylor and Willard Richards. A few visitors were allowed to come and go.

Despite repeated appeals for protection against threatened mob action, Governor Ford assured Joseph and his friends that their safety was secure, disbanded the militia, and left for Nauvoo, planning to return for a trial on the 29th. A small detachment of the Carthage Greys was left to guard the jail. On the afternoon of the 27th, at about five P.M., a mob with painted faces stormed the jail, the guards either conniving or assisting. Against the furious mob whose guns were firing into the room, those on the inside tried to hold the door shut and beat down the gun barrels with their canes. Joseph got off three shots with a small pepper box revolver. It was no use. Hyrum Smith was shot dead. John Taylor was hit with four balls and rolled under a bed. Miraculously, Willard Richards was only nicked on the ear. The shouts and cursing, the clatter of gunfire, the moans of the wounded or dying—it was a terrible moment. Leaping to the ledge of the window, Joseph was hit by gunshots from both inside and outside. "Oh, Lord, my God," he moaned, falling outward to the ground below. There he was shot several more times.

Joseph Smith's life was over.

* * *

Of the external facts there is really little dispute: Joseph Smith was born, married, had children, moved here and moved there. He said this and said that. Sometimes it is a challenge to reconstruct his words, or sort out the influence of scribes, but in this he was not different from other historical figures. We can say that he had followers who, to all appearances, accepted his claims, although they may have had different levels of understanding. It is rather easy to discover what his enemies, who were scarcely unwilling to speak out, thought of him. Where we run into difficulty, and inevitable disagreement, is in the area of motives. Why did he say and do these things? Did he believe what he was saying or was he putting us on? Who was he?

During his lifetime and ever since, different people have reacted in different ways. Jostling and clashing right down to the present have been competing images of the Prophet Joseph Smith.

## ENDNOTES

1. Gordon A. Madsen, "Joseph Smith's 1826 Trial: The Legal Setting," *Brigham Young University Studies* 30 (Spring 1990): 91–108.

2. Joseph Smith, *History of The Church of Jesus Christ of Latter-day Saints*, 6 vols. (Salt Lake City: Deseret News, 1948), 3:175.

3. Smith, 6:464.

4. *Nauvoo Expositor*, 7 June 1844.

# The Hostile View

2

"[Joseph Smith is] one of the blackest and basest scoundrels that has appeared upon the stage of human existence since the days of Nero and Caligula."

—Francis Higbee

"Such a rare human being is not to be disposed of by pelting his memory with unsavory epithets."

—Josiah Quincy

Deep water is what I am wont to swim in," wrote Joseph Smith in 1842.[1] The deep water included not only the outward trials of privation and pain and grief but also a verbal barrage of denunciation. What kind of psychological strength must one have to survive while being relentlessly portrayed in the most demeaning terms? Parents attempting to instill in their children a positive self-image would shudder at the prospect of such a negative barrage during the teenage years, the twenties, and thirties. Yet this is what Joseph Smith experienced.

Saving for a later chapter the hues with which biographers and historians would portray him, we shall here analyze what his detractors were saying during his lifetime. It is not sufficient, I think, simply to say that his opponents had a negative view, that they turned thumbs down on him. To identify the different components of the hostile image, it will be helpful to pay particular attention to the most common adjectives and nouns employed in the popular press whenever Joseph Smith was mentioned.

It was the First Vision experience of 1820, according to Joseph Smith's later account, that caused the first furor.[2] When he told this experience to a Methodist preacher, "he treated my communication not only lightly, but with great contempt, saying it was all of the devil, that there were no such things as visions or revelations in these days; that all such things had ceased with the apostles, and that there would never be any more of them." Smith went on to describe a more general reaction of "prejudice against me among professors of religion" and bitter persecution. When he used the term *persecution*, of course, he was not only expressing his subjective sense of being mis-understood but was linking himself with the early Christians, includ-ing the martyrs.

The word *persecute* carries baggage with it. When he adds the word *revile*, we immediately assume that the textual backdrop, even if unconscious, was Matthew 5:11–12: "Blessed are ye, when men shall revile you, and persecute you, and shall say all manner of evil against you falsely, for my sake. Rejoice, and be exceedingly glad: for great is your reward in heaven: for so persecuted they the prophets which were before you." The suspicion is confirmed as the words from Jesus' famous sermon are used in Joseph Smith's autobiographi-cal statement: ". . . while they were persecuting me, reviling me, and speaking all manner of evil against me falsely for so saying, I was led to say in my heart: Why persecute me for telling the truth?"

Direct evidence of opposition during the decade of the 1820s, while Smith was between ages fifteen and twenty-five, is not abun-dant. It is not hard to believe that community religious leaders, the two or three who may have heard about him, responded with curt rejection. These and perhaps a few other friends of the family would be "those who ought to have been my friends and to have treated me kindly, and if they supposed me to be deluded to have endeavored in a proper and affectionate manner to have reclaimed me." We sense the hurt. But in the meantime this boy of fifteen, sixteen, seventeen did not pout in a corner. He associated with "jovial company" and had a "native cheery temperament."

From about 1823 to 1829, the period of the Moroni visitations and, from 1827 on, the preparation of the Book of Mormon manu-script, the tongues were still wagging. It is not clear just how much Joseph Smith told. The experience of the First Vision was not trum-peted abroad; rather, after the initial scornful rejection by his minis-ter and perhaps others, he treasured it up in his heart, leaving even some family members with vague, confused memories. But between 1823 and 1827, he told some people, even outside his family, about the prospect of obtaining golden plates. Lacking the autobiographi-cal statement of 1838, in which he made the sequence clear enough for most purposes, earlier contemporaries could be pardoned for a tendency to mix up that precious treasure with the treasure Smith was digging for in the employ of Josiah Stowell. In any case, in his early adulthood Joseph Smith acquired the label of *money-digger*, with a freight of associated meanings that was entirely pejorative: charlatan, confidence man, superstitious oaf.[3]

Which brings us to the court trials. Not the many "vexatious lawsuits" of Smith's later life, but those in New York that occurred in 1826 and 1830. Although some later writers claimed that he was charged as an "impostor," there is no such crime. Attorney Gordon A. Madsen has studied the 1826 trial thoroughly.[4] Madsen concludes that Smith "was indeed charged and tried for being a disorderly person and that he was acquitted." He was not yet twenty-one. One important fact remains: he had enemies and critics well before the organization of the Church in 1830.

However, the publication of the Book of Mormon along with the organization of the Church, both in the spring of 1830, really brought Joseph Smith onto the public stage. Even prior to its publication, the book was being ridiculed. On 30 June 1830 the Palmyra *Reflector* disdainfully wrote that "the age of miracles has again arrived":

> . . . and if the least reliance can be placed upon the assertions, daily made by the "Gold Bible" apostles, (which is somewhat doubtful), no prophet, since the destruction of Jerusalem by Titus, has performed half so many wonders as have been attributed to that spindle shanked ignoramus JOE SMITH. This fellow appears to possess the quintessence of impudence, while his fellow laborers are not far behind . . . , denouncing dire damnation on such as may withhold their approbation from one of the most ridiculous impostures ever promulgated.[5]

*Ignorance, impudence, imposture*—already the labels were sticking.

When Abner Cole, editor of the Palmyra *Reflector*, wrote a

series on the new religion (under the pseudonym of Obadiah Dogberry), he added some details, all negative. Joseph Smith was "tall and slender—thin favored—having but little expression of countenance, other than that of dullness; his mental powers appear to be extremely limited, and from the small opportunity he has had at school, he made little or no proficiency." The defamation was extended to the entire Smith family: "We have never been able to learn that any of the family were ever noted for much else than ignorance and stupidity, to which might be added, so far as it may respect the elder branch, a propensity to superstition and a fondness for everything marvelous."

Cole went on the describe Joseph's mother as unstable religiously. Joseph was said to have made no "pretensions" to religion "until his late pretended revelation." The social context which Cole thought decisive was not religion but rather folk belief in money-digging and other popular superstitions. Not until after the appearance of the Book of Mormon did the religious element come in: "It is well known that Joe Smith never pretended to have any communion with angels, until a long period after the pretended finding of his book." Cole attempted to relate Joseph Smith to some predecessors, especially Joanna Southcote, described as a false prophet, and one Walters, "a vagabond fortune-teller . . . who then resided in the town of Sodus, and was once committed to the jail of this country for juggling . . . [and] was the constant companion and bosom friend of these money digging impostors."

Cole uses the word *prophet* but with the specific qualification that Smith was a "false" prophet. First he was called "the pseudo prophet Joe Smith Junior." He was compared not only to such "impostures" as the Morristown Ghost, Rogers, Walters the Magician, Joanna Southcote, and Jemima Wilkinson but also to Muhammed, here spelled Mohamet, thus introducing an identification that would be repeated many times in the future. Not that Joseph had the military leadership or the natural abilities of Muhammed; "it is only in their ignorance and impudence that a parallel can be found."[6]

As early as January 1831, therefore, before the move of the New York Latter-day Saints to Ohio, Joseph Smith was described by his detractors as ignorant, superstitious, impudent, and fraudulent. His followers too were considered ignorant and superstitious, easily taken advantage of. In short, they were "dupes." Some of those closest to him were not dupes but "pious reprobates," suggesting knowing collusion.

In March 1831, the Book of Mormon was called a "hoax": "Many may persevere in sustaining the Hoax, after they are convinced of the imposition, rather than acknowledge they were duped by so barefaced and contemptible an artifice."[7] The perpetrator of a hoax is of course a fraud or charlatan.

This same year, 1831, the Campbells entered the fray. A former associate of Sidney Rigdon, Thomas Campbell did not mention Joseph Smith, but the implication was clear when he denounced the "blasphemous pretensions" of Mormonism. Listing other groups such as the Quakers, the French prophets, and the Shakers, Thomas Campbell concluded: "If the Mormonite prophets and teachers can show no better authority for their pretended mission and revelations than those impostors have done, we have no better authority to believe them than we have to believe their predecessors in imposition."[8] *Imposture, pretense, imposition.*

About the same time, Thomas's son Alexander Campbell was publishing an extensive review of the Book of Mormon in his *Millennial Harbinger.*[9] Here Joseph Smith, described as a *liar* and a *knave*, with recurring adjectives such as *impudent* and *ignorant*, was again placed in the company of discredited predecessors: "Every age of the world has produced impostors and delusions."[10] *Delusion, fanaticism, pretension,* and *imposture*—words by which mainstream Christianity had dismissed Anabaptists and Quakers and more recently a series of idiosyncratic religious leaders—were now used against the Mormons. According to this view, Joseph Smith was of course the chief deluder, fanatic, pretender, and impostor.

In 1831 skeptical observer David I. Burnett wrote of "a feigned revelation purporting to be literally new." The Mormons in general he denounced as mainly "rabble." Joseph Smith was "a perfect igno-ramous [sic]," while others were "accomplices."[11]

A landmark in anti-Mormon literature was Eber D. Howe's 1834 book *Mormonism Unvailed*, whose subtitle conveyed the interpreta-tion: *A Faithful Account of That Singular Imposition and Delusion*.[12] Howe argued for the Spaulding theory of the Book of Mormon's ori-gin—that is, Smith purloined an unpublished romance written by Solomon Spaulding, a Presbyterian minister, and adapted it before publishing it as the Book of Mormon.[13] The book and the religion were thus an "artful imposition" on "credulous" believers. Smith was "our imposter." "No one but the vilest wretch on earth, disregarding all that is sacred, intrepid and fearless of eternity, would ever dared to have profaned the sacred oracles of truth to such base purposes."

In reprinted letters by former-Mormon Ezra Booth, one more negative label was added: *despot*. "Never was there a despot more jealous of his prerogative than Smith," we read, "and never was a fortress guarded with more vigilance and ardor against every invad-ing foe, than he guards those."[14]

It is in *Mormonism Unvailed*, too, that affidavits from Palmyra neighbors were reprinted. Since these betray a common authorship in some cases and are contradicted by other affidavits, they have been considered unreliable by Mormons. Later biographers, including Fawn Brodie, used them, and one recent book attempts to rehabilitate them. For our present purposes, what matters is that they were among the statements made about Joseph Smith, adding importantly to his negative image. The allegations against the entire Smith family were that they were *ignorant*, *lazy* or *indolent*, *intemperate*, *superstitious*, and *visionary*. We can add *dishonest*, for "their word was not to be depended upon." Joseph Smith and his father were both "considered entirely destitute of moral character and addicted to vicious habits."[15]

In 1842 John C. Bennett began going public, first in letters to newspapers and then in his book. Since his baptism in 1839, Bennett had enjoyed a meteoric rise. Quickly he became mayor of Nauvoo, chancellor of the "university," and a counselor in the First Presidency. His voice would have credibility—if he could overcome suspicions about his own honesty for having been a high-ranking Mormon himself. *The History of the Saints* (1842) carried a subtitle: *An Exposé of Joe Smith and the Mormons*. Claiming to have joined the Church as a subterfuge in the same way that Napoleon became a Muslim in Egypt, Bennett denounced Mormonism as "a frightfully corrupt system, that would enable them to give free course to their lust, ambition, and cruelty—a system than which, one more abominable the arch-enemy of mankind himself could not have invented."[16] This was not a dispassionate book.

But what does Bennett say about Joseph Smith? We start out with the now well established *impostor*. Smith was "one of the grossest and most infamous impostors that ever appeared upon the face of the earth." The moral degeneracy alluded to by earlier critics is made more specific as Bennett itemizes Mormon profanity, drunkenness, swindling, robberies, and the attempted assassination of Missouri's ex-governor Boggs. But by now, of course, polygamy had been introduced on a limited basis, proof for Bennett of his subject's depravity. Smith was now a "polluted monster," a "holy debauchee." Different levels of polygamy, "the Mormon seraglio," are described, and the misadventures of several women are reported. Thus in the negative image circulating among the public at large Joseph Smith now became also a *lecher*.

Even more threateningly, Bennett's Joseph Smith was, again, a *despot*. Ezra Booth had earlier raised this complaint, but now Bennett charged that Smith's objective was to erect "a despotic military and religious empire the head of which [was] emperor and pope."[17] Smith had a nefarious plan to take over Illinois, Missouri, Iowa, and other states by force of arms, exterminating those who would not convert to Mormonism. Why, Bennett asks, should this be surprising? Mormons were like other *fanatics* throughout history, most notably the Anabaptists of the Reformation era, described of course by citing the extreme example of the 1534 Muenster debacle.[18] The term *fanaticism* was much discussed and employed during the 1830s to describe "an overheating of the emotions that led otherwise normal people to entertain strange and enthusiastic doctrines."[19]

The comparison which Bennett did not originate (Abner Cole first introduced the idea as early as 1830) but perhaps did the most to popularize was between Joseph Smith and Muhammed.[20] Both called themselves prophets. Both, for Bennett, had been obvious impostors. Both allowed polygamy. (The term *seraglio* was employed by Bennett to conjure up the image of a Turkish harem.) Both had political ambitions and were willing to use military force. Thus a simple phrase such as "the Mormon Mahomet" summed up much of the negative stereotype.

The question of Joseph Smith's motives is quickly disposed of by all of these early hostile treatments. He was just no good, that's all; he was "a consummate knave." Bennett quotes the Reverend William Harris: Smith could not be "dupe of his own imposture," could not, in other words, have convinced himself that he was telling the truth. Why not? Because "his works plainly show that he is neither fool, nor a fanatic, but a deliberate designer"—and all "for the gratification of his own vanity and selfishness."[21] Thus the interpretation advanced by Fawn Brodie in the 1940s was very early considered and rejected.

My purpose here is not to give a quantitative analysis of anti-Smith statements but to give a sense of the different elements in the negative image as it developed. Practically all of it was in place by 1842. A fine-tuned description would trace the vocabulary of vilification through year by year, noting the influence of specific events, such as the failure of the Kirtland bank or the Missouri hostilities. The two major published landmarks were Howe's *Mormonism Unvailed* (1834) and Bennett's *History of the Saints* (1842), but many newspaper articles and speeches along the way used the same terms in a repetitious drumbeat of anti-Smith rhetoric.

If you did not have sufficient reason to dislike Joseph Smith already, one additional charge was hurled in the 1840s: *secrecy*. The introduction of the sacred endowment ceremony about this time in Nauvoo gave some basis to the charge, but it received apparent confirmation with the construction of the Nauvoo Temple and the performance of sacred ceremonies there at the end of 1845 and the beginning of 1846. In 1847 appeared a pamphlet by Increase and Maria Van Deusen, *The Mormon Endowment*, subtitled *A Secret Drama, or Conspiracy, in the Nauvoo Temple in 1846.*[22]

One might protest that this was a later development after Joseph Smith's death even if it was projected backward onto him. But the charge of secrecy began earlier, dovetailing into other aspects of the negative image: superstition, immorality, tyranny, and conspiracy. Even Bennett's 1842 book is based on the claim that the real evil of Mormonism and Smith's real character could not be publicly known; one had to become part of the inner circle to gain access to the secret designs.

One take on Joseph Smith from disbelievers might have seemed harmless enough. I refer to humor, seeing him as a figure of fun, a *clown*. The best example comes from the Reverend Henry Caswall, whose *The Prophet of the Nineteenth Century* was published in 1843. Some of Caswall's adjectives are unoriginal: "It is difficult to imagine a human being more corrupt, or more destitute of redeeming qualities. . . . [There is] little in his character besides unscrupulous audacity, reckless falsehood, low cunning, groveling vulgarity, daring blasphemy, and grasping selfishness."

Caswall describes an interview in which he asked Smith to identify a psalter. The answer: "What ain't Greek is Egyptian, and what ain't Egyptian is Greek." In this account the reader is treated to an amusing scene in which a sophisticated English visitor has fun at the expense of the naive, rustic Mormon leader, who is presented as linguistically incompetent, grammatically unaware, and yet pretentious.[23] One can imagine the chuckles. The unlikelihood that any such interchange actually took place does not negate the fact of its publication. It was possible, obviously, to see Joseph Smith as a figure of fun.

The uncommon humorous portrayal might have seemed a welcome relief from the relentless, unsmiling charges of depravity and criminality. But the humor, such as it was, could quite easily be harmonized with charges of ignorance and superstition. Leaving no room for respect or affection, it was perhaps not so harmless after all.

In sketching out this negative image of Joseph Smith with its different component parts, I have not meant to say that this was "*the non-Mormon image.*" There were some—one thinks of New York editor James Arlington Bennett—who admired Joseph, at least in many respects. There is the grudging admiration of Josiah Quincy (see chapter 3), often quoted selectively by Mormons. There were no doubt other non-Mormon friends or admirers of the prophet. What we have described is the most common anti-Smith image. Once circulating, of course, it became readily available as part of public discourse. One could accept it in whole or in part. I think it safe to say that among the public at large, among those who had any reaction to the subject at all, it was this anti-Mormon image that carried the day. Most of the time, in my judgment, this readily mobilized image was not a conclusion coming at the end of a sustained argument; it was so obvious as to need no basis in an elaborate lawyer's brief; with a disdainful snort, one simply assumed that all right-thinking people would agree and then, perhaps, cited examples of behavior, or rumors, showing Joseph Smith for what he really was. It may not be obvious to everyone that most people, even today, have their image in advance. It is contained in their set of assumptions about reality. Many will have been nodding their heads in agreement with the early negative terminology laid out in the present chapter.

As a postscript, one variation requires mention—that Joseph Smith was a *fallen prophet*, a label often used by apostates. With the human desire to preserve consistency, what other choices were there? Those who abandoned the faith could admit to having been taken in, to having been duped, but of course this meant admitting naiveté or foolishness. They could, like John C. Bennett, claim to have joined the Mormons simply in order to exposé the fraud—with fingers crossed, so to speak. But this did mean that they had lied and had betrayed those Mormons who for some period of time were their fellows. If the turncoat had not been sincere when a Mormon, was he sincere now or just trying to turn a profit by writing a best-seller or telling audiences what they wanted to hear?

The usual explanation from apostates was that they had believed the Mormon message as it was preached to them but later on found additional information they could not accept. Or as the new religion was developing, incremental additions were made that were simply unacceptable. Joseph Smith had thus been a prophet, but by adding details to the original message or behaving improperly had become a fallen prophet. Starting almost at the beginning of the history of the Church, this pattern of accusation replayed itself at repeated intervals. Some apostates could not accept the ordination of High Priests in 1831. As early as 1832, when "the Vision" was published in the *Evening and Morning Star* (now Section 76 in the Doctrine and Covenants), some were offended and left the Church. Then the Book of Commandments, published in 1833, became such a fixed anchor for some that when further revelations were brought forth, with the first edition of the Doctrine and Covenants published in 1835, they complained. They were getting teachings and organizational structure they had not bargained for. With the great financial crisis at Kirtland, Ohio, in 1837, the cry of "fallen prophet" was frequently raised, to be repeated by some in Missouri the following year. Near the end of Joseph Smith's life, those opponents who "seceded," the publishers of *Nauvoo Expositor*, explained: "We all verily believe, and many of us know of a surety, that the religion of the Latter-day Saints, as originally taught by Joseph Smith, which is contained in the Old and New Testaments, Book of Covenants, and Book of Mormon, is verily true."[24] But they denounced what they now considered the Prophet's dictatorial pretensions and gross immorality.

Such a conceptualization fell short of denying all validity to Joseph Smith's prophetic status. It enabled the apostates to defend their original conversions while disassociating themselves from later developments. Quite outside the usual anti-Smith stereotyping, this one tried to strike a middle position. But it was a position most difficult to maintain. Those who agreed were mainly limited to those who shared the same presuppositions and provocations— likely a small number. And even while trying to stop short of rejecting Joseph Smith in his entirety, those who denounced his later or current misdeeds, as they saw them, readily resorted to intemperate rhetoric. For Francis Higbee in 1844 Joseph was "one of the blackest and basest scoundrels that has appeared upon the stage of human existence since the days of Nero and Caligula."[25]

Not surprisingly, those seeing Joseph Smith as a fallen prophet were exploited to the hilt by anti-Mormons who did not think he was fallen for the simple reason that for them he had never been a prophet. The two groups of opponents fed on one another.

We have considered the development of the negative image in Joseph Smith's lifetime. It did not die but continued to be used by later anti-Mormons—right down to the present. Some later authors repeat the early charges under the trappings of scholarship by the simple device of citing the denunciations that were contemporary with Smith as a kind of primary source. They are of course primary sources—but of what? Of one of the images of Joseph Smith but, as we shall see, by no means the only one.

## ENDNOTES

1. Doctrine and Covenants 127:2.

2. Here I use the standard account now published in Joseph Smith, *History of The Church of Jesus Christ of Latter-day Saints*, ed. B. H. Roberts, 7 vols. (Salt Lake City: The Church of Jesus Christ of Latter-day Saints, 1932–1951), 1:1–17, and in the Pearl of Great Price (Salt Lake City: The Church of Jesus Christ of Latter-day Saints, 1981), section entitled "Joseph Smith—History."

3. The issue of money-digging and associated popular superstitions is treated most thoroughly in D. Michael Quinn, *Early Mormonism and the Magic World View* (Salt Lake City: Signature Books, 1987). One among many challenges to this thesis is Stephen D. Ricks and Daniel C. Peterson, "Joseph Smith and 'Magic': Methodological Reflections on the Use of a Term," in Robert L. Millet, ed., *"To Be Learned Is Good If . . ."* (Salt Lake City: Bookcraft, 1987), 129–47.

4. Gordon A. Madsen, "Joseph Smith's 1826 Trial: The Legal Setting," *Brigham Young University Studies* 30 (Spring 1990): 91–108.

5. Francis W. Kirkham, *A New Witness for Christ in America*, 2 vols. (Independence, MO: Zion's Printing and Publishing, 1942–1951), 1:278–79; also 2:55–56.

6. Kirkham, 1:283–95; also 2:63–77. In some instances, capitalized and italicized words of the original newspaper publications have been ignored. See also Russell R. Rich, "The Dogberry Papers and the Book of Mormon," *Brigham Young University Studies* 10 (Spring 1970): 315–19.

7. Kirkham, 2:76–77, quoting from the *Painesville* [Ohio] *Telegraph*.

8. Kirkham, 2:95.

9. Published in book form in *Delusions: An Analysis of the Book of Mormon* (Boston: Benjamin H. Greene, 1832), passages conveniently reprinted in Kirkham, 2:101–9.

10. "Delusions," in *Painesville Telegraph*, 8 March 1831, as quoted by Milton V. Backman, Jr., in *Joseph Smith: The Prophet, the Man* (Provo, UT: BYU Religious Studies Center, 1993), 89.

11. Kirkham, 2:111–13.

12. Painesville, OH: Printed and published by the author, 1834.

13. The best summary is Lester F. Bush, Jr., "The Spaulding Theory Then and Now," *Dialogue: A Journal of Mormon Thought* 10 (August 1977): 40–69.

14. Kirkham, 2:132.

15. Kirkham, 2:137. Hugh Nibley, *The Myth Makers* (first published in 1961), "Everybody knew him when . . .," in *Collected Works of Hugh Nibley* (Salt Lake City /Provo, UT: Deseret Book and F.A.R.M.S., 1991), 11:105–53. The basic treatment is Richard L. Anderson, "Joseph Smith's New York Reputation Reappraised," *Brigham Young University Studies* 10 (Spring 1970): 283–314. The attempted rehabilitation of the affidavits is Rodger I. Anderson, *Joseph Smith's New York Reputation Reexamined* (Salt Lake City: Signature Books, 1990), which in turn is critically reviewed by Richard L. Anderson in *Reviews of Books on the Book of Mormon* 3 (1991): 52–80.

16. John C. Bennett, *The History of the Saints; or, An Exposé of Joe Smith and the Mormons* 3d ed. (Boston: Whiting, 1842), 9.

17. Bennett, 2.

18. Bennett, 302ff.

19. Paul E. Johnson and Sean Wilentz, *The Kingdom of Matthias* (New York/Oxford: Oxford University Press, 1994), 150–51, which cites, among other sources, Amariah Brigham, *Observations on the Influence of Religion upon the Health and Physical Welfare of Mankind* (Boston, 1835).

20. Arnold H. Green and Lawrence P. Goldrup, "Joseph Smith, an American Muhammed? An Essay on the Parallels of Historical Analogy," *Dialogue* 6 (Spring 1971): 46–58; Hugh Nibley, "Eduard Meyer's Comparison of Mohammed and Joseph Smith" (Provo, UT: F.A.R.M.S., 1989).

21. Bennett, 57–58. Bennett, who quoted extensively from earlier anti-Mormon works, is here quoting William Harris, *Mormonism Portrayed* (Warsaw, IL: Sharp and Gamble, 1841), with a subtitle: *Its errors and absurdities exposed, and the spirit and designs of its authors made manifest.*

22. Syracuse, NY: N.M.D. Lathrop printer, 1847. For several later editions, including an expanded version in 1854, see Chad J. Flake, ed., *A Mormon Bibliography, 1830–1930* (Salt Lake City: University of Utah Press, 1978).

23. Henry Caswall, *The City of the Mormons; or Three Days at Nauvoo in 1842* (London: J.G.F. & J., 1842). For a witty dissection, see Nibley, *The Myth Makers*, in *Collected Works of Hugh Nibley*, 11:304-406.

24. *Nauvoo Expositor*, 7 June 1844, 1.

25. *Nauvoo Expositor*, 7 June 1844, 3.

# Jacksonian
# Hero

3

"Jesus, Buddha, Caesar, Cromwell, Washington, and Joseph Smith all knew, as true heroes must, their respective wildernesses, exiles, castigations by contemporaries, even their Elbas and Golgothas."

—Robert Nisbet

As odious as Joseph Smith appeared to the broad public, those who looked at him with different eyes could see him as a hero. To properly appreciate this aspect of his persona we must see him against the backdrop of nineteenth-century heroism. What had been inherited from previous centuries and their view of the heroic? How had this been modified by the half-century stretching from about 1775 to 1825? And how did Joseph Smith measure up against the heroic yardstick of his day? These are the questions we will explore in the present chapter.

The designation of hero can be applied to historical figures or literary figures. In either case the label makes no sense without certain minimum attributes. Different lists have been constructed of the essential attributes of a hero. In other words, it is by possessing these particular attributes, or most of them, that one qualifies for the label. Literary scholar Roy Porter sees as essential the following: (1) the hero is a dead human being—that is, not divine—and consequently possesses human failings. (2) The hero is the object of heightened admiration—not necessarily of worship but at least "the keeping alive of the venerated memory of the hero by the recounting of his biography in circles for whom his memory had social significance." (3) The hero is an extraordinary individual, with the ability "to perform extraordinary feats or miracles or to give inspired teaching." (4) The hero demonstrates his powers in warfare or some other kind of dangerous or violent situation, but the heroic potency "may be expressed in any number of ways that are viewed as extending the range of achievement for a particular society or group." (5) The traditions or stories of the hero, as transmitted, are "essentially folklore material and display the particular characteristics and structure of the folktale."[1]

Bill Butler, a historian of ideas, lists thirty different attributes of the divine or super hero.[2] Some of these—preceded by legends, of unknown parentage, conceived miraculously—seem to apply to the founders of major religions. Some of Butler's other points are derived from specific heroic figures but are by no means considered necessary for all heroes: "rescued or taught by wild or supernatural beings"; "consecrated by acquiring weapons"; "initiated by being given a name." Selecting from Butler's larger list, however, we find several features with possible applicability to our present subject: a life "more difficult than that of most people"; "a constant wanderer"; "larger-than-life actions, size, beauty, courage, intelligence"; possibly having to disguise himself; wielding "supernatural weapons"; having a sidekick; living a dangerous social life that "can bring death to his friends as often as to his enemies"; "a supernatural or sacrificial death."

No hero has all of these characteristics, but many of them will appear in the life of those who have been regarded as heroes in our human experience. Interestingly, while listing many modern variants of the heroic (the Mafia Don, the Kennedys, John Wayne, Clint Eastwood, Superman, and others), Butler sees them as all related ultimately to two sources: Heracles and Jesus Christ.[3]

Joseph Campbell, well known authority on myth in different cultures, sees as common to the hero a three-phase sequence of "a separation from the world, a penetration to some source of power, and a life-enhancing return."[4] Joseph Smith could fit these concepts (to the Grove, the encounter with God the Father and Jesus Christ, and return), and he is rather well described by some of Campbell's other general comments about heroes. "If we could dredge up something forgotten not only by ourselves but by our whole generation or our entire civilization, we should become indeed the boon-bringer, the culture hero of the day—a personage of not only local but world historical moment."[5] Not to others, of course, but to his followers the Mormon Prophet did exactly that. Again, his followers saw him as indeed "rendering the modern world spiritually significant."[6] But by ranging back and forth across the centuries and geographically from culture to culture, which some would see as his great strength, Campbell is unhelpful in setting a framework for heroism in the nineteenth century.[7]

Looming largest as historical hero in European and American consciousness at the beginning of the nineteenth century was Napoleon. A recent discussion of Napoleon as hero notes that he was not the culture-hero who defends society but more the outlaw adventurer with "boundless ambition," willing "to break with law and convention." Anxious to achieve the lofty status of hero, Napoleon needed to exhibit "the rebellious aura of the adventurer." His could not be a life of ease or convention. He was—or wished to be seen as—the Man of Destiny.[8] When Joseph Smith was growing up as a boy, Napoleon was winning some of his great battles, escaping from Elba to return to France in the Hundred Days, losing the battle of Waterloo, and then living out his life on St. Helena.

Another "hero" very familiar to the educated public by the 1820s was Lord Byron. A poetic genius, dashing, self-dramatizing, brave, willing to sacrifice his life, Byron strode across the stage of history, his life contrasting sharply with the humdrum existence of most people.[9]

Dixon Wecter, a historian of popular culture, has studied a sequence of Americans from Captain John Smith to Franklin Delano Roosevelt. In the late eighteenth century Benjamin Franklin, George Washington, and Thomas Jefferson had all been seen as heroes, to be followed in the nineteenth century by Daniel Boone, Davy Crockett, Abraham Lincoln, Robert E. Lee, and others.[10] Of these it will be most helpful for our present purposes to consider Old Hickory—Andrew Jackson.

Historian John William Ward has supplied the standard study of Jackson's image.[11] In 1815, when Joseph Smith was just nine years old, Jackson became a national hero as a result of the American victory in the battle of New Orleans. In the actual battle British troops were not noticeably cowardly (although their leadership put them in an impossible situation). Nor did the American troops display any particular skill in marksmanship. The fact remains, however, that when the shooting subsided, the British casualties were 2,000, while the Americans lost only 8 killed and 13 wounded.

The battle was one thing, its image another. Soon one heard that victory was due to American marksmanship. This version of the events received a fresh infusion of popularity in the 1820s through the song "The Hunters of Kentucky." Here is one stanza:

> But Jackson he was wide awake, and
> wasn't scared with trifles,
> For well he knew what aim we take
> with our Kentucky rifles;
> So he marched us down to 'Cyprus Swamp';
> The ground was low and mucky;
> There stood 'John Bull,' in martial pomp,
> *But here was old Kentucky.*

In essence, the claim was being made that uncorrupted nature, in the form of soldiers fresh from the forests and the fields, triumphed over the pomp of old Europe.

Not the beneficiary of a pampered childhood or an aristocratic education, Jackson had grown from infancy to maturity "as the forest trees grow." This very lack of training was significantly one of the important aspects of Jackson as hero. Lacking academic degrees and formal study, he nevertheless possessed (or was presented as possessing) strength of mind, even genius, an ability to cut through to the essential, to rise above petty detail to the broad generalization. As a newspaper correspondent put it, "His mind seems to be clogged by no forms."[12]

No dandy, no intellectual, Jackson faced as an opponent in the 1828 election John Quincy Adams, a Harvard professor. One of the criticisms of Jackson from his opponents was that he would embarrass the United States. "What will the English malignants . . . the Edinburgh and Quarterly reviewers . . . say of a people who want a man to govern them who cannot spell *more than about one word in four?*" As it turned out, Ward comments, the people, "didn't give much of a damn what the English malignants thought." [13]

Although Jackson may not have been particularly religious, to be an American hero for his generation required some connection with the divine. Soon after the battle of New Orleans a great *Te Deum* was celebrated. Then the Catholic Abbé extolled Jackson as God's representative: "To *Him*, therefore, our most fervent thanks are due for our late unexpected rescue, and it is *Him* we chiefly intend to praise, when considering you, general, as *the man of his right hand*, whom he has taken pains to fit out for the important commission of our defence."[14] An important part of Jackson's positive image as hero for his age was the assumption that God watched over him, assisted him, and even intervened in his behalf.

What of Joseph Smith? Could Joseph Smith be seen as a hero by the definitions presented above? With little effort, we find that (1) many of the traits of Joseph Smith were specifically such as to make him appear heroic; and (2) these are in large part traits observable in the man himself by witnesses and not merely imaginative constructs projected upon him by later generations of adulators. Consider the following:

1. He came from lower-class origins. More so than Jackson, certainly more so than William Henry Harrison, he could claim to have been born in a log cabin in Sharon, Vermont. He didn't stay there—heroes never do.

2. He challenged the establishment. This is too obvious to require evidence, but it may be worth reminding ourselves of how steadily he pursued his course, taking on, as it were, the entire world.

3. He exhibited courage, not only in the general willingness just mentioned but also in the physical sense. Two incidents immediately come to mind.

When still only seven years of age, as briefly noted in chapter 1, he became afflicted with a bone infection that ultimately required surgery. The first incision was eight inches on his lower leg. The second time the surgeon reopened the wound, he went deep as the bone. The third was even more excruciating, a boring into the bone of his leg, first from one side, then from the other, and then breaking off a piece of bone with a pair of pincers. This process was repeated three times in order to remove the necessary amount of infected bone. The boy refused to be tied down, saying that he could "tough it out" if his father would hold him in his arms. And he refused to take any wine to mitigate the pain.[15]

About twenty years later, after the Church had been organized, and while living on the Johnson farm near Kirtland, Ohio, Joseph Smith was awakened in the night by a mob of armed men who burst into the house, choked him into unconsciousness, dragged him outside, tore off his clothes, beat him, scratched him, smeared his naked body with hot tar, and rolled him in feathers. Staggering back home, he appeared at the door, only to frighten his wife Emma, who swooned when she saw what she thought was blood all over him. A blanket was thrown around him. All night his friends worked using lard to loosen the tar and then scrape it off, often removing pieces of skin with the tar. The next morning he appeared on schedule at a worship service, much to the surprise of two mob leaders who were in the congregation. Joseph preached a sermon, making no reference to his experience of the night before, and afterwards baptized three new members into the Church.[16]

Many such incidents could be adduced. To his followers they showed a courageous leader who drew upon unseen sources of strength.

4. Against incredible opposition he kept bouncing back. The incident just described is one example of his resilience, but his entire life can be seen as a series of experiences taking this form. At one of the lowest points in his life, his people having been expelled from Missouri, Joseph languished with a few associates in Liberty Jail. One might think he was down for the count. But during the crucial months of late 1838 and early 1839 we find instead that he was binding his fellow prisoners to him even more closely, putting forth teachings that inspired (and still do), regrouping his own and his people's resources (this with the indispensable aid of Brigham Young). In the immediate aftermath of his escape, he established a new center on the banks of the Mississippi River and then sent out apostle-missionaries, themselves in the depths of poverty, to far-away England.

5. Audaciously, he played for high stakes. This was inherent in his initial claim to exclusive religious authority, but also in such operatic actions as leading an "army," the so-called Zion's Camp, to the rescue of the beleaguered Saints in Missouri. However humble he was before God in a spiritual sense, there was nothing modest about Joseph Smith's undertakings and style, but then modesty is not a trait we readily associate with Alexander the Great, Napoleon, or Old Hickory.

6. He was a builder—of a church, of social institutions, of a city. It may have been enough for the heroes of past history and legend to defeat the dragon, to save their family or people, but the greatest of them had constructive achievements to their credit, as witness David of the Old Testament, Napoleon, and Andrew Jackson. Not at all satisfied simply to denounce the political, economic, and religious institutions of his day, Joseph Smith launched his own (or as he would say, God's) countersystems—political, economic, social, and especially ecclesiastical. Even if all did not succeed, he gave sufficient impetus to the new Church—and the ancillary Utopian aspects—that they were able to survive his death. If George Washington was *pater patriae*, the father of his country, Joseph Smith was *pater ecclesiae*, father of his church. Both Washington and Smith would insist on adding the words "under God."

7. Finally, let us consider Joseph Smith's personal style. Although some have extended the concept of hero to include the great intellectual and artistic geniuses of the past, it is hard to think of a recluse or a balding, bespectacled milquetoast as a true hero. Out in the public arena, the hero is able to be noticed, indeed to command attention, and to attract (and keep) followers. This flair, however we define it, Joseph Smith had. It was impossible to ignore him. Not perhaps handsome in the usual sense of the word, he was striking in appearance. Certainly he had his moments of private relaxation and casual conversation, even humor, but clearly when he spoke people listened, whether in the question-answer format that became common near the end of his life or in sermons and orations. Joseph Smith had charisma. He was a natural leader of men.

Listen to Apostle Wilford Woodruff, as early as 1836, writing in his journal after listening to Joseph Smith preach in the newly dedicated Kirtland Temple:

> There is not a greater man than Joseph standing in this generation. The gentiles look upon him & he is to them like bed of gold concealed from human view: they know not his principle, his spirit, his wisdom, virtue, phylanthropy, nor his calling. His mind like Enochs swells wide as eternity. Nothing short of a God can comprehend his soul.[17]

Or here is the testimony of First Counselor George Q. Cannon:

> Whether engaging in manly sport, during hours of relaxation, or proclaiming words of wisdom in pulpit or grove, he was ever the leader. His magnetism was masterful, and his heroic qualities won universal admiration. Where he moved all classes were forced to recognize in him the man of power. Strangers journeying to see him from a distance, knew him the moment their eyes beheld his person.

If this last claim seems exaggerated, George Q. Cannon cites his own experience when he landed at the pier in Nauvoo. Crowds of people were milling about, including many prominent Church leaders, but when Cannon spotted the Prophet he "knew him instantly."[18]

But, it may be said, this is loading the dice. Of course his followers—his dupes, if you prefer—saw him in glowing terms. It was quite possible for the non-Mormon, or at least the anti-Mormon, to see him as ridiculous, pompous, tyrannical. The answer, of course, is that all heroes could be seen in similar negative terms. We don't know what the Trojans were saying about Agamemnon, or the Philistines about Saul and David, but we do know of the hostile caricatures of George Washington, Napoleon Bonaparte, and Andrew Jackson. Heroism is very largely in the eye of the beholder.

But without certain characteristics an individual simply is not convincingly labeled a hero. Of humble origins, lacking formal education, not hampered by traditional forms, extraordinarily intelligent, ready with the repartee that showed his acuity, resolute of purpose, of penetrating eye, a natural leader, protective of women and children, somehow connected with or approved by God—such was the litany of attributes of Andrew Jackson, at least in the image held by his followers. Without exception such also were the attributes of Joseph Smith.

Even some outside observers recognized that Joseph was far from ordinary and might very well have a significance beyond their present estimate. As early as 1840 a visitor to Nauvoo remarked on the way in which leading people gathered to hear Joseph's pronouncements: "His bearing towards them was like one who had authority, and the deference which they paid him convinced us that his dominion was deeply seated in the empire of their consciences."[19] In 1842, the *New York Herald* editorialized: "This Joe Smith is undoubtedly one of the greatest characters of the age. He indicates as much talent, originality, and moral courage as Mahomet, Odin, or any of the great spirits that have hitherto produced the revolutions of past ages."[20]

Later, Josiah Quincy, mayor of Boston (after describing Andrew Jackson in terms far from adulatory), wrote of Joseph Smith:

> It is by no means improbable that some future textbook, for the use of generations yet unborn, will contain a question something like this: What historical American of the nineteenth century has exerted the most powerful influence upon the destinies of his countrymen? And it is by no means impossible that the answer to that interrogatory may be thus written: *Joseph Smith, the Mormon prophet.* And the reply, absurd as it doubtless seems to most men now living, may be an obvious commonplace to their descendants.

Quincy goes on to say that "such a rare human being is not to be disposed of by pelting his memory with unsavory epithets." Joseph

Smith, he wrote, was a "sturdy self-asserter," a "fine-looking man" of "commanding appearance." But he was more. Comparing Joseph to Elijah Potter of Rhode Island, Quincy wrote: "Of all men I have met, these two seemed best endowed with that kingly faculty which directs, as by intrinsic right, the feeble or confused souls who are looking for guidance."

Much too sophisticated to take the Mormon religion seriously, Quincy was not entirely complimentary. But he could not deny that the Mormons had an extraordinary leader. "Born in the lowest ranks of poverty, without book-learning and with the homeliest of all human names," Quincy concluded, Joseph Smith "had made himself at the age of thirty-nine a power upon the earth."[21]

But it was to his followers above all that Smith stood on the earth like a Titan. His willingness to think in grandiose terms was evidenced in 1843 when he proposed to the U.S. government that he be given the contract for enforcing the law on the overland trail to Oregon. Had this been accepted—and we know not whether it was even taken seriously—there might well have been a generation who thought of the entire country west of the Mississippi as Smith country. He would have been the Godfather over thousands of miles in the West. That he could even think in such terms tells something of the man.

In 1844, as if he didn't have enough problems already, Joseph Smith threw his hat into the ring for the presidency of the United States. We have the *Views of the Presidency*, his campaign pamphlet, that sets forth his dissatisfaction with much of the present social-political order.[22] He told Quincy that he might be the balance of power.[23] What would be the message, the pitch, of those out on the stump promoting his candidacy? Speaking to non-Mormons, they could not well emphasize that Joseph Smith was a prophet. That would be a turn-off. But they could, in addition to looking at his specific policy proposals, convey their own conviction that he was a towering human individual, capable of providing strong leadership—in short, a hero.

In this last year or two of his life we begin to see more of the trappings of distinction: ceremony and parades. On such occasions, he would appear uniformed, mounted on a handsome horse. This may seem a minor point, but within the long tradition of heroism it is worth remembering the importance of being seen on horseback. "Perhaps we have not really been able to believe in heroes since the triumph of the internal combustion engine," a Renaissance historian remarks as he notes the popularity of equestrian monuments in Renaissance Italy.[24] Once restored, this artistic representation, the man on horseback, was used endlessly for the military hero.

The changing mores of the nineteenth century made it possible to think of heroes as men in top hats (Abraham Lincoln) and other civilian attire, but the inherited image of the hero was usually that of a military man on horseback. Uniform and prancing steed—these were the attributes. After establishing a new city of Nauvoo, Illinois, Joseph Smith, already head of the Church, became its mayor and a commander of the Nauvoo Legion. If already he had seemed a hero, now he had all the external paraphernalia. He could wear his officer's uniform on public occasions, could lead the troops in parade, and could commission (or at least encourage) an artistic rendition of himself that is squarely in the tradition of the equestrian statue.

Already in Joseph Smith's lifetime the notion of hero was complex. Later it would fragment further. Thomas Carlyle's famous *On Heroes, Hero-Worship and the Heroic in History* (1841) discusses the hero as divinity, the hero as prophet, the hero as poet, the hero as priest, the hero as man of letters, and the hero as king.[25] In these terms, Joseph Smith stands forth not only as prophet-hero but as a political, economic, and military hero. Moreover, his intellectual (or revelatory) production was such that to his followers he was not merely the hero-as-man-of-action. In his single person he managed to refract several of the main components of heroic possibility.

Obviously, being a hero, a title Smith never claimed for himself, was subordinate to the claim of being "prophet, seer, and revelator." The latter implies designation by God; the former, merely traits of character, charismatic personality, and actions during a series of challenges. Thus it might have been possible to see Smith as a genuine hero—thinking, for example, of the putative voters in the 1844 presidential election—without accepting his prophetic claims. Even among his followers, one imagines, there were those still struggling with the religious aspect who were mesmerized by the hero.

As they looked upon Joseph Smith, especially as they remembered him, they saw someone who in a short lifetime had accomplished great things. He had been a crucial player in the cosmic plan of God. But there have been founders of movements who have been essentially recluses, working out their designs in their study and sending them forth via the written word. Such had not been the life, or the personal style, of Joseph Smith. With a flair for the dramatic, he had asserted his claims in a way that could not be ignored. Grandly he strode across the historical stage. For his followers, those unwilling to dismiss him as a mountebank, he was a prophet and much more. In part, for them, he was a true hero of the Jacksonian era.

The term *hero* has experienced a metamorphosis. Some have seen this as a result of decreasing admiration for the military. That explanation becomes less convincing when we reflect on the stature of Ulysses S. Grant, Robert E. Lee, Teddy Roosevelt, Generals Pershing, MacArthur, Patton, Eisenhower, and "Stormin'" Norman Schwarzkopf. Others find that heroism melts before modern investigative reporting and the glare of television cameras. Political philosopher Sidney Hook sees the hero as fundamentally incompatible with modern democracy.[26] A more profound explanation comes from George Roche, a college president, who says that heroes cannot exist in an age of moral relativism, confirming Hawthorne's earlier pronouncement that "a hero cannot be a hero unless in an heroic world."[27] At the very least, the hero himself cannot be a relativist.[28] The term is devaluated almost beyond recognition when people, asked to name their heroes, simply point to sports and entertainment stars.[29]

A recent analysis by sociologist Robert Nisbet sees six attributes as essential to the hero.[30] First, says Nisbet, there must be an "unshakable belief in one's own charismatic nature—that is, belief that one is on a mission not merely to instruct the world but to liberate it, from dogma and superstition, from torment and tyranny." Second, there is the "heroic deed," which can be a book. Third is "the hero's obsessive sense of coming, as it were, upon a midnight clear, all the world hushed in unconscious anticipation." Fourth is "the all-important exile or ostracism as the direct and immediate consequence of the great deed." Fifth, there must be enemies. "Without hostile opposition, above all treachery, one cannot possibly become a hero." Finally, says Nisbet, talent or genius is not enough; the hero must be "larger than life."

There is little difficulty in demonstrating that Joseph Smith fulfilled each of these requirements for heroism. In fact, in commenting on one of the attributes, Nisbet writes: "Jesus, Buddha, Caesar, Cromwell, Washington, and Joseph Smith all knew, as true heroes must, their respective wildernesses, exiles, castigations by contemporaries, even their Elbas and Golgothas."[31] He might have added "and their Liberty Jails."

For present-day Mormons Joseph Smith's religious titles—especially prophet, seer, and revelator—have become central while his heroic attributes are clouded over. Many who staunchly accept him as a prophet know little of his biography. But those in tune who have sufficient interest in history can still see him in the heroic mold. For example, here is a summary by biographer John Henry Evans:

> Here is a man who was born in the stark hills of Vermont; who was reared in the backwoods of New York; who never looked inside a college or high school; who lived in six States, no one of which would own him during his lifetime; who spent months in the vile prisons of the period; who, even when he had his freedom, was hounded like a fugitive; who was covered once with a coat of tar and feathers, and left for dead; who, with his following, was driven by irate neighbors from New York to Ohio, from Ohio to Missouri, and from Missouri to Illinois; and who, at the unripe age of thirty-eight, was shot to death by a mob with painted faces.
>
> Yet this man became mayor of the biggest town in Illinois and the state's most prominent citizen, the

commander of the largest body of trained soldiers in the nation outside the Federal army, the founder of cities and of a university, and aspired to become President of the United States.[32]

Such is the stuff of hero-worship.

In the past century, perception of the heroic Joseph was yet sharper. Eight years after Joseph's death William Willes expressed his admiration in the following verse:

Say, Who beheld the pious rage
'Mong sects in this *enlightened* age,
And saw them differ, foam, and rage?
    The Prophet, Joseph Smith.
Who made the resolution rare
To ask the Lord in secret prayer,
"Which sect did all the truth declare?"
    The Prophet, Joseph Smith.
Who was encompassed and assailed
By powers of darkness, yet ne'er quailed
And wrestled until he prevailed?
    The Prophet, Joseph Smith.
Who saw the Lord descend and say,—
"Hear thou my son, he'll show the way,
"If you will now his laws obey?"
    The Prophet, Joseph Smith.
Who took the Plates the angel shewed,
And brought them from their dark abode,
And made them plain by power of God?
    The Prophet Joseph Smith.
Who did receive the power to raise
The Church of Christ in Latter-days,
And call on men to mend their ways?
    The Prophet Joseph Smith.
Who bore the scorn, the rage, the ire,
Of those who preach for filthy hire,

Was called by them "Imposter, Liar?"
    The Prophet, Joseph Smith.
Who brought the truth of God to view,
And led God's faithful people through,
And built the city of Nauvoo?
    The Prophet, Joseph Smith.
Who fell by ruthless mobbers' hands?
Whose heart's-blood stained Columbia's land?
Who died fulfilling Christ's command?
    The Prophet, Joseph Smith.[33]

Whatever one may think of the author's literary skills, it is clear that for him Joseph Smith was a hero.

In the immediate aftermath of Joseph Smith's death, with no sense of incongruity, W. W. Phelps could write the words familiar to all Mormons:

Hail to the Prophet, ascended to heaven!
Traitors and tyrants now fight him in vain.
Mingling with Gods, he can plan for his brethren;
Death cannot conquer the hero again.[34]

## ENDNOTES

1. Roy Porter, "Heroes in the Old Testament: The Hero as seen in the Book of Judges," in H. R. E. Davidson, ed., *The Hero in Tradition and Folklore*, London: The Folklore Society, 1984), 90-111.

2. Bill Butler, *The Myth of the Hero* (London: Rider and Company, 1979).

3. Butler, 35.

4. Joseph Campbell, *The Hero with a Thousand Faces* (1st ed., 1949; Cleveland, OH: World Publishing Company, 1956), 35.

5. Campbell, 17.

6. Campbell, 388.

7. See Owen Jones, "Joseph Campbell and the Power of Myth," *Intercollegiate Review* 25 (Fall 1989): 13–24, for a criticism calling attention to some of the implications of Campbell's approach. For present purposes I see similar limitations in E. M.

Butler, *The Myth of the Magus* (Cambridge: Cambridge University Press, 1948). Butler traces the "magus" from ritual beginnings on through Zoroaster and Moses to Christ and eventually Madame Blavatsky. Joseph Smith might fall into this sequence in some ways, especially emphasizing the magic of his early life as Michael Quinn has done. There is some overlapping between Butler's *magus* and *hero* as I am using it here, but I prefer to see the heroic in starker terms, reserving for other chapters the discussion of Smith's extraordinary powers and divine calling. The following quotations might be useful as we think of Joseph Smith: "It has sometimes proved impossible not to be drawn into speculations on the possible basis of objective reality underlying the supernatural claims made by or for various magicians; but I have avoided doing so as much as I could. For the nature of the evidence, when there is any evidence to scrutinise, is generally valueless from the critical point of view. The hostile and friendly witnesses are equally biased; and few indeed and far to seek are the dispassionate observers. Lecky very truly said that where supernatural phenomena are concerned humanity believes in the teeth of the evidence, or disbelieves in spite of the evidence, but never because of the evidence." E. M. Butler, 11.

8. Shoshana Knapp, "Napoleon as Hero," in Sara M. Putzell and David C. Leonard, eds., *Perspectives on Nineteenth-Century Heroism* (Potomac, MD: Studia Humanitatis, 1982).

9. Peter L. Thorslev, Jr., in *The Byronic Hero: Types and Prototypes* (Minneapolis: University of Minnesota Press, 1962), discusses the tradition of literary, not historical, heroes, but also recognizes the influence of Byron's example.

10. Dixon Wecter, *The Hero in America: A Chronicle of Hero-Worship* (1st ed., 1941; Ann Arbor: University of Michigan Press, 1963). See also Marshall W. Fishwick, *American Heroes: Myth and Reality* (Washington, D.C.: Public Affairs Press, 1954), with chapters on Smith, Washington, Boone, and others. See especially Paul K. Longmore, *The Invention of George Washington* (Berkeley/Los Angeles/London: University of California Press, 1988).

11. John William Ward, *Andrew Jackson: Symbol for an Age* (1st ed., 1953; New York: Oxford University Press, 1962).

12. Ward, 53.

13. Ward, 65.

14. Ward, 104.

15. Lucy Mack Smith, *History of Joseph Smith* (1st ed., 1853; Salt Lake City: Bookcraft, 1958), ch. 15; Donna Hill, *Joseph Smith: The First Mormon* (Garden City, NY: Doubleday, 1977), 35–36.

16. Hill, 145–46.

17. *Wilford Woodruff's Journal*, ed. Scott G. Kenney, 9 vols. (Midvale, UT: Signature Books, 1983–1984), 19 April 1837.

18. George Q. Cannon, *Life of Joseph Smith, the Prophet* (1st ed., 1888; Salt Lake City: Deseret Book, 1964), 20.

19. Hill, 283.

20. *New York Herald*, 7 November 1842.

21. Josiah Quincy, *Figures of the Past* (Boston: Little Brown, 1883), 376–400.

22. "Joseph Smith's Presidential Platform," *Dialogue: A Journal of Mormon Thought* 3 (Autumn 1968): 17–36. Included in this section are Richard D. Poll, "Joseph Smith and the Presidency, 1844"; Martin B. Hickman, "The Political Legacy of Joseph Smith"; a photographic reprint of *General Smith's Views*; and editorial footnotes.

23. Quincy, 399.

24. Randolph Starn, "Reinventing Heroes in Renaissance Italy," *Journal of Interdisciplinary History* 17 (Summer 1986): 77.

25. Thomas Carlyle, *On Heroes, Hero-Worship and the Heroic in History* (1st ed., 1841). Compare D. Sonstroem, "Double Vortex in Carlyle's *On Heroes and Hero Worship*," *Philological Quarterly* 59 (Fall 1980): 531–40.

26. Sidney Hook, *The Hero in History: A Study in Limitation and Possibility* (1st ed., 1943; Boston: Beacon, 1955), ch. 11. More important themes of Hook's study—the influence or noninfluence of heroes and historical causation—are beyond the parameters of the present chapter.

27. George Roche, *A World without Heroes: The Modern Tragedy* (Hillsdale, MI: Hillsdale College Press, 1987), 7 and *passim*. Hawthorne is quoted in Russell Kirk's introduction, v.

28. "When the primordial sentiments of a people weaken, there invariably follows a decline of belief in the hero. To see the significance of this, we must realize that the hero can never be a relativist." Richard M. Weaver, *Ideas Have Consequences* (Chicago/London: University of Chicago Press, 1948), 31.

29. See symposium "Where Have All the Heroes Gone?" in *Critic* 335 (Fall 1976): 28–35. Also see F. R. Lloyd, "Home Run King," *Journal of Popular Culture* 9 (Spring 1976): 983–95; P. A. Hutton, "From Little Bighorn to Little Big Man: The Changing Image of a Western Hero," *Western Historical Quarterly* 7 (January 1976): 19–45; and W. M. Clements, "Savage, Pastoral, Civilized: An Ecology Typology of American Frontier Heroes," *Journal of Popular Culture* 8 (Fall 1974): 254–66.

30. Robert Nisbet, *Prejudices* (Cambridge, MA/London, England: Harvard University Press, 1982), 152–58.

31. Nisbet, 154.

32. John Henry Evans, *Joseph Smith, an American Prophet* (New York: Macmillan, 1933), v.

33. William Willis [Willes], "The Prophet, Joseph Smith," *Millennial Star* 14 (1852): 303–4.

34. William W. Phelps, "Praise to the Man," *Hymns of The Church of Jesus Christ of Latter-day Saints* (Salt Lake City: Corporation of the President, 1985), number 27.

# In the
# Book of Mormon

"His own visions and visitations are not more marvelous than those reported throughout the Book of Mormon, which, in fact, they closely resemble."

—Hugh Nibley[1]

Some critics of the Book of Mormon consider it simply a product of Joseph Smith, a pious fraud produced entirely within the context of early national America. Mormons have traditionally accepted Joseph's own account of the book's miraculous discovery and translation from ancient plates. Some have attempted to come up with a compromise, ranging from the natural, ingenuous insertion of King James language when it seemed appropriate to a more complex meld of ancient and modern into a targum-like sacred text. What all of these theories—the hostile one of fraud, the traditional one of believers, and the efforts at compromise—have in common is the recognition that somehow the words of the Book of Mormon passed through the brain of Joseph Smith.

Using that simple fact as a point of departure, I would like to explore some passages that must have seemed especially relevant to Joseph Smith. I am referring not to moral teachings but to descriptions that touched very close to the reality of his own life experience. No one can prove that he produced these passages (or thought, pronounced, or read them) with his own life in mind, but I think we can assume that he would have responded with special sensitivity to words that seemed close to his own experiences.

Perhaps before even considering the examples, I should make it clear that this reading does not imply a fabrication, with Joseph incorporating his own experiences into a text ostensibly dealing with ancient people.[2] In fact, some of his own peak experiences and tribulations that closely resonate with the Book of Mormon came after its publication. All I wish to suggest here is that, far more than those of us who are average readers, he would have been especially tuned in to many of the passages in the book.[3]

Of obvious relevance are passages that specifically refer to a future prophet. When Lehi, blessing his son Joseph, tells of a future seer who will also be named Joseph after his father (2 Ne. 3:15), we understand this to be a strikingly specific ancient prophecy from the sixth century B.C. referring to the nineteenth-century prophet. But here I have in mind not such an obvious, explicit reference but rather various descriptions made in the course of the Book of Mormon account that on the face of it do not apply to Joseph Smith.[4]

Let us start with the description of visions. Lehi's vision at the very beginning ("he thought he saw God") led to praise, "for his soul did rejoice, and his whole heart was filled" (1 Ne. 1:15). By the time he was dictating these words of the Book of Mormon to a scribe, Joseph had also experienced visions. Did his soul rejoice? Was his heart filled? Would he have reflected on the comparison, saying, in effect, "Yes, that is the way one feels after such a marvelous experience"? It is instructive to consider all the visions in the Book of Mormon in the same light: Would they have rung true to Joseph Smith? Would he have seen in them parallels to his own supernatural communications? We make mention of these revelatory experiences with humility and an advance awareness that our usual categories of thought may not suffice to explain them.

The Book of Mormon describes a future time—from the context, obviously referring to the generation of Joseph Smith—when there would be different churches, "when the one shall say unto the other: Behold, I, I am the Lord's; and the others shall say: I, I am the Lord's; and thus shall every one say that hath built up churches, and not unto the Lord" (2 Ne. 28:3). Is this unrelated to the circumstance of different competing religions in upstate New York, "some crying 'Lo, here!' and others 'Lo, there!' Some were contending for the Methodist faith, some for the Presbyterian, and some for the Baptist" (Pearl of Great Price, Joseph Smith—History [JS—H] 1:5). Is the frequent alignment of "contention" with unrighteousness and departure from the ways of God in the Book of Mormon unrelated to the sectarian strife of the early nineteenth century? As the words of the scriptural text passed through his mind and came from his lips, or afterwards as he read them, would Joseph Smith have been oblivious to the contemporary scene? It was the resurrected Savior who is quoted in the Book of Mormon as saying: "For verily, verily I say unto you, he that hath the spirit of contention is not of me, but is of the devil, who is the father of contention, and he stirreth up the hearts of men to contend with anger, one with another" (3 Ne. 11:29).

In addition to a general context of contending, incompatible claims, some of the elements of Joseph Smith's First Vision as he later described it were a strong desire, a recognition that God would communicate (prompted by the epistle of James), the request in prayer, and a gratifying sense of being forgiven for his sins. In the Book of Mormon we read of Nephi's great desire, his recognition that God granted revelations (1 Ne. 10:17–19), his request (19:3), followed of course by a sublime revelation. Later, Enos pled with the Lord, crying unto him "in mighty prayer and supplication." Finally came the voice of the Lord: "Enos, thy sins are forgiven thee, and thou shalt be blessed" (Enos 2–5). Are we to think that such passages struck no chord of response in Joseph Smith, who, recalling his First Vision in 1832, wrote, "I saw the Lord and he spake unto me saying Joseph my son thy sins are forgiven thee"?[5] In a sense, then, we have in the Book of Mormon, published in 1830, not a report of the 1820 First Vision, but descriptions of other visions that include several of its constituent elements.

Then there is the reaction of the unbelievers. In Lehi's case "the Jews did mock him" (1 Ne. 1:19). Indeed, mockery was the standard response. When Lehi had a dream-vision of the tree of life, the faithful disciples were far fewer in number than the inhabitants of "a great and spacious building" who were "in the attitude of mocking and pointing their fingers" in scorn (1 Ne. 8:27). Later Nephi foresaw a generation when the record (the Book of Mormon) would come forth, when, as noted above, there would be different competing churches. Their message would be, "Hearken unto us, and hear ye our precept; for behold there is no God today, for the Lord and the Redeemer hath done his work, and he hath given his power unto men. Behold, hearken ye unto my precept; if they shall say there is a miracle wrought by the hand of the Lord, believe it not; for this day he is not a God of miracles; he hath done his work" (2 Ne. 28:5–6).

It is hard to believe that Joseph Smith could have dictated these words or later read them without thinking of his own visions and, for example, the Methodist minister who "treated my communication not only lightly, but with great contempt" (JS—H 1:21).

How do believers react to ridicule? So desperate are we for approval, so responsive to peer pressure, that many, even after conversion ("after they had tasted of the fruit"), will become ashamed and fall away (1 Ne. 8:28). But Nephi, after his own vision, came to recognize the large and spacious building as "vain imaginations and pride of the children of men" (1 Ne. 12:18). He reaffirmed his own sincerity, that he was not faking or trying to win notoriety: "For the fulness of mine intent is that I may persuade men to come unto the God of Abraham, and the God of Isaac, and the God of Jacob, and be saved" (1 Ne. 6:4). And rather than being swayed by the amused and condescending ridicule of cultured despisers, he "heeded them not" (1 Ne. 8:33).

Would Joseph Smith have gone over such descriptions without thinking of the superciliously negative reaction to his own stubborn insistence that he had seen a vision? "Why does the world think to make me deny what I have actually seen? For I had seen a vision; I knew it, and I knew that God knew it, and I could not deny it, neither dared I do it; at least I knew that by so doing I would offend God, and come under condemnation" (JS—H 1:25).

One of the most basic premises of Joseph Smith from the First Vision onward was that God was still a God of miracles, that he did speak to his children according to their need and their faith, this in contrast to the common attitude that such divine intervention occurred only in Bible times. In the Book of Mormon, after Nephi had heard of his father's momentous dream and desired to see and know for himself, he wrote, almost as if insisting over and over again: "I, Nephi, was desirous also that I might see, and hear, and know of these things, by the power of the Holy Ghost, which is the gift of God unto all those who diligently seek him, as well in times of old as in the time that he should manifest himself unto the children of men. For he is the same yesterday, to-day, and forever; and the way is prepared for all men from the foundation of the world, if it so be that they repent and come unto him. For he that diligently seeketh shall find; and the mysteries of God shall be unfolded unto them, by the power of the Holy Ghost, as well in these times as in times of old, and as well in times of old as in times to come; wherefore, the course of the Lord is one eternal round" (1 Ne. 10:17–19).

Joseph Smith was ridiculed by ministers and critics who told him that "there were no such things as visions or revelations in these days; that all such things had ceased with the apostles, and that there would never be any more of them" (JS—H 1:21). Would not Nephi's fervent declaration have had direct application?

The Book of Mormon contains other passages describing the way prophets are received. For example, another Nephi was denounced by the Establishment, the judges, for wanting to "raise himself to be a great man, chosen of God, and a prophet" (Hel. 9:16). Ridicule and suspicion—these were the response of respectable people to the words of prophets. And anger. Samuel the Lamanite uttered these telling words:

> And now when ye talk, ye say: If our days had been in the days of our fathers of old, we would not have slain the prophets; we would not have stoned them, and cast them out. Behold ye are worse than they; for as the Lord liveth, if a prophet come among you and declareth unto you the word of the Lord, which testifieth of your sins and iniquities, ye are angry with him, and cast him out and seek all manner of ways to destroy him; yea, you will say that he is a false prophet, and that he is a sinner, and of the devil, because he testifieth that your deeds are evil. (Hel. 13:25–26)

It might be held that this is simply a restatement of how prophets are always received—a type established by such ancient prophets as

Jeremiah. But beyond that, I am here suggesting that Joseph Smith must have recognized significant points of close similarity to his own life experience.

In the course of his memorable dream, Lehi, after tasting the fruit that "filled my soul with exceedingly great joy" began to be "desirous that my family should partake of it also" (1 Ne. 8:12). Likewise Joseph Smith was anxious to share his great divine encounters with his family members. In the Book of Mormon narrative it is Father Lehi, Nephi, Sam, and eventually Jacob and Joseph (younger children born in the wilderness) who are the steadfast believers, while Laman and Lemuel personify doubt and murmuring. In a characteristic burst of sibling jealousy, they complain that their brother "has taken it upon him to be our ruler and our teacher" (1 Ne. 16:37). When he began to build a ship, they said, "Our brother is a fool" (1 Ne. 17:17).

The alignment was not always so stark. At one point even Lehi faltered (1 Ne. 16:20), and the elder brothers were able at times to submit sufficiently that Nephi "had great hopes of them, that they would walk in the paths of righteousness" (1 Ne. 15:5). But in the final analysis friction in the family led to schism.

What has all of this to do with Joseph Smith? How would he have recognized any of his own life in the scriptural account? The desire to share his convictions with other members of the Smith family was certainly present. We have no evidence of sibling rivalry, and the two older brothers, Alvin and Hyrum, did not reject their younger brother's claims. But perhaps for a time there was a concern in Joseph's mind about this possibility. Was Joseph ever called a fool? Did any family members protest that he, like Nephi, was following in the footsteps of a visionary father? Did the Smith family members, or some of them, complain of the "hard things" (1 Ne. 16:1) Joseph was telling them?

We are too lacking in detailed information about the Smith family dynamics during the decade of the 1820s to answer with certainty, and what we do know shows a rather incredible degree of family unity. Nevertheless, it seems highly unlikely that the Book of

Mormon passages now being considered were looked upon by Joseph as totally unrelated to his own family existence, as apprehension of possible reactions if not allusions to actual happenings. One can well imagine that in his family Joseph, like Nephi, spoke "in the energy of my soul" (1 Ne. 16:24).

The family of Joseph Smith, Sr., and Lucy Mack Smith was not always at the bottom of the social scale. There was some education, some degree of literacy, and for a while there was even the possibility of at least moderate wealth. But the expectations were disappointed, and most of the time—I am thinking of the move from Vermont to New York and the hard-scrabble existence of clearing fields and trying to pay off a mortgage during the fifteen years leading up to 1830— it must have seemed like bare survival. In Lucy Mack Smith's history we gain a picture of a family looked down upon, not quite acceptable in polite society, yet sincere, hardworking, religious, and conscious of a special destiny.

Would the depths of Joseph Smith's soul have been provoked by references in the Book of Mormon to "the pride of the world" (1 Ne. 11:36), "the vain imaginations and the pride of the children of men" (1 Ne. 12:18)? Lehi recalled that his son Joseph was born "in the wilderness of mine afflictions" (2 Ne. 3:1). Many times, especially after 1830, Joseph Smith must have felt that he was in the wilderness of his own afflictions.

Against this background, Joseph was faced with awesome challenges. Had he been able to look ahead from the spring of 1830, when the Book of Mormon was published and the Church was organized, how would he have reacted? It was not going to be a quick or an easy triumph. Accompanying the slings and arrows of persecution would come sickness, drivings from place to place, prison, and finally death.

Would he, then, have recognized some consolation in Lehi's great blessing on Jacob about the necessity of "opposition in all things" (2 Ne. 2:11)? Would he, too, have prayed that the Lord would consecrate his afflictions to his gain (2 Ne. 2:2)? And would he have been able to proclaim with Nephi, "I will go and do the things which the Lord hath commanded, for I know that the Lord giveth no commandments unto the children of men, save he shall prepare a way for them that they may accomplish the thing which he commandeth them" (1 Ne. 3:7)?

One of the recurring commonplaces in the Book of Mormon has to do with the inadequacy of words to express certain things. We should, it appears, recognize different levels to this problem. First is the distinction between speaking and writing, oral utterance as opposed to written accounts. It was quite possible to be "powerful" in the former while weak in the latter. Writing, as any teacher of composition knows, requires one to know about such practical matters as spelling, paragraphing, and punctuation. As found in the scriptures, too, mastery of some literary forms was included. Not just anybody who has the gift of gab is a skilled writer. And the words on a page are not presented by a human voice, with its pauses and emotional overtones. Here is Moroni's statement: "Thou hast also made our words powerful and great, even that we cannot write them; wherefore, when we write we behold our weakness, and stumble because of the placing of our words; and I fear lest the Gentiles shall mock at our words" (Ether 12:25).

Then, beyond this distinction, human language, oral or written, is inadequate to express the things of the spirit. Specifically, as prophets and mystics seem to agree, our human language systems, functional enough in workaday situations, are incapable of expressing that which lies outside their cultural context.

Again, what has all of this to do with Joseph Smith? In the late 1820s this young man was somehow producing a book of over 500 pages. He might have been quite articulate when talking to friends and family, but putting down something in writing was different. He was also experiencing additional encounters with God and angels— the revelations now found at the beginning of the Doctrine and Covenants. Can he possibly have been oblivious to his own frustrations when going over passages dealing with the specific problems of language, the difficulty of expressing the things of eternity, an awareness of weakness in writing, and an apprehension that future readers would "mock"? Again, in the same sense as before, we have "autobiographical" elements, unidentified as such, in the Book of Mormon itself.

The Book of Mormon tells of a series of prophets, great leaders chosen by God. Did Joseph Smith see himself as a modern equivalent of these men? It is hard to believe that he made no comparisons.

Consider Mormon and the skeletal account of his life we are given.[6] When he was "about ten" Mormon received a kind of calling from Ammaron, who said, "I perceive that thou art a sober child, and art quick to observe" (Morm. 1:2) When Joseph Smith was the same age, he was still recovering from the traumatic leg operation that had occurred when he was seven. He traveled to Salem and spent time with his Uncle Jesse. His mother remembered him as "remarkably well disposed." At age eleven Mormon was "carried by my father into the land southward" (Morm. 1:6) At the same age, in 1816, Joseph Smith accompanied his family in a move from Vermont to New York. When Mormon was fifteen, "being somewhat of a sober mind, therefore I was visited of the Lord, and tasted and knew of the goodness of Jesus" (Morm. 1:15). It was in his fifteenth year, as Joseph Smith later wrote, that he experienced the First Vision, seeing the Father and the Son (JS—H 1:7ff). When he was "about twenty-four" Mormon was to take the sacred plates from their hiding place in the hill Shim. Joseph Smith, who had turned twenty-four on 23 December 1829, was completing the translation of the Book of Mormon prior to its publication in the spring of 1830.

When Moroni took over the plates from his father, we find him addressing the future generation in which the record would come forth. It would come forth at a time when many disbelieved, did not believe in Christ, "imagined up" a god unto themselves, and despised those who believed in miracles. The similarity to Joseph Smith's time, at least as he experienced it, is obvious. But there are even interesting specifics. Consider some parallels.

## Mormon 9

27. Doubt not, but be believing, and begin as in times of old, and come unto the Lord with all your heart, . . .

## Mormon 8

26. . . . and it shall come in a day when it shall be said that miracles are done away . . .

14. . . . For he truly saith that no one shall have them to get gain; but the record thereof is of great worth; and whoso shall bring it to light, him will the Lord bless.

15. For none can have power to bring it to light save it be given him of God; for God wills that it shall be done with an eye single to his glory, for the welfare of the ancient and long dispersed covenant people of the Lord.

## Joseph Smith—History 1

11. . . . I was one day reading the Epistle of James, first chapter and fifth verse, which reads: *If any of you lack wisdom, let him ask of God, that giveth to all men liberally, and upbraideth not, and it shall be given him.* [the passage of course continues: *But let him ask in faith, nothing wavering.*]

21. Some few days after I had this vision, I happened to be in company with one of the Methodist preachers, who was very active in the before mentioned religious excitement; and, conversing with him on the subject of religion, I took occasion to give him an account of the vision which I had had. I was greatly surprised at his behavior; he treated my communication not only lightly, but with great contempt, saying it was all of the devil, that there were no such things as visions or revelations in these days; that all such things had ceased with the apostles, and that there would never be any more of them.

46. [Moroni] . . . Added a caution to me, telling me that Satan would try to tempt me (in consequence of the indigent circumstances of my father's family), to get the plates for the purpose of getting rich. This he forbade me, saying that I must have no other object in view in getting the plates but to glorify God, and must not be influenced by any other motive than that of building his kingdom; otherwise I could not get them.

By now, it seems unnecessary to ask the question: Could or did Joseph Smith see himself and his own experiences in the Book of Mormon?

In addition, of course, prophecies in the Book of Mormon refer to the future individual who will "bring forth" this sacred record: Ether 5:1–3 even seems to forget point of view. In his stance as a prophet standing alone, Moroni had been commanded to "seal up" both the record and the interpreters for a distant future generation. He quotes moving words from the Lord, including direct admonition to both Gentiles and the house of Israel: "Come unto me." But at this point, abruptly, we read: ". . . I have told you the things which I have sealed up; therefore touch them not in order that ye may translate; for that thing is forbidden you, except by and by it shall be wisdom in God. And behold, ye may be privileged that ye may show the plates unto those who shall assist to bring forth this work; And unto three shall they be shown by the power of God; wherefore they shall know of a surety that these things are true." These words put us squarely into the experience of Joseph Smith, who on the occasion of Moroni's first appearance to him had heard similar cautions about his motives and intimation that he would be able to show the plates to some individuals (JS—H 1:42, 46). Does Moroni not seem to be addressing Joseph Smith specifically? In any case, how can the words have been dictated by Joseph Smith in the late 1820s (or later read by him) without an acute awareness of their personal relevance? After all, Joseph was impecunious and, like all human beings, thought about financial security. And under some combination of circumstances only months before publication of the Book of Mormon in 1830 witnesses had testified of seeing the plates.

At the end of Joseph Smith's life, in Carthage Jail with death staring him in the face, he turned to the Book of Mormon. One has to wonder how this action fits with the claim that the whole thing was a fraud. If he would not then be prompted to admit that the jig was up and confess his gigantic confidence scheme, at the very least, one would suppose, he should have turned to the Bible looking for a passage about forgiveness. Instead he found his solace in the Book of Mormon, in Ether 12, where he read the following moving words:

"And it came to pass that I prayed unto the Lord that he would give unto the Gentiles grace, that they might have charity. And it came to pass that the Lord said unto me: If they have not charity it mattereth not unto thee, thou hast been faithful; wherefore, thy garments shall be made clean. And because thou hast seen thy weakness, thou shalt be made strong, even unto the sitting down in the place which I have prepared in the mansions of my Father. And now I, Moroni, bid farewell unto the Gentiles, yea, and also unto my brethren whom I love, until we shall meet before the judgment-seat of Christ, where all men shall know that my garments are not spotted with your blood." (Ether 12:36–38)

As quoted by John Taylor in Doctrine and Covenants 135 the word *Moroni* is replaced with the three dots of an ellipsis so that the reader would realize, in case it were not sufficiently obvious, that Joseph Smith in 1844 could utter the same words in his own right. If in Carthage Jail he read the entire Book of Mormon chapter he might well have recognized more than a little of his own life: the necessity for faith before receiving a "witness," rejection by people who would not believe because they saw not, the reaction of those who would mock ("Fools mock, but they shall mourn"), and the simple statement that at the judgment all would know that he (Moroni/Joseph?) had "seen Jesus, and that he hath talked with me face to face" (Ether 12:39).

Much in the Book of Mormon moves beyond such connections: the panoramic visions of the future, the history of wars and migrations, the religious teachings in memorable passages about such subjects as the resurrection of the dead. I have no desire to suggest that the book is *only* a reflection of Joseph Smith's life.[7] I can attest that other readers will find passages which reflect some of *their* feelings and life situation. Yet we have seen enough, I suggest, to be convinced that to a remarkable degree the Book of Mormon contains many passages that could easily be seen as describing not only the external circumstances but also some of the most sacred and intimate aspects of the nineteenth-century Prophet.

One explanation would be that in fabricating the book Joseph inserted some feelings based on his own experiences (although this does suggest, awkwardly for some, that he had genuine religious experiences). Another is that the process of translation was sufficiently flexible that words and feelings of his own were used precisely at the points where they were appropriate in describing other prophets who, human beings after all, had anticipated some of his experiences and emotions. I find it sufficient to say that, whether in the process of dictating it to his scribe or in later correcting, reading, or pondering it, Joseph Smith would encounter in the Book of Mormon more than a few passages that resonated powerfully in his soul.

## ENDNOTES

1. Hugh Nibley, *Tinkling Cymbals and Sounding Brass*, in *The Collected Works of Hugh Nibley* (Salt Lake City and Provo, UT: Deseret Book and F.A.R.M.S., 1991), 11:65.

2. I do not therefore accept the assumptions and conclusions of the following, although I note some of the same passages: William D. Morain, "The Sword of Laban: Joseph Smith, Jr. and the Unconscious," paper presented at Mormon History Association, Ogden, UT, May 1993; Robert D. Anderson, "The Sword of Laban: The Book of Mormon as Autobiography," paper presented at Sunstone Symposium, Salt Lake City, August 1993, and "The Autobiography of Joseph Smith in Third Nephi," paper presented at Sunstone Symposium, Salt Lake City, August 1994.

3. Unlike John L. Brooke, *The Refiner's Fire* (Cambridge: Cambridge University Press, 1994), who sees the Book of Mormon as an "autobiography" of the Prophet, I leave room for a genuine ancient history, an honestly lived life, and a shock of recognition.

4. For a listing of nine prophecies, not my subject matter in this chapter, see Richard Wadsworth, "Does the Book of Mormon Prophesy of the Prophet Joseph Smith?" *Ensign* 19 (April 1989): 52-53.

5. *The Personal Writings of Joseph Smith*, ed. Dean C. Jessee (Salt Lake City: Deseret Book, 1984), 6.

6. A comparison of Mormon and Joseph Smith is also found in *Church News*, 22 October 1988.

7. For parallels between the Book of Mormon and Joseph Smith's life, Robert Anderson, "Toward an Introduction to a Psychobiography of Joseph Smith," *Dialogue: A Journal of Mormon Thought,* 23 (Fall 1994), has a simple explanation: the book was a disguised, perhaps unintentional autobiography. This interpretation, as stated, is unconvincing. It does not recognize possibilities of recognition rather than a simple one-directional influence; does not account for life experiences of Joseph Smith with Book of Mormon similarities that occurred after the book's publication; and forces comparisons that do not hold up under scrutiny. Moreover, the bulk of the Book of Mormon text is untouched by such an interpretation. My interpretation here emphatically leaves room for the authenticity of the Book of Mormon.

# The Prophet:
# "Like Unto..."

"You could not discover the limits of the self even by traveling along every path: so deep a logos does it have."

—Heraclitus

I am Joseph, the prophet," said Joseph Smith as he introduced himself to Newel K. Whitney in Kirtland, Ohio, in February 1831. To the question "How did Joseph Smith think of himself and his life's mission?" the short answer is "as a prophet." Of course that term could be cynically applied to him, as it was to Robert Matthews (Matthias the Prophet), meaning a self-proclaimed prophet obviously suffering from delusions of grandeur or some form of mental illness.[1] Others meant to put Joseph Smith in the company of Muhammed, a prophet to his people but, in the view of middle-class Americans of the past century, one with a false message.

In common parlance, a prophet is one who prophecies in the sense of foretelling future events. Deuteronomy 18:21–22 is well known for offering this as the test of the prophet's legitimacy: does or does not the thing foretold by the prophet come to pass? To the extent that insight into the future was part of Joseph Smith's role, then, he satisfied the expectation. He came across to his followers as a latter-day John the Revelator, telling in detail of the judgments to come.[2]

More basic is the fact that the prophet proclaims the word of God to his generation, itemizing its sins, calling it to repentance, with the wrath to come either implied or explicitly described.[3] An hour's reading in the revelations of the Doctrine and Covenants should demonstrate clearly enough that Joseph Smith supplied copious evidence of both kinds of message: he foretold coming events, and he delivered "a voice of warning" to the modern world.

Joseph Smith also brought forth additional scriptures, thus enlarging the usual prophetic role. Besides the revelations of the Doctrine and Covenants, he translated the Book of Mormon and the Book of Abraham from ancient documents. (*Translation* cannot be understood in the usual sense, for he did not claim to know the original language of these texts and could accomplish the task only "by the gift and power of God.") An enormous scholarly literature exists on these scriptures that the Mormons accept along with the Bible. The simple point here is that written scriptures were among the most important productions of this prophet.

But beyond simply itemizing different aspects of his prophetic role, there is a more satisfying way, I believe, to get at what the term *prophet* meant to Joseph Smith. Looking back across the centuries, he was aware of other prophets. Which, if any, of these did he identify with? Of course he had his own uniqueness, his own setting, but, looking back, he could find shared experiences that made it possible to see earlier prophets as role models, as anticipators. To some degree he was "like unto" them. In the last chapter we remarked on a few such connections between Joseph Smith and Book of Mormon characters. To further grasp this dimension of his prophetic role, let us turn our attention to some of the ancient biblical patriarchs and prophets.

*Enoch.* We do not know much about Enoch from the Bible. Seven generations removed from Adam, he "walked with God" and "God took him" (Gen. 5:24). At the age of twenty-five Joseph Smith added more details, including a great panoramic vision from Enoch's vantage point of the future course of world events (Moses 5 and 6).[4] Without attempting a comprehensive analysis, let us simply observe that the City of Zion, far in the future from the point of view of ancient Enoch, would be built up in the last days and would join Enoch's righteous city. "And the Lord said unto Enoch: Then shall thou and all thy city meet them there, and we will receive them into our bosom, and they shall see us; and we will fall upon their necks, and they shall fall upon our necks, and we will kiss each other . . ." (Moses 7:63).

Since the New Jerusalem, the latter-day Zion, was to be built up in Jackson County, Missouri, under the leadership of Joseph Smith, it is clear that some kind of parallelism is envisioned. One characteristic of Enoch's righteous society was that there were no poor among them; Joseph Smith, anxious to establish justice in his day, strove mightily to get his followers to follow a system of communalism (not communism), which he, significantly, called the Order of Enoch.[5]

The first Zion, having been lifted up to heaven, would somehow rejoin the latter-day Zion. Enoch would meet his counterpart, the great prophet-seer-revelator-translator (D&C 107:92) of the last dispensation. There may even be a subtle suggestion that Enoch had appeared to his latter-day successor: "He is a ministering Angel to minister to those who shall be heirs of Salvation and appered [sic] unto Jude as Abel did unto Paul."[6]

Clearly Joseph Smith admired the ancient great-souled patriarch,[7] but deeper than admiration is the sense of identity, of performing parallel roles. We are not at all surprised to discover that one of the code names used to designate Joseph Smith in the early revelations was that of Enoch.[8]

*Abraham.* Also highly significant for the latter-day prophet was the ancient patriarch Abraham. The Book of Abraham, now part of the Pearl of Great Price, adds many details not found in the Bible and reinforces the central importance of Abraham. That Joseph Smith breezily made up the additional biographical incidents seems unlikely in view of the striking confirmation in other extrabiblical sources published only in the late twentieth century.[9]

Parallels between the lives of Abraham and Joseph Smith are also noticeable. Joseph Smith's prayer, leading to the First Vision at age fourteen, writes E. Douglas Clark, "echoes young Abraham's prayer at the same age. . . . Both men had been foreordained; both received the priesthood, preached the gospel, and encountered formidable opposition; both spoke face to face with divine messengers and God himself; both possessed a Urim and Thummim, translated ancient records, and wrote scripture; and both founded an influential community of believers."[10]

Clark goes on to point out other connections, including an appearance by Abraham to Joseph Smith. "A central purpose of the restoration is to make Abraham's promises effective for his descendants, who through temple ordinances may receive the blessings of Abraham." Despite his special mission, Joseph Smith claimed no monopoly on these blessings; all Saints "are commanded to come to Christ by 'doing the works of Abraham,' whose life constitutes a pattern."[11]

*Joseph.* The naming of Joseph Smith after the biblical Joseph, who was sold into Egypt, is alluded to in the Book of Mormon. Lehi, blessing his son Joseph (another individual with this same name), quoted ancient Joseph's prophecy of a future seer: "And his name shall be called after me; and it shall be after the name of his father. And he shall be like unto me . . . " (2 Ne. 3:15). The Book of Mormon was published in 1830; here was a passage referring to Joseph Smith, then twenty-four years old. To claim that he would in any significant way be like the ancient Joseph seems rather audacious.

That ancient Joseph was a type of Christ is one of the long-standing truisms of Christian biblical exegesis. Mormon religion professor Joseph Fielding McConkie has listed fifteen similarities between Joseph and Jesus.[12] But, remarkably, ancient Joseph also typified and foreshadowed his nineteenth-century namesake. Apostle Neal A. Maxwell has noted some of the similarities between ancient Joseph and nineteenth-century Joseph Smith. Both had "inauspicious beginnings"; both had visions when young; both were hated; both "knew sibling jealousy or other ill feelings"; both were "falsely accused"; both were "generous to those who betrayed them"; both were "jailed and knew what it was to be in a 'pit'"; both prophesied; both knew separation from family and friends; both were "amazingly resilient in the midst of adversity."[13] Others have also listed and commented upon the many parallels between the two Josephs.[14]

It would be claiming too much to say that Joseph Smith consciously saw to it that his life replayed much of the ancient Joseph's experience, but at times he was conscious of similarities. Writing from Liberty Jail, he said, "I feel like Joseph in Egypt."[15]

*Moses.* There is no greater Old Testament figure than Moses, who led the children of Israel out of Egypt. Teaching the Israelites anciently, Moses declared, according to the account preserved in Deuteronomy: "The Lord thy God will raise up unto thee a Prophet from the midst of thee, of thy brethren, like unto me; unto him shall ye hearken" (Deut. 18:15). The exegesis of this passage in Jewish and Christian traditions is interesting to trace. Christians have typically seen it as referring to Jesus Christ (see Acts 3:22–23).

Interestingly, in Joseph Smith's description of the early visits to him by the angel Moroni, in which the messenger quoted passages of scripture, one of those was Acts 3:22–23. "He said that that prophet was Christ; but the day had not yet come when 'they who would not hear his voice should be cut off from among the people,' but soon would come" (JS–H 1:40).

The Book of Mormon, too, states very clearly that Jesus fulfilled the prediction of being one "like unto Moses." Speaking to the Nephites in the western hemisphere, the resurrected Lord proclaimed: "Behold, I am he of whom Moses spake, saying: A prophet shall the Lord your God raise up unto you of your brethren, like unto me; him shall ye hear in all things whatsoever he shall say unto you" (3 Ne. 20:23).

But this is not quite the end of it. Others too could emulate Moses or look to his life as a foreshadowing of their later experience. Thus Nephi, demonstrating to his murmuring brothers that God's powers could do marvelous things, listed a series of remarkable parallels between the family of Lehi and the ancient followers of Moses. The exodus began with God's call; a miracle had occurred at the Red Sea; manna had been supplied in the wilderness; water had gushed forth from a rock; although led by God, the ancient Israelites too had murmured; nevertheless God had both chastised and led them; finally they reached the promised land. The Lehites were like unto the children of Israel, and by strong suggestion both Lehi and Nephi were like unto Moses (1 Ne. 17:23–32).[16]

It is not entirely surprising to read that the future prophet whose name would be Joseph after his father's would be "great like unto Moses" (2 Nephi 3:9). After ancient Joseph prophesied that Moses, or "a Moses," would have judgment in writing but would not be "mighty in speaking" and that God would raise up a "spokesman"—referring of course to Aaron—he went on to make a similar prophecy about the future prophet Joseph, son of a Joseph (2 Ne. 3:17–18). Sidney Rigdon was in 1833 declared a "spokesman" unto the people and unto Joseph Smith. (D&C 100:9). In 1844, almost in passing, Joseph remarked, "Moses was a stammering sort of a boy like me."[17]

As early as September 1830 the comparison was made: "But, behold, verily, verily, I say unto thee, no one shall be appointed to receive commandments and revelations in this church excepting my servant Joseph Smith, Jun., for he receiveth them even as Moses" (D&C 28:2).

In 1834, as the Missouri Saints were being driven from their homes, a revelation spoke of the future redemption of Zion: "Behold, I say unto you, the redemption of Zion must needs come by power; Therefore, I will raise up unto my people a man, who shall lead them like as Moses led the children of Israel" (D&C 103:15–16). That this individual was the President of the Church should have been made clear early in 1835 by these words: "And again, the duty of the President of the office of the High Priesthood is to preside over the whole church, and to be like unto Moses" (D&C 107:91). But it is not going too far, I think, to say that it was Joseph Smith, the founding prophet of the last dispensation, who was preeminently likened unto Moses.[18]

In describing an 1836 blessing in Kirtland, Joseph Smith wrote: "I then took the seat, and father annoint[ed] my head and sealed upon me the blessings, of Moses, to lead Israel in the latter days, even as Moses led them in days of old."[19] The following year, at a meeting in the Kirtland Temple, according to Wilford Woodruff's diary, "Elder Brigham Young one of the twelve gave us an interesting exhortation & warned us not to murmer against Moses (or) Joseph or the heads of the church."[20]

In important ways, like Brigham Young after him, Joseph Smith could be seen as a Moses to his people.

*John the Baptist.* John the Baptist, as portrayed in the New Testament, is a rather enigmatic figure. He does not loom large in terms of the amount of attention given to him. Yet he was clearly too imposing to ignore, and Jesus granted him more than a little importance. Scholars have suggested that the rivalry between his followers and those of Jesus continued for many years. Religion professor Robert Matthews has given the most thorough Latter-day Saint appreciation of this "bright and shining light."[21]

As he thought of John the Baptist, Joseph Smith might well have identified with his roughness. Lacking the outward sophistication of the world, the Baptist spoke from the wilderness. His message to his generation was direct: repent. All his life Joseph was acutely aware of his own disadvantages, his lack of education. He well knew that he would not cut a figure in the drawing rooms of New York and Philadelphia. Yet he had something to say and fearlessly raised his voice of warning to the world.

John the Baptist also of course died a martyr. To the extent that he had premonitions about his own violent death, Joseph might well have thought of this comparison along with other biblical apostles and prophets.

Most importantly, John the Baptist was a forerunner, he who prepared the way of the Lord and testified of him. As we all remember, a connection was drawn between him and Elias. Was he the Elias whose return had been predicted? Yes and no. Reading the New Testament passages, we recognize that there was ambiguity on this matter, no doubt reflecting disagreement in the first century. John both denied and admitted that he was Elias. Traditional exegesis has fastened onto the fact that he was a forerunner, a herald of the Messiah.

That Joseph Smith is drawn into this same pattern of thinking is obvious on the surface: for him the Second Coming of the Lord was nigh. As a kind of parallel or latter-day version of the Baptist, Joseph was forerunner and herald. The similarity was made quite explicit in the revision and expansion of the Bible now known as the Joseph Smith translation. His translation of Matthew 17:11–14 contains Jesus' response to the question of whether he himself was Elias:

> And again I say unto you that Elias has come already, concerning whom it is written, Behold, I will send my messenger, and he shall prepare the way before me; and they knew him not, and have done unto him, whatsoever they listed. Likewise shall also the Son of Man suffer of them. But I say unto you, Who is Elias? Behold, this is Elias, whom I send to

prepare the way before me. Then the disciples understood that he spake unto them of John the Baptist, and also of another who should come and restore all things, as it is written by the prophets.

"And also of another"—this is of course Joseph Smith himself. As religion professor Robert L. Millet has written, "Joseph Smith was the final great Elias before the Messiah, an Elias of the Restoration."[22]

*Paul.* The Apostle Paul, seen by some as the real founder of Christianity, may not be an obvious model for Joseph Smith. Yet after describing the ridicule and rejection of people in his neighborhood who heard of his First Vision, Joseph later wrote: "I have thought since, that I felt much like Paul, when he made his defense before King Agrippa and related the account of the vision he had when he saw a light, and heard a voice; but still there were but few who believed him; some said he was dishonest, others said he was mad; and he was ridiculed and reviled. But all this did not destroy the reality of his vision. . . . So it was with me." (JS—H 1:24–25).

As problems accumulated in his life, Joseph wrote: "deep water is what I am wont to swim in. It has all become a second nature to me; and I feel, like Paul, to glory in tribulation" (D&C 127:2). Later, only a month before his death, Joseph Smith, who had been reading from 2 Corinthians 11, wrote: "I, like Paul, have been in perils, and oftener than anyone in this generation. As Paul boasted, I have suffered more than Paul did. I should be like a fish out of water, if I were out of persecutions."[23]

Richard L. Anderson, a longtime student of Paul, has been struck by more than a few similarities between that New Testament apostle-prophet and Joseph Smith.[24] Both had a "first vision." Both delayed giving a description of the event. Both had revelations of the resurrected Lord. Both put forth insightful doctrinal instruction but did not claim to know all the answers. Testifying courageously on the basis of their firsthand experiences, both were "considered blasphemers by their contemporaries." Both had visions of the degrees of glory. Both prayed for their contemporary believers and worked to help them understand how to live Christian lives. Both sacrificed beyond measure for the work. Both bore powerful testimonies. Both anticipated martyrdom. Widely separated in time, culture, and incidental trappings, the lives of Paul and Joseph Smith nevertheless possessed "dramatic common denominators."

To find significant parallels and even points of identity with others would no doubt be possible. Daniel, Peter, John, and Nephi are just a few of the possibilities that suggest themselves. Striking parallels with the Book of Mormon prophet Mormon have already been pointed out in chapter 4. But most important by far is the partial conflation of Joseph Smith with Jesus Christ.

*Jesus Christ.* Joseph Smith of course did not consider himself superior or even equal to Jesus Christ. Jesus was divine, the only begotten Son of God. Joseph was human. Joseph accepted the divine Sonship of Jesus Christ, his divine role as Creator, and his unique atonement, never claiming any such significance for himself. Nevertheless, there are more than a few points at which Joseph Smith made comparisons between himself and Jesus, and other Mormons were not ashamed to do the same. Before declaring any such comparison blasphemous, let us see what specifically was meant.

First of all, both Joseph Smith and Jesus went through great difficulty and persecution. This is a general observation true of all the prophets and of course predicted by Jesus to be the lot of his followers: "Blessed are ye, when men shall revile you, and persecute you." (Matt. 5:11). At one of Joseph's moments of greatest trial, in Liberty Jail in 1839, he was prompted to ask the following deeply introspective question: "The Son of Man hath descended below them all. Art thou greater than he?" (D&C 122:8). The implied answer of course is that Christ had suffered and sacrificed far more, but it is significant that the comparison did come to mind.

The end of Joseph Smith's life provoked further comparison with Jesus. In each case there were traitors. In each case there was a voluntary submission. And in each case there was a claim of innocence. Neither Joseph nor his followers ever claimed that he was atoning for the sins of the world. What they were saying, in effect, is that on a lesser level Joseph Smith was experiencing something akin to what Christ experienced.[25]

But unmistakable similarities are there. Both Jesus and Joseph were born in lowly surroundings. Both had rather short lives. Both were prophets.[26] Both founded churches—Jesus his church in "the meridian of time," Joseph the same church restored in "the fullness of time." In the thought categories of Latter-day Saint dispensationalism, these were the two greatest outpourings of God's revelations and authority. Joseph Fielding McConkie lists ten points of identity.[27] As Francis M. Gibbons, General Authority and writer, has pointed out, differences as well as similarities exist, but the similarities are there.[28] In important ways Joseph Smith was like unto Christ.

In a further effort to avoid misunderstanding, we shall return to this comparison in chapter 7.

*Conclusion.* What are we to make of such parallels across time? It seems to me that two different frames of reference are useful here. First is typology. The word has different meanings but here refers to a conception of human time that saw a relationship between an earlier person or event and a later one. More specifically, as developed by Christians in the patristic period, following leads laid down in the New Testament itself, Old Testament persons, events, or even objects were seen as foreshadowing the New Testament. Most commonly it was Christ himself who was typified by such personages as David or Joshua, but even Noah's ark could be seen as a type pointing to Christ's atoning sacrifice on the cross or the church he established.[29]

The typological understanding of human experience was pervasive in the Middle Ages, but it continued for many generations longer. Far more than we had earlier thought, typological thinking was still widely accepted in colonial and early national America.[30] And the idea is explicitly spelled out in the Book of Mormon.[31] I am arguing here that the typological mindset, far from being confined to the Bible and the Book of Mormon, extended on into Joseph Smith's self-concept and self-presentation. Like John Bunyan, who earlier in *Grace Abounding* had seen himself as an antitype of Moses,[32] Joseph

Smith saw himself as having been prefigured by prophets from the distant past. For his generation he was an Enoch, a Moses, a Joseph, a Paul, and, to a lesser degree, even a Jesus.

The second frame of reference I wish to invoke is that of identity as projected or created in autobiography. To determine who or what one *is*, is far from a simple matter.[33] Part of the problem is determining which categories, labels, or roles one will select as most determinative of one's essence, or, more likely, experience as inevitable, as imposed from outside. As several recent studies have conclusively pointed out, autobiography as a literary form has had for its characteristic task self-fashioning, invention of the self, and at times a conscious modeling on the lives of earlier prototypes.[34]

Did Joseph Smith set out with malice aforethought to imitate the earlier heroic figures? Was his life a conscious playing out of a role he had selected for himself? If such questions are simply another way of charging him with charlatanry, perhaps we should be cautious, remembering the honorable tradition of *imitatio* as a way of elevating our individual lives.[35] And it is worth stating something rather obvious: it is far easier to select a noble individual of the present or the past as one's ideal than it is to replicate that life to any significant degree. However motivated, Joseph was living a life—acting out a role or roles—of immense, archetypal scope.

I have not here attempted to make a case that Joseph Smith *was* a prophet. Instead, I have probed some aspects of his self-concept, which were then conveyed to his followers. Clearly he identified strongly with certain figures from the deep past—Enoch, Abraham, Joseph, Moses, John the Baptist, Paul, and Jesus—with whom he was connected by invisible threads. He thought of himself as, like them, a prophet, and for his followers that was what he was.[36]

ENDNOTES

1. Paul E. Johnson and Sean Wilentz, *The Kingdom of Matthias* (New York/Oxford: Oxford University Press, 1994).

2. Two of the most specific works on this subject are Nephi L. Morris, *Prophecies of Joseph Smith and Their Fulfillment* (2d ed.; Salt Lake City: Deseret Book, 1926); and Duane S. Crowther, *The Prophecies of Joseph Smith* (Salt Lake City: Bookcraft, 1963).

3. Abraham J. Heschel, *The Prophets* (New York: Jewish Publication Society of America, 1962).

4. For scriptural references I use standard citation form for the Bible and for the other three "standard works" of The Church of Jesus Christ of Latter-day Saints. Section numbers of the Doctrine and Covenants as well as chapter-verse for the Book of Mormon are slightly different for the editions of the Reorganized Church of Jesus Christ of Latter Day Saints. Although the RLDS Church does not accept the Pearl of Great Price in its canon, it does not deny, I think, that Joseph Smith somehow produced the books of Moses and Abraham, which were first published in early Mormon periodicals.

5. Commenting on deed-forms found in the papers of Edward Partridge, B. H. Roberts said: "The first of the following deed-forms was used in consecrating property to the Church; the second, in securing the stewardship to those entering into the law of consecration and stewardship, sometimes called the order of Enoch, because it was the law under which the Patriarch Enoch and his people lived." Joseph Smith, *History of The Church of Jesus Christ of Latter-day Saints*, ed. B. H. Roberts, 7 vols. (Salt Lake City: The Church of Jesus Christ of Latter-day Saints, 1932–1951), 1:365; hereafter abbreviated as *HC*. See also Leonard J. Arrington et al., *Building the City of God: Community and Cooperation among the Mormons* (Salt Lake City: Deseret Book, 1976); and Leonard J. Arrington, "Early Mormon Communitarianism: The Law of Consecration and Stewardship," *Western Humanities Review* 7 (Autumn 1973): 341–69.

6. Sermon of 5 October 1840. Andrew F. Ehat and Lyndon W. Cook, eds., *The Words of Joseph Smith* (Provo, UT: BYU Religious Studies Center, 1980), 41.

7. "The reason why I feel so good is because I have a big soul. There are men with small bodies who have got souls like Enoch. We have gathered our big souls from the ends of the earth." *HC*, 6:300.

8. As in Doctrine and Covenants 92, 96, and 104. See early editions or versions as published in *HC*, 1:352, 2:54. On the general topic, including current fascination with the apocryphal Book of Enoch, see Hugh Nibley, *Enoch the Prophet* (Salt Lake City and Provo, UT: Deseret Book and F.A.R.M.S., 1986). For comparisons with the Enoch of the kabbalah, see Harold Bloom, "The Religion-Making Imagination of Joseph Smith," *Yale Review* 80 (April 1992): 29–30, 32.

9. Hugh Nibley, *Abraham in Egypt* (Salt Lake City: Deseret Book, 1981); and Hugh Nibley, "A New Look at the Pearl of Great Price," *Improvement Era* 71–73 (January 1968–May 1970).

10. *Encyclopedia of Mormonism*, 4 vols. (New York: Macmillan, 1992), 1:8.

11. *Encyclopedia of Mormonism*, 1:8.

12. Joseph Fielding McConkie, *His Name Shall Be Joseph* (Salt Lake City: Hawkes Publishing Co., 1980), 78–79.

13. Neal A. Maxwell, "A Choice Seer," *Ensign* 16 (August 1986): 6–15.

14. McConkie, 80–83; Ann N. Madsen and Susan Easton Black, "Joseph and Joseph: 'He Shall Be Like unto Me' (2 Nephi 3:15)," in *The Old Testament and the Latter-day Saints* (Salt Lake City: Randall Books, 1986), 25–40.

15. Neal A. Maxwell, *But for a Small Moment* (Salt Lake City: Bookcraft, 1986), 106–7.

16. George S. Tate, "The Typology of the Exodus Pattern in the Book of Mormon," in Neal A. Lambert, ed., *Literature of Belief: Sacred Scripture and Religious Experience* (Provo, UT: BYU Religious Studies Center, 1981), 245–62.

17. *HC*, 6:478.

18. John A. Widtsoe, *Evidences and Reconciliations*, 3 vols., 2d ed. (Salt Lake City: Bookcraft, 1951), 1:197.

19. *The Personal Writings of Joseph Smith*, ed. Dean C. Jessee (Salt Lake City: Deseret Book, 1984), 145.

20. Entry for 10 January 1837 as transcribed in Dean C. Jessee, ed., "The Kirtland Diary of Wilford Woodruff," *Brigham Young University Studies* 12 (Summer 1972): 382.

21. Robert J. Matthews, *A Burning Light: The Life and Ministry of John the Baptist* (Provo, UT: Brigham Young University Press, 1972).

22. Robert L. Millet, "Joseph Smith among the Prophets," in Susan Easton Black and Charles D. Tate, Jr., eds., *Joseph Smith: The Prophet, the Man* (Provo, UT: BYU Religious Studies Center, 1993), 19.

23. *HC*, 6:408.

24. Richard L. Anderson, "Parallel Prophets: Paul and Joseph Smith," *Ensign* 15 (March 1985): 12–17.

25. "All prophets to one degree or another are in the similitude of the Savior. Prophets stand as living types or models of the Christ." McConkie, 216.

26. On Jesus as prophet, see John 6:14.

27. McConkie, 218–19.

28. Francis M. Gibbons, "The Savior and Joseph Smith—Alike Yet Unlike," *Ensign* (May 1991): 32–33.

29. The most important single study is Henri de Lubac, *Exégèse médiévale: les quatre sens de l'écriture*, 4 vols. (Paris: Aubier, 1959- ). But see also Paul J. Korshin, *Typologies in England, 1650–1820* (Princeton, NJ: Princeton University Press, 1982).

30. Sacvan Bercovitch, *Typology and Early American Literature* (Amherst: University of Massachusetts Press, 1972); Sacvan Bercovitch, *The Puritan Origins of the American Self* (New Haven, CT: Yale University Press, 1975); Ursula Brumm, *Die religiöse Typologie im amerikanischen Denken* (Leiden: Brill, 1963).

31. In addition to the George S. Tate article previously cited, see Bruce W. Jorgensen, "The Dark Way to the Tree: Typological Unity in the Book of Mormon";

and Richard Dilworth Rust, "'All Things Which Have Been Given of God . . . Are the Typifying of Him': Typology in the Book of Mormon"—both in *Literature of Belief: Sacred Scripture and Religious Experience*, ed. M. Gerald Bradford (Provo, UT: BYU Religious Studies Center, 1981).

32. See chapter on "The Hermeneutic Imperative" in Linda H. Peterson, *Victorian Autobiography: The Tradition of Self-Interpretation* (New Haven, CT: Yale University Press, 1986), especially 6–7, 10, 21.

33. See P. Gleason, "Identifying Identity: A Semantic History," *Journal of American History* 15 (Winter 1984): 365–85; G. F. Macdonald, ed., *Perception and Identity* (Ithaca, NY: Cornell University Press, 1979); and R. K. Fenn, "Religion, Identity and Authority in the Secular Society," in Roland Robertson and Burkart Holzner, eds., *Identity and Authority: Explorations in the Theory of Society* (New York: St. Martin's, 1979).

34. See especially Stephen J. Greenblatt, *Renaissance Self-Fashioning: From More to Shakespeare* (Chicago: University of Chicago Press, 1980); Paul J. Eakin, *Fictions in Autobiography: Studies in the Art of Self-Invention* (Princeton, NJ: Princeton University Press, 1985); and Peterson, *Victorian Autobiography: The Tradition of Self-Interpretation*. On modeling see especially Karl F. Morrison, *The Mimetic Tradition of Reform in the West* (Princeton, NJ: Princeton University Press, 1982); also Glenn W. Olsen, "St. Augustine and the Problem of the Medieval Discovery of the Individual," *Word and Spirit* 9 (1987): 129–56, with bibliographical leads. A seminal article is Georges Gusdorf, "Conditions and Limits of Autobiography," reproduced in translation in James Olney, ed., *Autobiography: Essays Theoretical and Critical* (Princeton, NJ: Princeton University Press, 1980), 28–48.

35. From a lengthy scholarly literature on the imitation of Christ I cite one example: John D. Laurance, *Priest as Type of Christ: The Leader of the Eucharist in the Salvation History according to Cyprian of Carthage* (New York: Lang, 1984).

36. Writes Kenelm Burridge in *New Heaven, New Earth* (1960): "If we are confronted with evidence of a divine revelation, we cannot think it irrelevant or irrational or fantasy or wishful thinking. We must take it seriously and try to account for what actually occurs. Even if our private assumptions do not admit of such a thing as divine revelation, we must admit that for others it does exist." Quoted by Marvin S. Hill in *Journal of Mormon History* 3 (1976): 104–5.

# In the Mormon Folk Memory

"We fear that many things that are reported as coming from the Prophet Joseph, and other early elders in the church, by not being carefully recorded or told with strict regard for accuracy, have lost something of their value as historical data."

—Joseph F. Smith

At his death in 1844, Joseph Smith's life span had lasted less than thirty-nine years, his leadership of the church he had organized, only fourteen years. Yet his impact on his followers continued. Their grief-stricken numbness in mid-1844 was soon followed by fond recollections, as those who had known him sat around the fireplace and exchanged stories. In the East, in the Midwest, and especially in Utah those who had known Joseph Smith told and retold the stories of their experiences with him. Some of the accounts were told in sermons, some in letters. As years passed, old-timers who remembered the Prophet were called upon to give their recollections in meetings and celebrations or write a piece for the newspaper or one of the Church magazines. Not surprisingly, there was some repetition as the stories were told and retold, as they were improved upon, and as published versions were picked up and transmitted orally. Those who remembered were soon outnumbered by those who knew Joseph only by reputation. But the telling of stories continued. This was the posthumous Joseph Smith as he lived in the collective memory of his people.

We are handicapped by being unable to listen to the actual voices of those who in the late nineteenth century told these stories. Limited to the written word, we are a step away from the ideal terrain for folklore research. However, by drawing upon sermons—which in Mormon usage were unstructured and conducive to spontaneous recollections—as well as diaries and letters we get close to the real-life situations in which these stories were told. Also, since the published stories were almost always an extension of previously told stories in the oral tradition, and since, once they were published, they had a feedback effect in being picked up and told again and again, there is no need to exclude published legends from present consideration.[1]

It is not my intent to provide an exhaustive catalogue of all stories told about Joseph Smith.[2] Rather, my purpose is to provide a simple but usable taxonomy and a selection of examples. Also, I have attempted to assess the value of this material for both the biographer and the historian.

## Human Qualities

In many stories Joseph Smith's warm and endearing qualities as a human being were mentioned. Contrary to the negative image of "old Joe Smith" that was promulgated during his lifetime—an image that combined the conniver, the fraud, the despot, the exploiter, and the rake—these storytellers seemed to say, "No, he was a good person. Here is what I remember about him."

In the Mormon collective memory Joseph emerges as a loving husband and father, someone who was kind to children. Margaret Burgess, daughter of William McIntyre, told of a touching incident when Joseph came to the McIntyre home, took the starving baby from its sick mother "to his own home where his wife gave it nourishment from her own breast, she having buried her own babe." When the McIntyre infant died, Joseph "grieved as if he had lost one of his own," embraced "the little cold form," and said, "Mary, oh my dear little Mary." Margaret also remembered when as a toddler she wandered into a side lane and became stuck in the mud. Joseph saw her there, came over, lifted her out, cleaned the mud from her shoes with tufts of grass, wiped the tears from her face with his handkerchief, and carried her home to her mother.[3] Story after story attests to the Prophet's generous and affectionate attitude toward children, demonstrating that he was open to the impulses of the heart and identifying him with the simple virtues of childhood.[4]

Contrary to the early efforts of his detractors to portray him as a lazy ne'er-do-well, Joseph Smith was remembered by his people as a hard worker.[5] He was remembered as a neat and responsible house-holder. Jesse W. Crosby told how Joseph "always left his fence clear of everything that might gather fire, such as underbrush, loose limbs, and tall strong weeds." In his wood yard "logs were neatly piled and all trash cleared away. If he did not finish the log on which he was chopping the remnant was laid back on the pile and not left on the ground for a stumbling block. The chips he made he picked up himself into a basket and put them in a wooden box which stood in the woodyard, or carried them into the house to be burned." His fields "were always in good condition and yielded well." When visitors came, "their teams were fed the best of hay and his barn was full." The reminiscence continues, "No other orchard had as fine fruit as did his." And "if an inferior cow was by any means shoved onto him it would be but a short time before she became a first class milker."[6] In pioneer Utah, where there was apparently a certain amount of littering and poor upkeep—witness Brigham Young's repeated scoldings—it was valuable to recall such a Joseph Smith, the master householder and manager, at the center of a charming scene reminiscent of the Dutch masters.

## Physical Strength

Closely related to the human qualities were stories of Joseph's great physical strength. He was not quite Paul Bunyan in these stories, perhaps, but some of his friends would have put him in the same league with Daniel Boone and Davy Crockett. This was the Joseph of exuberant spirits, who could wield an ax with the best of men.[7] He would bat a ball into the next county,[8] win any contest at stick pulling,[9] and straighten a bent axle-tree that had resisted the efforts of several other men.[10]

His prowess at fighting and defeating tough braggarts started when he was a boy and continued into manhood, when he was said to be able to defeat all comers in wrestling.[11] In one interesting variant of the champion wrestler, Joseph's human qualities were revealed as he threw down Howard Coray, a friend who was smaller and lighter, broke his leg, and then—full of remorse—carried the injured man to safety and tenderly nursed and blessed him.[12] In another variant it was not Joseph who won the wrestling match but Joseph who, standing on the side, inspired young Mormon Philemon Merrill with faith sufficient to throw down a bully.[13] Nauvoo, the city of Joseph, was no place for rivermen—half-hoss, half-alligator though they might be—to intimidate God-fearing people.

One of the most interesting examples of Joseph's superhuman strength was when, as the story goes, he carried an exhausted friend (probably Oliver Cowdery) through the darkness and swamps away from the pursuing mob to safety—an all-night ordeal that conjures up images of Aeneas carrying Anchises from burning Troy.[14]

On another occasion Joseph found himself in a stagecoach, the driver of which had gone into an inn for a drink. When the horses took fright and started to run with increasing speed, the Prophet calmed the excited passengers. Then, in the manner of a Western movie hero, he went through the window, pulled himself up into the driver's seat, gathered the reins, and brought the horses under control.[15]

The nineteenth-century American hero was a man of physical strength. George Washington could throw a dollar across the Potomac; Abraham Lincoln was a champion rail-splitter—these were the qualities admired by Americans in their heroes. Frail asceticism was not in their catalogue of heroic virtues.[16] Joseph Smith, the six-foot giant, fit the stereotype, and stories of his deeds helped to perpetuate the image.

## Supernatural Glow

As some of the Saints looked back, what they remembered about their prophet, in addition to incidents showing strength, affection, and cheerfulness, was a kind of supernatural glow. His eyes looked right through them.[17] When he spoke, his words were so powerful that they shook the very souls of his listeners.[18] When he touched them or shook their hand, they were electrified.[19] When he was in a moment of ecstatic communion with the divine, or after emerging from a revelatory experience, his face glowed in an unforgettable manner.[20] At least this was the way the Saints remembered him. Not miracles in the sense of extraordinary deeds, these were clues, visible to the natural eye or otherwise accessible to the physical senses, seen as evidence of the Prophet's supernatural powers.

## Miracles

Even when they might not remember any actual words uttered by Joseph, his faithful followers in later years could recall certain incidents when he had performed miracles. I have in mind here not prophecies, which were basically verbal, but rather acts showing supernatural forces at work.

According to one of these stories, Joseph once said he had something that needed to be done that very night. He turned to a young man and asked if he would do it, and the young man said he would before morning. The young man "testified that he did do the job although he had to travel five hundred miles to do it—500 there and 500 back." Impossible? The teller of this story explained:

> I do not doubt but that if Joseph Smith required such a thing to be done, said it must be done, and delegated a man to do it who was willing, it would be done, and that by the person being wafted through the air by the power of God, equal to translation; whether the person went in body or in spirit, whether the distance was 500 or 5000 miles, it would be all the same. If he required such a thing it would be because God required it and all things are possible with God. That is my faith in the Prophet Joseph Smith.[21]

The Zion's Camp expedition of 1834 provided the setting for other recollected miracles.[22] In 1884 Zera Cole recounted that one night the company was camped on a prairie far from water. The weather was warm and the men and animals were thirsty.

> Joseph called for a shovel and as if surveying for the most convenient place for all started in to digging a hole like a well with his own hands, about the size of a wash tub, and but little deeper when water came up

and filled the hole, so that all the man and horses had plenty to drink. The ground seemed as dry, when they camped, as prairies generally are.[23]

If Moses could bring forth a gushing well by striking the rock of Horeb with his staff, it seemed reasonable to the Mormon faithful that their prophet would have similar powers.

Healings were the most frequent example of miracles. Especially memorable were those occurring at Nauvoo in July 1839.[24] In 1859 Charles R. Dana recalled the occasion in 1841 when his wife was sick "nigh unto death." He went in search of Joseph and, eyes full of tears, asked him to come administer to her. At first Joseph, who was pre-occupied with another matter, said he could not but on second thought said he would come presently. Here is Dana's account of what happened:

> My heart leaped for joy. I hurried home. I had not much more than got there before Bro. Joseph came bounding over the bottom like a chased roe. He asked me, "How long has she been so sick?" He then walked the house for some minutes. I began to fear that he considered her past recovery, but he finally went to the fire, warmed his hands, throwed his cloak off, went to the bed, laid his hands on her, and while in the midst of his administering to her he seemed to be baffled. The disease or evil spirit rested upon him, but he overpowered it and pronounced great blessings upon her. After he took off his hands he turned to me and said, "That sister will get well, take good care of her." . . . She began to amend from that hour. I firmly believe that if he had not been called in that she would have died.[25]

Not that Joseph Smith, any more than Jesus Christ, healed every person of every ailment, but his miraculous healings were frequent enough and impressive enough to be a source of faith and encouragement to his followers.

*Doctrinal Sayings*

If the remembered deeds and miracles were inspiring to the Saints, more substantive in content were the Prophet's words, his sayings. Many of these were expressed not in writing or even in sermons but in individual conversations. As the Saints remembered him, Joseph gave answers to all kinds of doctrinal questions, some important, others seemingly trivial. Toward the end of the century Oliver B. Huntington attributed to Joseph Smith the saying that the ark of Noah was built in or near South Carolina; that houses previously inhabited by wicked people should be thoroughly cleaned, fumigated, and dedicated by prayer, lest the wicked spirits afflict the new inhabitants; and that "every living thing that knows enough to run when you point your finger at it, will be resurrected."[26] Such utterances were essentially oracular. One of the most curious of such statements, again coming from Huntington, is the following:

> The inhabitants of the moon are more of a uniform size than the inhabitants of the earth, being about 6 feet in height. They dress very much like the quaker style and are quite general in style, or the one fashion of dress. They live to be very old, coming generally near a thousand years.[27]

Oliver Huntington wrote that he heard this from Philo Dibble, who was accustomed to going up and down through the communities of Utah giving lectures on Church history.

One question with important doctrinal implications has to do with the Mormon belief in a Mother in Heaven, most commonly known from one verse in Eliza R. Snow's hymn "Oh, My Father." As late as 1916 Susa Young Gates recalled what she had earlier heard from Zina D. Huntington Smith Young. It seems that Zina had lost her mother under trying circumstances and, full of intense grief, asked the prophet whether she would know her mother on the other side.

> "Certainly you will," was the instant reply of the Prophet. "More than that, you will meet and become

acquainted with your eternal Mother, the wife of your Father in Heaven."

"And have I then a Mother in Heaven?" exclaimed the astonished girl.

"You assuredly have. How could a Father claim His title unless there were also a Mother to share that parenthood?"[28]

These Huntingtons—Zina was Oliver's sister—got around. A fascinating family having close ties with both Joseph Smith and Brigham Young, they enjoyed talking about such things and seem to have seen it as their personal mission to preserve the choice experiences and sayings of Joseph Smith.

One question of special interest to many Mormons was the location of the Lost Tribes of Israel, who, as part of the winding-up scene, were expected to return. What had Joseph to say on this subject? In 1884 Abraham H. Cannon noted in his diary that he had called upon Eliza R. Snow, who said she had heard Joseph Smith say, "When the ten tribes were taken away, the earth was divided, so that they occupy a separate planet from this."[29] Martha Cox heard the same story from her father, who told her that the Prophet had said to him "that at the north pole the earth is convex or cup shaped with the deepest sea resting there. The planet that belonged to that part of the world would in time return to its place, strike the earth at that part, completing the sphere."[30] All of which led Eliza R. Snow to compose a hymn, three stanzas of which follow:

> Thou, earth, wast once a glorious sphere
>> Of noble magnitude,
> And didst with majesty appear,
>> Among the worlds of God.

> But thy dimensions have been torn
>> Asunder, piece by piece,
> And each dismembered fragment borne
>> Abroad to distant space . . .

And when the Lord saw fit to hide
The "Ten Lost Tribes" away,
Thou, earth, wast severed to provide
The orb on which they stay.[31]

The whole "doctrine," besides resting on the recollection of Eliza
Snow and Martha Cox, was found in the family tradition of Patriarch
Homer M. Brown, who in 1924 told in lavish detail of a conversation
between his grandfather, Benjamin Brown, and the Prophet.[32]

The trouble was that others remembered differently. In 1886,
when asked what the Prophet had said regarding the Ten Tribes,
Anson Call wrote: "I have heard Joseph say that the ten tribes were
in the northern interior of the earth, and that they retain their tribe
relations and their strength and manhood, that they have not dwin-
dled, as we have, for they have been favored of the Lord, and have
retained their organizations and understood well the redemption and
have ever had in their midst the true prophets of the Lord."[33] Did
Joseph Smith make both statements? Or only one? Or neither? Or
did he use a crucial word like "perhaps" or "possibly" that was forgotten in the later traditions?[34] In any case, one of the problems of
oral tradition as a source of doctrinal truth is well illustrated.

The pithiness of many of these sayings, especially those that were
passed on in successive generations, probably reveals something of
Joseph Smith's preaching style. The aphorism—the oracular, single-
sentence utterance containing a truth, a principle, or an alleged fact—
is familiar in some of the sections of the Doctrine and Covenants.[35]
After his arrival in Nauvoo, starting in January 1840, the Prophet participated occasionally in a kind of study group, minutes of which were
kept by William Patterson McIntyre. Although various people participated in the discussions and gave reports on special topics, it is interesting to note that on almost every question Joseph had the last word
and gave his views in a series of short pronouncements.[36] The constant
questions coming from the Saints, who assumed that he had answers to
all questions, must have reinforced whatever natural tendencies he had
in this direction. To say that his typical style was conducive to apho-
ristic declarative statements is not to claim that all the remembered

sayings are genuine, for it is precisely such short sentences that could be easily distorted or misremembered. More important, perhaps, is the fact that later recollections often failed to include the context, the question or situations that evoked the Prophet's answer. And one has to suspect that an occasional tongue-in-cheek mood was lost, if not on his hearers, at least by those in later generations who passed on the Smith apocrypha with utter seriousness.

## Practice and Policy

Where recalling what Joseph Smith had said or done became more crucial was on matters of practice and policy. In 1883, when the School of the Prophets was organized (or reorganized), the only survivor of the original School of the Prophets that existed at Kirtland in the 1830s was Zebedee Coltrin. Coltrin was called in and asked to explain the procedures. Did they have the ceremony of washing of feet? Did they kneel when praying or did they raise their hands? And what was the manner of administering the sacrament in Joseph's day? On this last question, Coltrin answered:

> The Sacrament was also administered at times when Joseph appointed, after the ancient order; that is, warm bread to break easy was provided, and broken into pieces as large as my fist, and each person had a glass of wine and sat and ate the bread and drank the wine; and Joseph said that was the way that Jesus and his disciples partook of the bread and wine; and this was the order of the church anciently, and until the church went into darkness.[37]

Similar questions were raised regarding procedures in the Kirtland Temple. It is significant that Church leaders, nearly forty years after the Martyrdom, still felt obligated to find out Joseph Smith's way of doing something. Yet after finding out the facts as best they could, the brethren did not feel obligated to follow Joseph on every jot and tittle, for they recognized that often he had acted in haste due to the exigencies of the time.

The importance of remembered conversations is illustrated by the policy prior to 1978 of not ordaining blacks to the priesthood, a practice which went back to the early years of the Church, but with at least a slight degree of inconsistency.[38] Some Church members, troubled by the apparent discrimination, cited the great vision of Peter that extended the gospel to the Gentiles as evidence of God's desire to treat all races alike. In 1879, a small group met in Provo, Utah, to attempt to establish what Joseph Smith had taught. Present were Abraham O. Smoot (a Kentuckian), President John Taylor, Brigham Young, Jr., Secretary L. John Nuttall, and Zebedee Coltrin. The whole discussion was based on the recollection of Coltrin. All the way back in 1834 Coltrin and John P. Greene had argued over the question and took the matter to Joseph, who (according to Coltrin) said, "Brother Zebedee is right, for the Spirit of the Lord saith the Negro has no right nor cannot hold the Priesthood."[39] Although this recollection did not determine policy in this case, it did much to reinforce it. The exclusionary policy came to an end, of course, in 1978 with a revelation "extending priesthood and temple blessings to all worthy male members of the Church."[40]

*Prophecies*

Many of Joseph Smith's remembered sayings were predictions about the future. Some of these predictions were canonical, written down as revelations in the 1820s or 1830s. Some were fulfilled in his lifetime; some, such as the prophecy of a war between the states to begin in South Carolina, were fulfilled later. Some, such as the prophecy that the Mormons would return to claim their "inheritances" in Jackson County, Missouri, are yet to be fulfilled.[41] The study of the Prophet's prophetic utterances is a specialty in itself and has been the subject of at least three books.[42] The prophetic recollections passed on by word of mouth were usually not the great cosmic utterances but rather short statements, often one-liners, easily remembered. All were fulfilled to the satisfaction of the narrator; in fact, this was usually the point of the story.

In one of these miniprophecies, as it was later remembered, Joseph once told W. W. Phelps and his wife that they never should taste death. Well, they died. Was this then an unfulfilled prophecy? Not in the mind of true believers. Here is the explanation later given:

> The manner of the fulfillment of that promise is rather singular. They supposed, and so did all that knew of the promise, that they were to never die, but the Lord does business in his own way and his way is not as the way of a man.
>
> Before Brother Phelps died he lost all his judgment, lost all his mind reason, consciousness and all sense. He knew nothing, not even his name, nor how to eat, thus being unable to taste of anything; not even death. His mind gradually dwindled, withered and dried up. His wife was killed instantly, so quickly that she had not time to taste of death. She was killed as she was dipping up a bucket of water from the ditch, a gust of wind hurled a board from a house and it struck her on the neck breaking it instantly. She never tasted of death nor even felt the blow.[43]

Another sepulchral prediction was the Prophet's prediction to Mrs. William Huntington that "her flesh should never see corruption." This was first taken to be a promise that she would never die, but of course she did. When the "old burying ground" in Nauvoo was moved outside the city, however, it was necessary to disinter her body, which was found to be "full, plump and looked natural in feature without a 'smell of corruption or decay.'"[44] Again, according to this report, the prophet was vindicated.

One of the favorite, noncanonical Joseph Smith prophecies was that the day would come when the Constitution of the United States would hang, as it were, by a thread and that it would be saved by the elders of the Church. Usually the first reference to this prophecy is cited as Brigham Young's sermon on the Fourth of July 1854.[45] In

1855 Jedediah Grant remembered something similar although the imagery was slightly different: "What did the Prophet Joseph say? When the Constitution shall be tottering, we shall be the people to save it from the hand of the foe."[46] Three years later, in 1858, Orson Hyde made a slight but important correction: "I believe he said something like this—that the time would come when the Constitution and the country would be in danger of an overthrow, and said he, 'If the Constitution be saved at all, it will be by the elders of this Church.'"[47] In 1870 Eliza R. Snow, citing her own memory, repeated the basic prophecy without Hyde's qualification: the Constitution would hang by a thread and the Mormons would "rise up" and save it and "bear it off triumphantly."[48]

It will be illuminating to consider the probable basis for these later recollections. It is easy to demonstrate that Joseph Smith had great respect for the U.S. Constitution, especially venerating its provision for freedom of religion; that he was disappointed and disillusioned with the failure of the state and national governments to protect the Saints in Missouri and Illinois; that he was contemptuous of many office holders and politicians of his day; that he had grim forebodings about the future, in which he saw, among other things, increased mob violence and the outbreak of a war between the states; that, being unable to endorse any of the major candidates in 1844 and seeing no other alternative, he put himself forth as a candidate for the Presidency; and that, in long-range terms, he saw some kind of political kingdom which would, in effect, be controlled by the Mormon leaders but would include non-Mormons and would protect all people in their rights. This whole congeries of ideas reflecting Joseph Smith's point of view in the Nauvoo period, roughly from 1840 to 1844, would seem to provide a plausible basis for expecting him to say something of the kind—the Constitution was in danger, would totter or hang by a thread, and would be saved by the Church—although it seems likely, from a naturalistic perspective, that he was thinking either in terms of his possible election in 1844 or, more likely, the establishment of a Mormon theocracy in Nauvoo or elsewhere that would become stronger and stronger, a bastion of security while the rest of the country was collapsing in violence and warfare.[49]

Interestingly enough, primary documents in the Church Archives reveal that the basic assertions about the failure of the Constitution did not have to await the disappointments and disillusionment of 1842 and 1843 or the organization of the political kingdom and Joseph's decision to be a candidate in 1844. The following was written by Orson Pratt on 21 January 1841:

> He [Joseph Smith] says . . . The government is fallen and needs redeeming. It is guilty of Blood and cannot stand as it now is but will come so near desolation as to hang as it were by a single hair!!! Then the servants goes to the nations of the earth, & gethers the strength of the Lord's house, a mighty army!!! And this is the redemption of Zion, when the Saints shall redeemed that government & reinstated it in all its purity and glory!!! That America may be an asylum for the remnant of all nations.[50]

This curious statement is third hand. Orson Pratt was recounting to George A. Smith what Parley P. Pratt had written in a letter. The original germ is probably found in a sermon delivered by Joseph Smith on 19 July 1840. Unfortunately there are no verbatim transcriptions of most of his sermons, but the following notes, apparently taken at the time by Martha Jane Knowlton, suffice to make the point:

> We shall build the Zion of the Lord in peace until the servants of that Lord shall begin to lay the foundation of a great and high watch Tower. . . . Then the Enemy shall come as a thief in the night and scatter the servants abroad. When the seed of these 12 Olive trees are scattered abroad they will wake up the Nations of the whole Earth. Even this Nation will be on the very verge of crumbling to pieces and tumbling to the ground and when the constitution is upon the brink of ruin this people will be the Staff up[on] which the

Nation shall lean and they shall bear the constitution
away from the very verge of destruction.

The same sermon contains fulsome prophecies about the future glory
of Nauvoo. "It is evident that the prophecies about Nauvoo, like
Jackson County before it," Dean C. Jessee has wisely remarked, "were
contingent upon human conditions and failings."[51]

The Constitution-by-a-thread prophecy therefore rests on an
actual statement made by Joseph Smith in the year 1840, not long
after the failure of his effort to obtain help from the U.S.
Government. What may be more interesting is the fact that it was
not until after 1850 that this prophecy began to be a favorite among
members of the Church.

From that time forward, I believe, the prophecy was cited whenever the nation seemed on the verge of calamity or the Saints felt
threatened by national policies. Thus the Utah War seemed a possible fulfillment, as did the Civil War. When the anti-polygamy campaign got underway during the 1860s, 1870s, and especially in the
1880s, the Saints saw themselves as beleaguered defenders of the
Constitutional principle of freedom of religion. What was more natural than to recall over and over again something like this: "The
Prophet told us this would happen. The Constitution would hang by
a thread, but if we just stand for our rights, eventually we will save it."

In the twentieth century, the uses of the Constitution-by-a-
thread prophecy have been what might be expected: those who decry
the political trends of the times—the New Freedom, the New Deal,
and the welfare state—have seen everything from the progressive
income tax to the Supreme Court decision on prayer in the schools
as fulfillment of the first part of the prophecy. Psychologically, it
served the triple purpose of providing confirmation of the Prophet
(he had told them all this would happen), reassurance for the future
(the Constitution would be saved), and enhancement of their self-
importance (they would be the ones to save it). A prophecy with
possibilities of such frequent application is understandably one of the
favorites in the lexicon of remembered sayings of Joseph Smith.[52]

## Occasion for Stories

Although these stories were in circulation at all times, they were stimulated and encouraged by certain events. In the 1860s, for example, when the Reorganized Church of Jesus Christ of Latter Day Saints sent missionaries (including the sons of Joseph Smith, Jr.) to Utah, it was natural that certain recollections would come to the fore. Later, the litigation over ownership of the Temple Lot in Independence, Missouri, resulted in many statements about the early Church.[53] Every year on Joseph Smith's birth and death anniversaries, 23 December and 27 June, the thoughts of some turned to the Prophet, often in sacrament meeting talks or testimonies. The 6 April date for the organization of the Church is another such occasion. And in 1880 began a series of jubilee (fifty-year) commemorations—of the organization of the Church, Zion's Camp, the founding of the Relief Society, the Prophet's death, the arrival in the Salt Lake Valley—in connection with which recollections would very naturally be expressed.

Of course the number of those who remembered Joseph Smith, who had had direct encounters with him, steadily decreased. In 1873, Brigham Young, speaking in Logan, said:

> I believe I will do myself the favor, and gratify myself so far as to ask those of my brethren and sisters now present, who were personally acquainted with Joseph Smith, to raise their right hands. (A very few hands up.) There is a few, but very few, not above one to twenty, and perhaps not more than one to fifty in this congregation who ever saw Joseph Smith.[54]

By the 1890s those who had been in their twenties at the Prophet's death were roughly in their seventies; those who had been children, roughly in their fifties and sixties. Life expectancy being less then than now, these survivors were not numerous. It was natural to pay some deference to them. Undoubtedly they thought it important to repeat for the edification of their family and friends whatever it was that they remembered about the Prophet and probably enjoyed doing so, for it enhanced their own importance in the eyes of others. All of this helps explain the character of many of the stories—the plethora of childhood recollections of the kindly Prophet, for example. Thinking in these terms, we can readily perceive that the life span in which the firsthand experiences were told stretched from 1844 to about 1914, with some tendency to cluster in the generation following the death of Brigham Young in 1877.

Certain characters loom especially large in the telling and retelling of these stories. Philo Dibble, Edward Stevenson, Jesse W. Crosby, Anson Call, Zebedee Coltrin, and Oliver B. Huntington— these were the old-timers who did most to keep stories about Joseph Smith in circulation during the 1880s and 1890s. To some extent they had indeed had direct experiences, and they were among the handful of survivors who saw it as their role to keep alive the memory of their departed leader. In addition, of course, Mormon leaders such as Brigham Young, Heber C. Kimball, Wilford Woodruff, and others also enjoyed recalling their experiences with Joseph Smith.

## Value of Material

What is the value of these stories? In a certain genre of faith-promoting discourse—sermons, magazine articles, and even books— they continue to be cited as evidence of the Prophet's awesome qualities without any hint that their reliability might be suspect. But even among the Mormons some of the stories were too strong for ready belief. In 1898 the *Improvement Era* carried the following editorial, probably written by Joseph F. Smith, member of the First Presidency and son of the martyr Hyrum Smith:

> We fear that many things that are reported as coming from the Prophet Joseph, and other early elders in the church, by not being carefully recorded or told with strict regard for accuracy, have lost something of their value as historical data, and unwarranted additions have sometimes been made to the

original facts, until it is difficult to determine just how far some of the traditions which have come to us may be accepted as reliable representations of what was said or what was done.[55]

Even though presented in a faith-promoting way, in other words, the stories about Joseph Smith could not be uncritically accepted at face value.

But what *can* these sayings and stories reveal about Joseph Smith? Are they to be rejected out of hand? The sensible approach, I think, is to be suspicious of them if they stand alone. Some of the stories cancel each other out, and others, as we have seen, are suspiciously consistent with the self-interest of the person doing the telling. If they can be pinned down close to the actual time and place they were supposed to have occurred, if they are consistent with the rest of what is known about the Prophet, and especially if there is confirmation from other evidence, they may have some use. The responsible biographer will use this material with caution. Mormons have rightfully protested when unfriendly biographers have accepted uncritically the affidavits taken from Joseph Smith's neighbors in 1833 and later; they were collected without adequate controls. It would be ironic to turn around and accept at face value the sayings and stories passed on by word of mouth fifty or a hundred years later.

But the stories and sayings of Joseph Smith as told after his death are indeed valuable source material, not for the life of the Prophet but for the popular mind of his people. They are a valuable source for studying the history of a religion originating with a prophet. Apparently, despite Joseph Smith's protestations to the contrary,[56] the words of a prophet assume a sacrosanct quality. The prophet is seen as having answers to everything; there is no conceivable question regarding past, present, or future on which he could not, in theory at least, provide an answer. Inevitably his followers cling to his words. Recollections of what he said on different occasions become more than simple woolgathering or idle conversation; they carry the potential, if accepted, of being authoritative. "Whatever he told us came from the Lord we accepted," recalled

Mercy Thompson in 1893, "and when he said the word of the Lord was thus and so, we knew it was so, and believed it without witnessing it ourselves, for we knew he would not tell us anything came from the Lord that did not come from the Lord."[57]

Mormonism in its first hundred years thus offers an illuminating case study of the transmission of testimony and some of the problems that can emerge as those who were acquainted with the founding prophet gradually die off and finally—as someone has said about the post apostolic period of early Christianity—none remains who can say, "I saw."

## ENDNOTES

1. One modern folklorist who has drawn heavily on printed material is Richard M. Dorson, as in *Jonathan Draws the Longbow* (Cambridge, MA: Harvard University Press, 1946). Stories about historical figures are considered fair game for the modern folklorist, who takes an enlarged view of his discipline. For further discussion of this question see Richard M. Dorson, *American Folklore and the Historian* (Chicago: University of Chicago Press, 1971) and *Folklore: Selected Essays* (Bloomington: Indiana University Press, 1971).

2. The single most convenient and available collection of stories told about Joseph Smith is Hyrum L. Andrus and Helen Mae Andrus, comps., *They Knew the Prophet* (Salt Lake City: Bookcraft, 1974). An older compilation is Edwin F. Parry, comp., *Stories about Joseph Smith the Prophet* (Salt Lake City: Deseret News Press, 1934). A primary source full of similar material is the journal of Oliver Boardman Huntington, typescript, Brigham Young University and LDS Church Archives. Other stories appeared in sermons published in the *Journal of Discourses*, 26 vols. (Liverpool and London: Latter-day Saints' Book Depot, 1854–1886), hereafter abbreviated as *JD*. A useful collection of Mormon folklore, although inadequate for the present topic, is Austin Fife and Alta Fife, *Saints of Sage and Saddle* (Bloomington: University of Indiana Press, 1956).

3. "Stories from the Notebook of Martha Cox," MS, LDS Church Archives; Parry, 23–27.

4. Among many references to Joseph Smith's fondness for children are the following: Parry, 31; Andrus and Andrus, 46, 99, 101, 102, 120, 127, 151, 154, 166. See also Leonard J. Arrington, "The Human Qualities of Joseph Smith, the Prophet," *Ensign* 1 (January 1971): 35–38.

5. Andrus and Andrus, 1, 5.

6. "Stories from the Notebook of Martha Cox"; Andrus and Andrus, 143.

7. Parry, 43.

8. Andrus and Andrus, 103, 140; Parry, 97.

9. Andrus and Andrus, 89, 103.

10. Andrus and Andrus, 89, 103.

11. Andrus and Andrus, 80, 89, 112, 117; Parry, 27–29.

12. Andrus and Andrus, 135.

13. "Philemon's Faith," *Friend* 3 (August 1974): 47; compare Parry, 87.

14. Andrus and Andrus, 14, 15; Oliver B. Huntington, 161.

15. Parry, 88.

16. See Dorson, *American Folklore*, 201; Dixon Wecter, *The Hero in America: A Chronicle of Hero-Worship* (New York: C. Scribner's Sons, 1941).

17. Andrus and Andrus, 34, 42, 43, 59, 68, 107; compare Gary L. Bunker and Davis Bitton, "Mesmerism and Mormonism," *Brigham Young University Studies* 15 (1975): 146–70.

18. Andrus and Andrus, 44, 59, 111, 120, 164, 172; *Young Woman's Journal* 16 (1905): 556.

19. *Young Woman's Journal* 16 (1905): 556; *Juvenile Instructor* 29 (1894): 132.

20. Andrus and Andrus, 23, 34, 42, 43, 59, 68, 107; *JD*, 9:89; *Young Woman's Journal* 16 (1905): 556.

21. Oliver B. Huntington, 8–9.

22. *JD*, 19:38.

23. Oliver B. Huntington, 23, 34; Parry, 29.

24. Wilford Woodruff, *Leaves from My Journal* (Salt Lake City: Juvenile Instructor Office, 1881), ch. 19.

25. Charles R. Dana Autobiography, 1841, holograph, LDS Church Archives.

26. *Young Woman's Journal* 2 (1891): 466–67; 5 (1894): 490.

27. Oliver B. Huntington, 166, 168.

28. Susa Young Gates, *History of the Young Ladies' Mutual Improvement Association* (Salt Lake City: Deseret News, 1911), 16.

29. Abraham H. Cannon Diary, photocopy of holograph, LDS Church Archives, 4; also in University of Utah Marriott Library Special Collections. On the Ten Tribes see Walt Whipple, "A Discussion of Many Theories concerning the Whereabouts of the Lost Ten Tribes," unpublished paper, LDS Church Archives.

30. Biographical Sketch of Martha Cox, 104, holograph, LDS Church Archives.

31. First published in *Deseret News*, 31 May 1851. The same idea was expressed earlier by Apostle Parley P. Pratt in the *Millennial Star* 1 (February 1841): 258.

32. Narration given to Theodore Tobiason by Patriarch Brown of Forest Dale, October 1924, LDS Church Archives.

33. Anson Call to John M. Whitaker, 30 January 1886, LDS Church Archives. A generation later Israel Call, son of Anson, wrote that he heard his father say "on a number of occasions that the Prophet told him in company with others that the ten tribes were on a portion of this earth that had been taken away." Robert W. Smith, *The Last Days* (Salt Lake City: Pyramid Press, 1947), 215.

34. "I heard him say, 'Peradventure, the Ten Tribes were not on this globe, but a portion of the earth had cleaved off with them and went flying into space.'" Bathsheba W. Smith, in Andrus and Andrus, 123.

35. D&C, sections 130, 131.

36. Minute Book of William Patterson McIntyre, LDS Church Archives.

37. Salt Lake Stake, School of the Prophets Minutes, 3 October 1883, LDS Church Archives.

38. Lester E. Bush, Jr., "Mormonism's Negro Doctrine: An Historical Overview," *Dialogue: A Journal of Mormon Thought* 8 (1973): 11–68.

39. Bush, 31.

40. D&C, Official Declaration 2.

41. Just what constitutes "fulfillment" of a prophecy is, of course, subject to interpretation. The Civil War prophecy (now Section 87 in the LDS Doctrine and Covenants) was received in 1832, first published in 1851, and included in the Doctrine and Covenants in 1876. Although it was and is widely viewed as having its fulfillment in the American Civil War, the nullification ordinance passed by the South Carolina legislature in 1832 could be seen as a "rebellion," and the statement that "war shall be poured out upon all nations" must extend beyond the Civil War itself. When a version of this chapter was published in a periodical, the RLDS editor added his own footnote to the statement about the return to Jackson County: "Members of the Reorganized Church dispute this point."

42. Nephi L. Morris, *Prophecies of Joseph Smith and Their Fulfillment* (Salt Lake City: Deseret Book, 1920); W. Cleon Skousen, *Prophecy and Modern Times* (Salt Lake City: Griffen Patterson Co., 1948); and Duane S. Crowther, *The Prophecies of Joseph Smith* (Salt Lake City: Bookcraft, 1963).

43. Oliver B. Huntington, 165.

44. Oliver B. Huntington, 165–66.

45. Journal History, 4 July 1854. The Journal History is a multivolume collection of sources located in the LDS Church Archives.

46. Daniel Tyler, *The Mormon Battalion*, 350, as cited in Preston Nibley, "What of Joseph Smith's Prophecy That the Constitution Would Hang by a Thread?" *Church News* [section of *Deseret News*], 15 December 1948.

47. JD, 6:152.

48. *Deseret News Weekly*, 19 January 1870, as cited in Preston Nibley.

49. Klaus J. Hansen, *Quest for Empire: The Political Kingdom of God and the Council of Fifty in Mormon History* (East Lansing: Michigan State University Press,

1967); Marvin S. Hill, *Quest for Refuge: The Mormon Flight from American Pluralism* (Salt Lake City: Signature Books, 1989).

50. Orson Pratt to George A. Smith, 21 January 1841, LDS Church Archives.

51. Dean C. Jessee, ed., "Joseph Smith's 19 July 1840 Discourse," *Brigham Young University Studies* 19 (Spring 1979): 390–93.

52. JD, 7:15; 12:204; 21:8, 31–32; 10:318, 357; 22:143; 23:226, 239; 26:39, 142; *Juvenile Instructor* 31:524, 544; *Conference Reports* [pub. Salt Lake City], October 1938, 196; October 1942, 58; April 1850, 154; October 1952, 18; Richard R. Vetterli, *The Constitution by a Thread* (Salt Lake City: Paramount Publishers, 1967).

53. *Abstract of Evidence, Temple Lot Case*, 2 vols. (Lamoni, IA, 1893).

54. JD, 16:67.

55. "Editor's Table," *Improvement Era* 1 (March 1898): 372.

56. "I told them that a prophet was a prophet only when he was acting as such." Joseph Smith, *History of The Church of Jesus Christ of Latter-day Saints*, ed. B. H. Roberts, 7 vols. (Salt Lake City: The Church of Jesus Christ of Latter-day Saints, 1932–1951), 5:265.

57. *Abstract of Evidence, Temple Lot Case*, 2:346.

# The Visual
# Image

7

"The Lord seeth not as a man seeth; for man looketh on the outward appearance, but the Lord looketh on the heart."

1 Samuel 16:7.

**P**hysical appearance is infinitely less important than other qualities, but perhaps we should concede that being short and fat—vertically challenged and with an overgenerous circumference—would be hard to imagine in our heroic latter-day prophet. The fact is, quite simply, that Joseph Smith was over six feet tall, of sturdy build and upright posture, with blue eyes and light brown hair. More important than these outward traits was a personality that was jovial, confident, assertive. He exuded warmth, fellowship, camaraderie, love. Combine all of this, and you have—if there is an inspiring message—charisma. Physically strong and imposing, Joseph Smith had a charismatic personality.

But what did he *look* like? And, not the same question, how has he been portrayed by artists and illustrators from his time to the present?[1]

Surprisingly, the word pictures that have come down to us are not consistent. It depended a great deal, apparently, whether you looked at Joseph Smith through the eyes of a believer or those of a detractor. In some instances the negative descriptions come not from seeing the man but from viewing a picture of the man. To some degree, I suppose, we can simply chalk up these divergences to the familiar phenomenon, as William James put it, of seeing things not as they are but as we are—that is, our perception is shaped by our own values, expectations, and apperceptive mass.

But some of the differences are not so easily explained. Hugh Nibley could not resist presenting some of the so-called primary verbal descriptions as follows (I omit his footnotes):

> He is described by eyewitnesses in 1830 as being "tall and slender—*thin favored.*" Mr. Dogberry calls him "spindle shanked"; here is a remarkable description by Harding, who "describes him as having been a tall,

long-legged and tow-headed youth, who seldom smiled, hardly ever worked and never fought, but who was hard on truth and bird's nests." . . . Thurlow Weed's description of Smith from that time is of "a stout, round, smooth-faced young man." Tall he may have been, but how he could have been "thin-favored" and stout and round at the same time is not so obvious. And just two years later another eye-witness who claims to have known Smith very well says he is "a man of mean and insignificant appearance, between forty and fifty years of age." Later on we are told that "the gait of this person was heavy and slouching, his hands were large and thick, his eyes grey and unsteady in their gaze." A year after this was published, another opus describes the prophet as "a tall, elegant-looking man with dark piercing eyes, and features, which if not handsome, were imposing." Another calls him "a man of commanding appearance, tall and well-proportioned. "A noble-looking fellow," says another, "a Mahomet every inch of him." . . . Another visitor says Smith had dark hair and eyes and a "strong rugged outline of face" with features exactly like those of Oliver Cromwell. Charles Francis Adams described him as "a middle-aged man with a shrewd but rather ordinary expression of countenance."

. . . While one illustrious visitor says he could not see Smith's eyes since the man refused to look people in the face, others speak of his "penetrating eagle eyes." Some think Smith's huge, fat, enormous awkward hands worthy of special mention, while others comment on the remarkably *small* size of his hands. One says that he had "a Herculean frame and a commanding appearance," another that he was sloppy and slouching, "very lank and loose in his appearance and movements."[2]

To say the least, the verbal descriptions are not uniform or even consistent.

Had he lived a few years longer, we would have photographs that would help. Consider Abraham Lincoln, whose picture was taken by Matthew Brady and others, or Brigham Young, who we can see staring at us from a photograph taken during one of his trips to St. George. These examples remind us, however, that photography too had its limitations. It captured just one instant in time, obviously, its accuracy limited by the equipment, the amount of light, and of course the angle and intent of the photographer.

An early photographic process using silver-coated metallic plates that were sensitive to light, named after its inventor, a Frenchman, was the daguerreotype. RLDS historians Ronald Romig and Lachlan Mackay have recently claimed to have identified a daguerreotype of the Prophet.[3] But thus far they have failed to convince most informed scholars. Ephraim Hatch, who has carefully studied Joseph's facial configuration, thinks Joseph Smith is not the individual represented in the daguerreotype.[4] Other alleged daguerreotypes have turned out, upon examination, to be photographs of paintings.[5]

Advanced biomedical visualization techniques hold out the possibility of a firmer conclusion, but anyone who has watched attorneys in court arguing over DNA evidence knows that we may never have absolute certainty about this daguerrotype.

Fortunately we have more than verbal descriptions to rely upon. Without question, the most valuable single piece of evidence is the death mask taken soon after Joseph's death. It captures the general physiognomy: the forehead, the cheekbones, the chin, angles and ratios that can be measured with calipers and reduced to precise quantity. We can be grateful to George Cannon, who under adverse circumstances applied the plaster of Paris, waited for it to harden, and then carefully removed it.[6]

But a death mask does not tell us everything. It captures a moment, not exactly the best, in the continuum of time. Would the appearance be different five years earlier? Would it be slightly but importantly different if taken when the person was alive, the facial muscles not sagging? In a death mask we have the face alone, not the entire head. The way in which the subject held himself, the angle of neck, the lively movement, the all-important eyes—none of this comes through. We have only to ask ourselves whether such an impression made of our face after death, without benefit of the mortician's art, when stress, sickness, or advanced age may well have taken their toll, would capture our true appearance.[7] The answer is yes but also no.

In 1995 computer expert Shannon M. Tracy published the result of his work on the basis of a computer-aided design program.[8] A three-dimensional digitization of the death masks enabled him to make a 3-D model on the computer. He also used photographs of the skulls of Joseph and Hyrum Smith that were exhumed in 1928. For the size of the bodies, the clothing worn by Hyrum at the time of death proved invaluable. The resulting computer image is admittedly subjective for the bodies but much more precise for the heads. Departing from scholarly conventions, Tracy describes his own emotional state at each step of his research. Nevertheless this conscientious work is a major breakthrough in showing the appearance of both Joseph and Hyrum Smith at the time of their death in 1844.

It is interesting to note how close Tracy's Joseph Smith is to the earliest portraits painted by Sutcliffe Maudsley. In 1842, Maudsley did a drawing of Joseph Smith that was reproduced on the map of Nauvoo. The same year, apparently, a portrait was painted by David Rogers.[9] Maudsley did profiles of Joseph and Hyrum in 1844. In 1845, just the year after the Martyrdom, Robert Campbell did a watercolor and ink work entitled *General Joseph Smith Addressing the Nauvoo Legion*. Two years later, full-length profiles of both Joseph and Hyrum ("after Sutcliffe Maudsley") were reproduced in London and New York.[10]

Another important image is the Joseph Smith portrait within the group portrait by W.W. Major. While he came to Nauvoo after Joseph's death and must have used Maudsley as a source, his picture is far more lifelike than his source. Perhaps he spoke to those who knew Joseph.

There is enough agreement in these earliest representations, I believe, that we can say we know about what Joseph Smith looked like. Enough people still remembered him to make it implausible that anything seriously inaccurate would have been accepted without an outcry. It is important to remember, however, that the Joseph of 1830 was not the Joseph of 1842 or 1844. While there is continuity in our appearance, we do change year by year as we age.

One of the most pronounced features, as the death mask reveals clearly, was Joseph Smith's nose. It is not too large for his face, but the angle of the bridge was such that his was a "Roman" nose. The chin is not receding, but it is not the opposite either, not a lantern jaw. His facial structure, the experts tell us, was convex.

Cartoonists love such unusual physiognomies, for they can exaggerate certain features to create their caricature. The earliest such efforts, the drawings in Howe's *Mormonism Unvailed* (1834), do not capitalize on Joseph Smith's real appearance, but after midcentury those who wanted to caricature him could come up with this:

JOSEPH SMITH.

Mormons would of course not be satisfied with such unflattering representations of their prophet. Some remembered him, but memories fade. With a new generation and with new converts coming into the fold, many must have wished to know how to visualize Joseph Smith. But heavily engaged in the challenges of pioneering the new environment in the West, Church leaders did not see art as their highest priority.

In 1853, Charles De Bault did a crayon sketch from an oil painting hanging in the Nauvoo House:

Brigham Young, anxious to have a visual representation of Joseph Smith in the new Utah environment, personally commissioned Danquart Weggeland to paint a portrait for the Bountiful Tabernacle. Completed in 1862 and dedicated 4 March 1863, the Bountiful Tabernacle thus included a mural that, following a common Northern European tradition, appeared to be a sculpted bust of the Prophet.

During the Brigham Young period—he died in 1877—there was not much more to go on, although Frederick Piercy's lithograph was published in 1853, and in 1860 Jules Rémy and Julius Brenchley reproduced a double portrait of Joseph and Hyrum Smith based on Maudsley but credited to David Rogers's 1842 painting.[11]

In the generation stretching from about 1880 to World War I, a burst of activity occurred as several artists attempted to capture Joseph Smith. Some of these works were widely exhibited, even copyrighted and run off in quantity. For example, C.C.A. Christensen, a forceful if primitive artist, did works showing such sacred events as the First Vision, the receiving of the plates from Moroni, and the restoration of the Aaronic Priesthood.[12] In an ambitious series now called Mormon Panorama, Christensen sought to narrate the events of early Mormon history. When Joseph Smith appeared—as in "Joseph Preaching to the Indians"—he was being seen in action, not posed for a portrait.[13]

About 1880 appeared a profile, attributed to Danquart Weggeland, that is unapologetically idealistic. Joseph, without blemish, looks to the left with clear gaze, his linen impeccable, hair freshly shampooed. But he is recognizable. This work remains a favorite. About the same time, Weggeland did a signed drawing of the Prophet.

There must have been a market for this kind of thing, for in 1885 photographer Charles W. Carter copyrighted a frontal bust and sold it in quantities. For a long time, this was thought to be a photograph of Joseph Smith, but it has become clear that it is Carter's photograph of a daguerreotype of a painting.[14]

Also in 1885, thousands of Latter-day Saints were able to enjoy—and perhaps cut out for home framing—a steel engraving prepared by Danquart Weggeland and published in *The Contributor*:

In 1888 John Hafen, who later became noted for his "impressionistic" landscapes, painted two pictures of Joseph Smith in uniform, one on horseback, the other addressing the Nauvoo Legion. These illustrative works in grisaille were the basis of published illustrations and produced for that purpose.

About 1890, William Armitage painted a huge version of *Joseph Smith Preaching to the Indians*. Hung in the Salt Lake Temple, it was not available to be examined by the generality of the population. Now it hangs in the Museum of Church History and Art:

A kind of culmination in the portrait painting of this generation was reached in 1910 with the completion of a large portrait by Lewis A. Ramsey. Although the original hung in the Salt Lake Temple, it was reproduced and made available to be displayed in chapels throughout the Church. It was such a reproduction that I gazed upon time and time again as a boy while attending meetings in the old Blackfoot, Idaho, Second Ward.

By the early twentieth century, the time was ripe for memorializing Joseph Smith in three-dimensional sculpture. Cyrus Dallin had contacted John Taylor in 1884 to produce a statue of Joseph Smith. Rejected, he tried again in 1890. Again denied, he was hired to produce portrait busts of the First Presidency. It was another artist of the first rank, Mahonri Young, who, after showing clay studies completed while he studied in Paris, was commissioned to do the life-size sculpture of Joseph Smith, completed in 1910, that now stands in Temple Square.

In 1947, a centennial year, Torlief Knaphus completed an impressive full-scale work. Originally commissioned for Temple Square, it now stands at the Wilford Wood Museum in Bountiful, Utah.

Before midcentury, two other notable sculptors were drawn to the subject. Avard Fairbanks, whose distinguished artistic career spanned seven decades, produced a bas-relief profile and several works on the sacred visions of the Prophet.[15]

Mormons could not leave Joseph Smith alone as a subject for their art. Among sculptors who more recently have tried their hand at representing Joseph are Dee Jay Bawden, William Whitaker (a painter as well as a sculptor), and Florence Hansen.[16] Castings of Hansen's pair of figures, Joseph and Emma, stand in the Monument to Women Garden in Nauvoo, Illinois, and in the plaza south of the Church Office Building in Salt Lake City, Utah.

Hansen has also prepared small busts of the Prophet and Emma, producing multiple copies as the market demands.

Not attempting a complete catalogue, I must mention four late twentieth-century painters. Alvin Gittins, a highly regarded portraitist at the University of Utah, was true to what is known from the death mask, but by capturing Joseph at an unusual angle and with a slight tilt of the head he shows us a less conventional prophet, with a touch of quizzical humanity.[17]

William Whitaker, already mentioned for a sculpted bust, has produced drawings and paintings of Joseph Smith.

Gary Smith, a productive Alpine artist, became obsessed with the subject of Joseph Smith's martyrdom, completing a series of major works on that subject. (These I have considered in my *The Martyrdom Remembered*). But he has also created the following *Translation of the Book of Mormon*.[18]

Theodore Gorka, a convert from South Carolina, took pains to preserve the necessary proportions but also obviously wished to preserve a larger-than-life Joseph.[19]

The production goes on and on. New buildings called forth works, such as those by Edward Grigware in the Los Angeles Temple, Ken Riley in the Independence Visitors Center, and Dale Kilbourn in the Nauvoo Visitors Center.

Church magazines encouraged or solicited works on Joseph Smith. Usually showing the Prophet in some kind of action, these works have come from the brush of such artists as Robert Barrett, Dean Fausett, Ted Henninger, G.W. Handrahan, Al Rounds, and Greg K. Olsen.[20] What kind of Joseph Smith was being marketed and reinforced? I think we can say that he is intended to be heroic but also loving, humane, courageous, vigorous, and, in certain works, the recipient of divine revelation. If such a portrayal is selective, it is also inevitable and very similar to the kind of artistic tradition we find with such figures as Washington, Jefferson, and Lincoln.[21]

The Museum of Church History and Art, in addition to serving as a repository and exhibit center for many of the works mentioned here, displayed an ambitious exhibit on Joseph Smith in 1985.[22] It has also sponsored international art competitions, thus providing another stimulus for works on different subjects, including Joseph Smith. A prize-winner and purchase award winner of the competition in 1987 was a distinctive, symbol-laden portrait by Pino Drago:

None of us can ever be perfectly captured even by modern photography, much less by an artist. It is not only that our span of years
is inadequately represented by a single view, but even changing
moods and states of mind are hard to capture. The great portraitists
made an effort to capture a single instant of emotion in such "psychological portraits" as *Mona Lisa*. Yusef Karsch, one of the best-
known commercial portrait photographers, could not be satisfied
with a quick shot as his subject posed. He expended great effort in
capturing the right mood.

In 1894, Joseph F. Smith, President of the LDS church and
nephew of Joseph Smith, said, "I never saw a likeness of Joseph
Smith. We have none that look like him or does him justice."[23]
Joseph F., who was only eight years old when his father and uncle
were killed in Carthage Jail, was certainly aware of many purported
likenesses of Joseph Smith. What this statement intends, I believe, is
found in the second sentence, which explains what he meant by the
first: he had seen no painting or sculpture that *did him justice*. Later,
while he must have appreciated the full-length sculpture completed
by Mahonri Young in 1910, one doubts that Joseph F. Smith would
describe even that as fully adequate to the subject.

No painting, no photograph, does *justice* to its subject. In the
case of Joseph Smith, we don't hear the sound of his voice, feel his
human warmth, see the way he moved and held himself, sense his
ability to relate—none of this is captured, although some of the
paintings made efforts to do so. He had a kind of magnetism. (That
of course is the old word, adapted from the faddish "animal magnetism" of the nineteenth century.) Drawing from the vocabulary of current popular culture, we would say that Joseph Smith put out vibes.
Different people reacted differently.

Of the many statements by contemporaries, let us conclude with
the carefully worded evaluation of Boston's mayor, Josiah Quincy:

> Pre-eminent among the stragglers by the door stood
> a man of commanding appearance, clad in the cos-
> tume of a journeyman carpenter when about his

work. He was a hearty, athletic fellow, with blue eyes standing prominently out upon his light complexion, a long nose, and a retreating forehead. . . .

A fine-looking man is what the passer-by would instinctively have murmured upon meeting the remarkable individual who had fashioned the mould which was to shape the feelings of so many thousands of his fellow-mortals. But Smith was more than this, and one could not resist the impression that capacity and resource were natural to his stalwart person. I have already mentioned the resemblance he bore to Elisha R. Potter, of Rhode Island, whom I met in Washington in 1826. The likeness was not such as would be recognized in a picture, but rather one that would be felt in a grave emergency. Of all men I have met, these two seemed best endowed with that kingly faculty which directs, as by intrinsic right, the feeble or confused souls who are looking for guidance. This it is just to say with emphasis; for the reader will find so much that is puerile and even shocking in my report of the prophet's conversation that he might never suspect the impression of rugged power that was given by the man.[24]

Our Boston sophisticate, much like a modern news anchorperson, wants to make it clear that he certainly does not take seriously the beliefs of this man, but he feels obliged to acknowledge "commanding appearance," "kingly faculty," and "rugged power," all of which the artists have captured only partially.

For the Latter-day Saints who knew and followed Joseph Smith, his appearance was fully consonant with his being a prophet of God.

# ENDNOTES

1. Ephraim Hatch, "Joseph Smith Portraits," unpublished paper in LDS Church Archives; Ephraim Hatch, "What Did Joseph Smith Look Like?" *Ensign* 11 (March 1981): 65–73; Marba C. Josephson, "What Did the Prophet Joseph Smith Look Like?" *Improvement Era* 56 (May 1953): 311–15, 371–75; William B. McCarl, "The Visual Image of Joseph Smith" (Master's thesis, Brigham Young University, 1962); Junius F. Wells, "New Portrait of the Prophet Joseph," *Juvenile Instructor* 45 (April 1910): 155; Lorie Winder Stromberg, "In Search of the Real Joseph Smith," *Sunstone* 5 (November-December 1980): 30–34; Roger Lanius and Joseph C. Hupp, "The Joseph Smith Portraits: What Do We Know about Them?" *Restoration Trail Forum* 4 (November 1978): 1-4; Reed Simonsen and Chad Fugate, *Photograph Found: A Concise History of the Joseph Smith Daguerreotype* (Centerville, UT: Privately published, 1993).

2. Hugh Nibley, *Tinkling Cymbals and Sounding Brass* (Salt Lake City and Provo, UT: Deseret Book and F.A.R.M.S., 1991), 179–80.

3. Ronald Romig and Lachlan Mackay, "No Man Knows My Image," unpublished paper, dated May 1994, copy in possession of Randall Dixon, LDS Church Archives.

4. Hatch, "Joseph Smith Portraits." See also Hatch, "What Did Joseph Smith Look Like?"

5. Hatch, "What Did Joseph Smith Look Like?" 71–73.

6. John Q. Cannon, *George Cannon, the Immigrant* (Salt Lake City: Deseret News Press, 1927), 131.

7. Hatch, "Joseph Smith Portraits," ch. 4 "The Death Mask" argues convincingly, I think, that we can rely on the death mask in all essentials. He quotes the opinion of several medical authorities, including especially the renowned orthodontist Dr. Reed Holdaway.

8. Shannon M. Tracy, *In Search of Joseph* (Orem, UT: Kenning House, 1995).

9. Naida R. Williamson, "David White Rogers of New York," *Brigham Young University Studies* 35 (Spring 1995): 73–90.

10. Glen M. Leonard, "Picturing the Nauvoo Legion," *Brigham Young University Studies* 35 (Spring 1995): 95–135.

11. Frederick Piercy, *Route from Liverpool to Great Salt Lake Valley* (London: LDS Book Depot, 1855); Jules Remy and Julius Brenchley, *Voyage au pays des Mormons*, 2 vols. (Paris: Dentu, 1860); Jules Remy and Julius Brenchley, *A Journey to Great Salt Lake City*, 2 vols. (London: Jeffs, 1861).

12. Richard L. Jensen and Richard G. Oman, *C.C.A. Christensen, 1831-1912: Mormon Immigrant Artist*, An Exhibition at the Museum of Church History and Art (Salt Lake City: The Church of Jesus Christ of Latter-day Saints, 1984).

13. C.C.A. Christensen, *Joseph Smith Preaches to the Lamanites*, *Ensign* 5 (June 1975): 80.

14. Hatch, "Joseph Smith Portraits," discussion of daguerreotypes, including Carter's photographs.

15. Eugene F. Fairbanks, *A Sculptor's Testimony in Bronze and Stone: Sacred Sculpture of Avard T. Fairbanks* (Salt Lake City: Publisher's Press, 1972).

16. Dee Jay Bawden, *Ensign* 13 (December 1983), inside back cover, *Ensign* 16 (June 1986), inside front cover.

17. *Ensign* 9 (May 1979), inside front cover.

18. *Ensign* 13 (December 1983), inside front cover.

19. *Joseph Smith in Nauvoo, 1840*, *Ensign* 11 (May 1981): front cover.

20. Robert Barrett, *Ensign* 16 (August 1986): front cover, *Ensign* 20 (September 1990): inside front cover; Dean Fausett, *Church News* 57 (26 December 1987), 14; Ted Henninger, *Ensign* 7 (November 1977): front cover; G. W. Handrahan, *Ensign* 20 (April 1990): inside front cover; Al Rounds, *Ensign* 21 (April 1991): inside front cover; Greg K. Olsen, *Ensign* 20 (April 1990): front cover, *Ensign* 21 (May 1991): inside front cover.

21. Wendy C. Wick, *George Washington an American Icon: The Eighteenth-Century Graphic Portraits* (Washington, D.C.: Barra Foundation, 1982; Noel E. Cunningham, Jr., *The Image of Thomas Jefferson in the Public Eye: Portraits for the People, 1800-1809* (Charlottesville: University Press of Virginia, 1981); Harold Holzer, *Washington and Lincoln Portrayed: National Icons in Popular Prints* (Jefferson, NC: Mcfarland and Company, 1993).

22. *Church News* 55 (2 June 1985), 8–10; *Ensign* 15 (August 1985): 76.

23. Early Mormon Writings, CD ROM, as cited in Romig.

24. Josiah Quincy, *Figures of the Past* (Boston: Robert Brothers, 1883), 380–82.

# Apotheosis

8

"His home's in the sky; he dwells with the Gods,
Far from the furious rage of mobs.
He died; he died—for those he lov'd,
He reigns; he reigns in realms above."

—John Taylor[1]

*A*potheosis, based on the Greek *theos*, means becoming divine, being raised to the status of godhood. Mormons continue rightly to insist that Joseph Smith was a human being. He is not to be confused with Jesus Christ, is not one of the three divine persons of the Godhead, and is not worshipped. Mormons do not address prayers to him. Technically and narrowly speaking, therefore, apotheosis may not be the accurate description of his final trajectory. But, remembering that throughout this volume we are concerned with image—with what people thought or now think about Joseph Smith—the term is pretty close.

During his life, as we have seen, Joseph Smith was described as a prophet. But he was not just *a* prophet, certainly not one of the minor, relatively insignificant prophets. He was on the level of the greatest of the Old Testament prophets—Isaiah, Ezekiel, Jeremiah. More than this, as we have seen, he was like unto Enoch, Joseph, Moses, John the Baptist, Paul, and Jesus. The external similarities are there, but the important point here is that these comparisons of role were in the minds of Joseph Smith and his followers.

No doubt unbelieving contemporaries would have jeered at such claims, which must have seemed not merely presumptuous but wildly incongruous. His followers were not amused by such scoffing. They considered themselves as better judges of Joseph Smith's true value, and often they put their lives on the line for him and for what he taught.

Who else had been prefigured by the earlier biblical figures? Who else was like unto Moses? Why, Jesus Christ, of course. Almost any Christian biblical commentary on Deuteronomy 18 will explain that the future prophet "like unto me [Moses]" was Jesus of Nazareth, which coincides with the New Testament gloss (Acts 7:37) and even with the Book of Mormon (3 Ne. 20:23). When Joseph Smith was presented in this same role of being like unto Moses, as noted earlier in chapter 5, he was assuredly not just another prophet; in some sense, he shared that connection with Jesus Christ. Can we appreciate the breathtaking audacity, or the fearsome responsibility, of being placed in the company of these two other individuals in all of human history? Moses, Jesus Christ—and Joseph Smith.

Of course everything depends on what we mean by "in some sense." Conceivably this juxtaposition of three names, each tied to a biblical passage, could mean not much more than a claim for greatness: Moses was great, so was Jesus, so was Joseph Smith. The precise role of each would remain to be spelled out. In chapter 5 we delineated some of the ways, beyond a generalized greatness, in which these lives were similar.

If Joseph Smith replicated to some degree the life of Christ, this is tantamount to at least a partial apotheosis, for Jesus Christ was of course divine. (If non-Christians wish to interpose an objection, I will concede the obvious: we are referring to image, to the view of believers, to Christology.) To say that a person is Christlike may mean simply that he or she is uncommonly charitable, dedicating energies to serving others. But the comparison could mean more.

When in Liberty Jail in 1839, Joseph Smith cried out: "O God, where art thou? And where is the pavilion that covereth thy hiding place?" (D&C 121:1). We do not need the cross-reference to be reminded of Jesus at the ninth hour saying "Eli, Eli, lama sabachthani? that is to say, My God, my God, why hast thou forsaken me?" (Matt. 27:46). Psalm 22 may well have had many other applications by persons who felt abandoned, but here, within limits, was a psychological sharing. Writing from the jail, Joseph recorded God's answer:

> And if thou shouldst be cast into the pit, or into the
> hands of murderers, and the sentence of death
> passed upon thee; if thou be cast into the deep; if the
> billowing surge conspire against thee; if fierce winds

become thine enemy; if the heavens gather black-
ness, and all the elements combine to hedge up the
way; and above all, if the very jaws of hell shall gape
open the mouth wide after thee, know thou, my son,
that all these things shall give thee experience, and
shall be for thy good.

The Son of Man hath descended below them all.
Art thou greater than he? (D&C 122:7–8)

There it is: the comparison with Jesus. True, the very point here is
that he was not Jesus and had not done what Jesus had done, but it
is at least worth noting that the comparison was going through
Joseph Smith's mind.

Coming out of Liberty Jail, he made his way to Illinois, where on
the banks of the Mississippi his beleaguered followers were waiting.
During the busy months that followed he exerted enormous leadership strength by such dramatic measures as sending most of the
Twelve Apostles to England and purchasing land for the founding of
the new city of Nauvoo. In the midst of all this, sickness attacked the
weakened people. In July and August he administered to the sick.
Here is B. H. Roberts's description of the events of 22 July:

President Smith's house was crowded with sick
whom he was trying to nurse back to health. In his
dooryard were a number of people camped in tents,
who had newly arrived, but upon whom the fever
had seized. Joseph himself was prostrate with sickness, and the general distress of the saints weighed
down his spirit with sadness. While still thinking of
the trials of his people in the past, and the gloom
that then overshadowed them, the Spirit of God
rested upon him and he was immediately healed. He
arose and began to administer to the sick in his
house, all of whom immediately recovered. He then
healed those encamped in his dooryard, and from
thence went from house to house calling on the sick

to arise from their beds of affliction, and they obeyed and were healed.[2]

The dramatic description continues and is verified by several eyewitnesses.

Several reactions are possible. For the moment, let us restrict ourselves to asking which comparisons would come to mind. For Roberts, this was nothing less than a modern fulfillment of New Testament promises (James 5:14–15; Mark 16:17), the power of healing having been restored to earth (D&C 84). A Catholic viewing the same phenomenon might think of St. Charles Borromeo administering to the plague victims in Milan, who had himself been venerated as a modern version of New Testament apostolic power. But who in the New Testament was the great Healer if not Christ himself?

Let us consider some of the titles that were used to describe Smith's role. We have already mentioned *prophet*, closely related to *seer* and *revelator*. He was also a *priest*, technically a *high priest*, referring to his priesthood authority. And he was *king*, this referring to his role of rulership over the kingdom of God on earth.[3] It will immediately occur to the perceptive reader that it is Jesus Christ who traditionally is described as bringing together the three titles or functions of prophet, priest, and king. Latter-day Saints join other Christians in singing about Jesus Christ "He lives, my prophet, priest, and king."

At the end of his life, as he was taken to Carthage Jail in June 1844, Joseph said, "I am going like a lamb to the slaughter; but I am calm as a summer's morning; I have a conscience void of offense towards God, and towards all men." I wonder if Mormons reading these famous words have remembered that the prime example of the spotless lamb being led to the slaughter is Jesus Christ. Specifically in Isaiah 53 the Suffering Servant, the man of sorrow who was bruised for our iniquities, "is brought as a lamb to the slaughter."

Did Joseph Smith voluntarily give up his life for his people? Instead of escaping, he, with strong premonitions of impending death, voluntarily turned himself in to the authorities. The important point here is that some of his people perceived him going to Carthage in order to prevent a rape of Nauvoo. Not that he wanted to die. He went to Carthage because he had to, having given up the idea of escape. But even a reluctant submission called up the following comparison to Heber C. Kimball:

> Judas, when he lost the faith, received the power of the devil, and betrayed the Son of God into the hands of murderers. Joseph Smith in like manner was betrayed into the hands of wicked men, who took his life.[4]

Immediately after the martyrdom the language sometimes came close to traditional Christian language about Christ. Here, for example, is Joseph Smith the intercessor:

> Unchanged in death, with a Savior's love
> He pleads their cause in the courts above.

And again:

> He died; he died—for those he lov'd,
> He reigns; he reigns in the realms above.[5]

While not truly confusing the prophetic mission of Joseph Smith and the unique atonement of Jesus Christ, Mormons did sometimes see a similarity—but not an identity—between the two.

Mormons do not believe that Joseph Smith atoned for the sins of mankind, but they did not always use good judgment when making these comparisons. Here is a recollection of Brigham Young:

> When Martin [Harris] was with Joseph Smith, he was continually trying to make the people believe that he (Joseph) was the Shepherd, the Stone of Israel. I have heard Joseph chastise him severely for it, and he told me that such a course, if persisted in, would destroy the kingdom of God.

Fortunately, such claims, when carried to an extreme in this way, were quickly repudiated. It is therefore irresponsible to suggest that they ever represented the official view of the Church. In the same sermon, Young was able to say:

> This people never professed that Joseph Smith was anything more than a Prophet given to them of the Lord, and to whom the Lord gave the keys of the last days, which were not to be taken from him in time, neither will they be in eternity.[6]

Despite several interesting similarities, Young seems to say, in the end the difference was profound.

In describing the death of Joseph, John Taylor wrote: "Joseph Smith, the Prophet and Seer of the Lord, has done more, save Jesus only, for the salvation of men in this world, than any other man that ever lived in it" (D&C 135:3). Once again we have the two placed in conjunction. The superior, unique contribution of Jesus Christ is recognized, but it is not trivial that here Joseph Smith is placed second *only* to Jesus Christ.

How did the Saints picture Joseph Smith after his death? Did they consider that he had simply joined the great mass of humanity in the grave, or as the scripturally informed might explain, in the spirit world awaiting the resurrection and final judgment? No. They could not help but think of him as occupying a status of elevated significance. Let us notice three aspects of the postmortal activity of Joseph Smith, as his people thought of him.

First, he ascended to the highest levels and continued to observe the experiences of his people on earth. This idea was expressed most memorably in the hymn "Praise To the Man," mentioned earlier in other connections. The closing words of its first verse are:

> Mingling with Gods he can plan for his brethren.
> Death cannot conquer the hero again.

We have already commented on the word *hero* in the last line. In the penultimate line we find Joseph not languishing in a spirit prison, not even preaching the gospel to the departed spirits, but mingling with Gods and planning for those on earth.

Second, he communicated to Church leaders, thus performing the role of intermediary. In a sense, this began on 8 August 1844, when in a great showdown Sidney Rigdon's bid to lead the Church was refused by the body of Saints gathered at Nauvoo. For when Brigham Young spoke a manifestation occurred: "It did not appear to be Brigham Young; it appeared to be Joseph Smith that spoke to the people—Joseph in his looks, in his manner, and in his voice; even his figure was transformed so that it looked like that of Joseph, and everybody present who had the Spirit of God, saw that he was the man whom God had chosen to hold the keys now that the Prophet Joseph had gone behind the veil, and that he had given him power to exercise them."[7] Just what happened we do not know except that many present on the occasion were satisfied that Brigham Young now rightfully assumed the leadership role previously held by Joseph Smith.

During the months to follow, at several crucial points during the journey west, Brigham Young had dreams in which Joseph Smith appeared to him. On 17 February 1847, for example, he had a tender dream in which Joseph said, "Tell the people to be sure to keep the Spirit of the Lord and follow it, and it will lead them just right."[8] We can if we wish explain this as a result of continuing obsession with the departed leader, but Brigham accepted it as a genuine communication. Again the minimal point remains intact: whatever we might think about the reality, the experience had validity in the minds of Brigham Young and his followers. For them, Joseph Smith was still interested in their welfare and was still, under God, able to convey the divine will.

Third, Joseph Smith would participate in the final judgment, not as a poor mortal standing in the dock, but as judge. Here is Brigham Young, speaking in 1859: "No man or woman in this dispensation will ever enter into the celestial kingdom of God without the consent of Joseph Smith."[9] In 1882 George Q. Cannon delivered an important discourse on the keys of presiding over the last generation, explaining about Joseph Smith: "He will sit as a judge to judge those who have received or those who have rejected his testimony. He will stand as a swift witness before the judgment seat of God against this generation."[10] In context, it is clear enough that Joseph is subordinate to Christ, but the fact remains that he would, in the Mormon view, play a role of judge in the last judgment.

If this does not add up to apotheosis in the complete sense, it is something close to it. Joseph Smith was not your ordinary human being, not even your ordinary prophet. He was hobnobbing with the Gods.

All of which may understandably scandalize nonbelievers. It was bad enough, they would say, that Joseph Smith claimed revelations. These further claims are simply beyond the pale. He should have been consigned to an insane asylum, some might think, or at the very least be roundly condemned for blasphemy. But to find something distasteful or offensive does not make it disappear. I leave to others the denunciation of this nineteenth-century American for his outrageous self-dramatization, if that is the way they wish to see it. Heaven knows he received an abundance of such condemnation during his lifetime. Our purpose here is simply to describe the image of Joseph Smith as he lives in the hearts and minds of his followers.

To avoid misunderstanding, however, two mitigating considerations should be mentioned. First, when all is said and done, Joseph Smith did not claim that he was God or Christ. Indeed, the scriptures he brought forth—the Book of Mormon, Doctrine and Covenants, Pearl of Great Price—are altogether Christocentric. Since his death, his followers have made the same distinction: they do not see him as God or as Christ. They do not worship him. In Catholic usage the term *venerate* is used to describe the special respect given to the Blessed Virgin and the saints. This same term might appropriately be used to describe the Mormons' feelings towards Joseph Smith, except that they do not even address prayers to him, as Catholics do to Mary and the saints. The claims to special status are there, all right, but when all is said they fall short of the kind of deification found in some Eastern religions. "We admire and thank Joseph Smith," a recent speaker said, "but we worship and adore Jesus Christ."

Furthermore, and this may surprise some readers, if Joseph Smith saw an extraordinarily exalted status for himself and if his followers subscribed to that perception, he presented an almost equally attractive prospect for all human beings who were willing to qualify. If he could receive revelations from God, so could they. He did not claim a monopoly. If he was a prophet, priest, and king, so might they be. Their status of prophet, bearing the testimony of Jesus or receiving divine guidance for their own callings, would not conflict with his. The wide sharing of priesthood authority among all worthy males (and, as often explained, among women in that they shared it with their husbands and fathers)—this was truly a priesthood of all believers. If their status as kings and queens was deferred until after death in the temple ceremonies, so too was his own. These prerogatives, whatever they might mean, Joseph Smith did not selfishly grasp exclusively to himself.

Even when we talk about the achievement of godhood, apotheosis in the technical sense, Joseph had not so much achieved it as he was on the road toward it with special distinctive claims. But anyone familiar with Mormon theology will recognize that such a destiny is available to all in the eternities ahead. The possibility of not only coming into the presence of God but of actually becoming a god, having been perfected in Christ, was spelled out by Joseph Smith in his final revelations and discourses and was expressed apothegmatically by Lorenzo Snow: "As man is, God once was; as God is, man may become." In proclaiming the awesome possibility, Joseph Smith did "not wish to humanize God but to deify man, not as he now is, but as he may become."[11] It was thus that Joseph Smith elucidated the full meaning of being "heirs of God, and joint-heirs with Christ" (Rom. 8:17).

ENDNOTES

1. John Taylor, "The Seer," *Times and Seasons*, 1 January 1845.

2. B. H. Roberts, *Comprehensive History of The Church of Jesus Christ of Latter-day Saints*, 6 vols. (Salt Lake City: Deseret News, 1930), 2:19.

3. Melodie Moench, "Joseph Smith: Prophet, Priest, and King," Task Paper (Salt Lake City: Historical Department of the Church, 1978).

4. Heber C. Kimball, *Journal of Discourses*, 26 vols. (Liverpool and London: Latter-day Saints' Book Depot, 1854–1886), 2:107. Discourse of 13 August 1853.

5. John Taylor, "The Seer." (Nauvoo: Times and Seasons, 1844).

6. Brigham Young, *Journal of Discourses*, 2:127. Sermon of 17 April 1853.

7. *Journal of Discourses*, 23:364.

8. Elden J. Watson, ed., *Manuscript History of Brigham Young, 1846–1847* (Salt Lake City: Privately published, 1971), 530.

9. *Journal of Discourses*, 7:289.

10. *Journal of Discourses*, 23:361.

11. Lowell L. Bennion, *The Religion of the Latter-day Saints* (Provo, UT: LDS Department of Education, 1962), 31.

# Joseph Smith
# and the Scholars

"It is the vice of scholars to suppose that there is no knowledge in the world but that of books."

—William Hazlitt

Not contemporary with Joseph Smith were the later scholarly
works published about him. Each of these, however elaborate the
scholarly apparatus, portrayed an additional image of the Mormon
leader.

Most people whose lives would be worthy biographical subjects
are never discovered by scholars. Typically, even those whose lives
have been the subject of research and writing wait a generation or
more for their biographer. It is an indication of the interest in Joseph
Smith, therefore, that only eight years after his death Charles
Mackay's The Mormons (1852) appeared, carrying the subtitle "With
memoirs of the life and death of Joseph Smith, the 'American
Mahomet.'"[1] Mackay's work was based on primary sources and he
tried to be evenhanded. It was not a bad beginning.

A year later Lucy Mack Smith's Biographical Sketches of Joseph
Smith the Prophet, and His Progenitors for Many Generations (1853)
was published in Liverpool.[2] Ostensibly by the Prophet's mother,
this work is a strange amalgam of self-serving recollections, infor-
mative details, and unacknowledged quotations from what had by
then become the official history. Not so much a biography as a primary source that later biographers would use, it is nevertheless a
landmark.[3]

In 1878 Edward Tullidge brought out his Life of Joseph the
Prophet. Published first in New York and in 1880 in Independence,
Missouri, this book became entangled in the rivalry between the
Utah Mormons and the still young Reorganized Church of Jesus
Christ of Latter Day Saints, to which Tullidge temporarily gravi-
tated.[4] It is a favorable account of its subject that would not alien-
ate believers, but it is not only that. Examples of Joseph's human
frailties are in evidence throughout. Most interestingly, Tullidge
used a new model for explaining the Mormon prophet—that of

spiritualism. This faddish movement, which had been going for about thirty years, was attracting many Americans. Some Mormon apostates found it appealing.[5] Tullidge thought he was paying Joseph Smith a compliment by describing him as a medium able to establish contact with the unseen world.

In 1888 George Q. Cannon published *The Life of Joseph Smith, the Prophet* in Salt Lake City.[6] A journalist and publisher as well as a counselor in the Church's First Presidency, Cannon was a leader in the Sunday School movement and was trying to create material that could be used for indoctrinating young Mormons. Organized chronologically and, within the framework of faith, giving much detail about the life of Joseph Smith, Cannon's work is the ancestor of many subsequent Mormon biographies of Joseph that have certain features in common. They get the basic external facts straight, uncritically include the material we earlier described as "folk tradition," and essentially bear testimony to Joseph Smith's divine calling.

General histories—Bancroft, Whitney, Linn—contained partial biographies. Then in 1902 appeared *The Founder of Mormonism: A Psychological Study of Joseph Smith, Jr.* by Isaac Woodbridge Riley, his published Yale doctoral dissertation.[7] The discipline of psychology was still new, which didn't stop Professor George Trumbull Ladd from making the following introductory statement: "At the time when the subject of the study [Joseph Smith] lived, there was little or no disposition or fitness for considering such manifestations of abnormal psychological development from the scientific point of view." If anything, this was to be a thoroughly modern, enlightened study.

Many themes or ideas developed by later scholars were first advanced by Riley.


*The Smith family.* The narrative of Solomon Mack is presented as proof that in the family "dreams are warnings, visions are messages from on high." Add the history of Lucy Mack Smith—"an unthinking credulity," "a positive hankering after the supernatural"—and we are able to conclude that "Joseph's mental outfit is seen to be largely a matter of inheritance." The mother is diagnosed as having melancholia, "a positive intolerance of the sects," and "a marked aloofness from denominationalism." A study of Joseph's genealogy discloses to Riley "serious hereditary weakness" and indeed through his mother "a liability to neural instability."[8]

*Dreams*. Dreams are seen as basic to the Smith family's religious understanding. Lucy had hers, of course, and she recounted seven dreams of her husband, Joseph Smith, Sr. Riley gives his quick and facile dream analysis. Having read his *Encyclopaedia Brittanica* (9th edition), Riley pronounces the Smiths as not entirely primitive, for they did not confuse their dreams with daytime experiences, but as "intermediate," for they were not sufficiently advanced to explain the dreams from the material and physical point of view. "Theirs was the mystic view: dreams are warnings from on high, visions are symbolic messages sent to guide the soul."[9] Riley is able to give the "scientific" explanation. The Smith dreams were either hallucinations or illusion. Sensory perceptions were involved in both, especially the visual, which led all dreams to be considered "visions."

*Influence of the environment on Joseph Smith*. Influences include a ridiculed, rudimentary education. Likely reading material available to Joseph is discussed, but "there is no positive evidence as to his youthful literary pabulum."[10] Especially important was the confusion and wrangling among religious sects, whose shared "sombre theology brought an intense melancholy."[11] Such were the preconditions of Joseph Smith's "peculiar psychic experience"—the First Vision followed by the appearances of the angel Moroni. The religious environment also provides Riley with his preliminary explanation of the early visions: "They may be put in terms of psychic functioning, and may be largely explained by the influences of suggestion and hypnotism."[12] They are not even unusual: Joseph's conversion occurred a year before the average; "the accompanying dreams and visions put him in the rarer third of youth who have dreams and hallucinations." Josiah Royce's analysis of John Bunyan is seen as at least partly valid for Joseph Smith.

*Pathological explanations.* Putting all of this together, I. Woodbridge Riley does not accuse Joseph Smith of prevarication. Joseph had experiences, all right. But "the apparent objective manifestations were actually subjective symptoms."[13] If we were to ask what about the divine aspects or the religious content, our scholar sees no problem: "The theophanic portions of his visions are precisely what occur in a certain form of visual disturbance akin to vertigo."[14] In addition to *vertigo*, other diagnostic terms advanced as explanations are: *ophthalmic migraine, melancholic depression,* and *epileptic convulsions* (or *convulsive paroxysms*) and *seizures.*

To Riley's credit, he advances epilepsy only as a "working hypothesis."[15] The "infrequency of the youthful attacks" meant that Joseph was afflicted with the ailment only in an "attenuated form." Furthermore, at about age 21 he had a "spontaneous cure." Yet, all things considered, Riley is convinced that "the psychiatric definition of the epileptic fits the prophet to a dot."[16]

Riley is willing to acknowledge that Joseph Smith considered his translations to be inspired. "For all that, his mystic writings may be resolved into their elements of Bible knowledge, petty information and every-day experience."[17] The Book of Mormon, in short, was "an imaginative elaboration of presentative material." Always up to date, Riley finds that the use of the Urim and Thummim comports comfortably with "a recent experimental study of visions." If Joseph saw Greek or Hebrew letters, or was able to reproduce them, this may have been due to a youthful glance at a Bible in the original tongues, for he was "a good visualizer."[18] The production of the Book of Mormon text was "a veritable piece of automatic writing."[19] The "usual clairvoyant and telepathic embellishments were added."[20]

Generally, even though providing what were then modern psychological explanations, Riley was willing to concede that Joseph Smith had genuine experiences and thought he was inspired. Where was the dividing line between self-deception and conscious duplicity?[21] Without acquitting Joseph of the latter, Riley's interpretation is primarily one of physical-psychological experiences combined with a simpleminded family milieu.

*Hypnotism*. But what about the others who believed Joseph? What about the witnesses of the Book of Mormon? In a chapter on "Joseph the Occultist," Riley explains the witnesses by "hypnotic hallucination." For their own vision to occur there had to be "preparatory manipulation." More broadly, all of the early Latter-day Saints, one gathers, were similarly disposed. Once they accepted Joseph as prophet, he would have "untold influence."[22] "Given, then, such an influence and sensitive subjects, and mental suggestion could produce anything [*sic*] in the way of illusion."[23] As for the testimony of the eight witnesses, there are only two possible explanations: pure fabrication or collective hypnosis. Favoring the latter explanation, Riley does not accuse his subject of fraud. Joseph didn't know what he was doing. "To his overwrought imagination, these [achievements] appeared true apostolic gifts."[24]

Not a full biography, Riley's *The Founder of Mormonism* was a provocative, bold attempt to explain the enigmatic Mormon prophet. Drawing upon *fin de siecle* psychological literature, he provided an explanation that was not exactly complimentary but did allow a certain honesty in Joseph. Its major thesis, that the Prophet had epilepsy, has not fared well in the twentieth century. Riley's book tells more about the state of medical and psychological understanding at the turn of the century and about the mind-set of the author than it does about Joseph Smith.

At exactly the same time that Riley was writing his book, William James was preparing and delivering in Edinburgh the lectures published as *The Varieties of Religious Experience* (1902). A classic in scholarly study of religion, *Varieties* has a broader approach and comes from a more important thinker. Yet interesting similarities exist between the James and Riley. In a famous first chapter, or lecture, James makes it clear that the origin of a religion in psychological illness in no way precludes its validity. He has nothing but disdain for what he calls "medical materialism," the reductionist view that a religion is explained by pathology. His brief reference to Joseph Smith is scarcely worth mentioning,[25] but clearly James's general attitude, consistent with his own philosophical pragmatism, would be primary interested not in the origins of the religion but in its results—its consequences in the lives of the believers. This may not be far from Riley's willingness to concede that Joseph Smith's revelations were genuine *for him*.

In 1933 John Henry Evans, a Mormon, published his *Joseph Smith, an American Prophet*.[26] Not a biography in the usual sense, the book offered many vignettes from Joseph's life in rough chronological sequence. Evans could be counted upon to be positive, although he did call attention to weaknesses in his subject. Many quotations from contemporary documents were included. The author, an English teacher, had a lively style, approximately on the *Reader's Digest* level, and knew how to retain interest. After going over Joseph's life in 200 pages, the author devotes about 100 pages to "the Prophet's religious philosophy" and then in a final section grapples with the challenge of explanation. Addressing the possibility of self-deception and hypnotism of others, Evans wrote:

> But the plates did not exist? Very well. Then the man who said they did was an egregious liar, and could not have been a prophet. For see what we must believe if we suppose that he only fancied the plates to be real. We must believe that he *imagined* he took them out of the hill; that he *imagined* he carried their fifty pounds home from the hill; that he *imagined* he was attacked three times on the way home; that he *imagined* he had to hide them here and there, to keep them from being stolen; that he *imagined* he had them before him for months, while he worked on them every day; that he not only *imagined* he showed them to eight men, but that these eight men also *imagined* they saw and felt the plates. If that does not tax one's credulity, it would be extremely hard to find anything that would.[27]

This work does not pretend to be coolly indifferent. Published by an eastern publisher and distributed nationally, it looked like it might well serve the purpose of a basic introduction for the indefinite future.

To satisfy Mormon readers who wanted a more consistently chronological narrative, Preston Nibley, an assistant LDS Church Historian, published *Joseph Smith the Prophet* in 1944.[28] Clear, straightforward, unimaginative, this biography marches through Joseph Smith's life, giving the sequence of events as they had come to be accepted by Mormons. There is no bibliography. There are no footnotes, although parenthetical references indicate the source of most quotations. Polygamy is unmentioned. A book for the already convinced, Preston Nibley's biography was ready to reign unchallenged in the Mormon market.

Then came a bombshell. With considerable fanfare in the national media, publisher Alfred Knopf of New York City brought out Fawn M. Brodie's *No Man Knows My History: The Life of Joseph Smith the Mormon Prophet.*[29] Former Church Historian Leonard Arrington and I have evaluated this work elsewhere, in the context of Mormon historiography.[30] We do not agree with its conclusions, its basic interpretation, but think it silly to deny that it possesses positive qualities. In 1945 the most thoroughly researched biography of Joseph Smith yet to appear, it decisively repudiates the theory that he had plagiarized the Book of Mormon from a romance by Solomon Spaulding. It conveys the energy of the Prophet and some of his unpredictability. Beautifully written, *No Man* captures the reader's interest and holds it fast through chapter after chapter. National reviewers were profuse in their plaudits.

The Joseph Smith portrayed by Brodie was an impostor, to be sure, but he was an engaging one. He was not even totally dishonest, for he managed to convince himself that he was telling the truth. This idea was not original with Brodie—remember the "self-deception" possibility acknowledged by Riley. For the nonbeliever such an interpretation might even appear unduly generous. For Brodie herself, who had jettisoned her Mormon beliefs in favor of an atheistic naturalism, there was no way of putting him on the stage as a genuine prophet of God, but she could show him as a charismatic leader, as an audacious claimant of divine religious authority. For most readers this was good enough, and to this day her book is widely read and recommended.

Mormons, who of course could not calmly accept such an interpretation, were quick to respond. The biographies of Preston Nibley and John Henry Evans were reprinted. A direct refutation of Brodie appeared in an issue of the weekly *Church News*.[31] In 1946 the learned Hugh Nibley employed rapier-like wit against Brodie in his *No Ma'am, That's Not History*.[32] Possibly weakened by its sarcasm and overkill, this lengthy review had important substantive points to make. Brodie was chided for her selective use of evidence, for her hasty, uncritical, and unconvincing use of parallels, for simple factual errors, and for her insistence on a gradual evolution in Joseph Smith's development that, Nibley demonstrates, often clashes directly with the evidence. Above all, he scolds her for pretending to know what was in people's minds. "So Brodie knows that Emma knew that Joseph knew what Emma thought! Is this *history?*"[33] Later, when Brodie's psychobiographies of Thomas Jefferson and Richard Nixon were torn to shreds by critics, it was easy to point out that her work on Joseph Smith had used the same dubious approach.[34]

Another defender standing in the breach, sword in hand, to defend his prophet was John A. Widtsoe, learned educator and Mormon apostle, whose several articles appeared in *The Improvement Era*. Then, in fulfillment of an assignment from the President of the Church, he published *Joseph Smith: Seeker After Truth, Prophet of God* in fifty-seven chapters.[35] Consistently respectful of his subject, Widtsoe lays out his evidence on topic after topic, occasionally locking horns directly with Brodie. While useful on many specific points and definitely worth reading, Widtsoe is now out of date on several issues.

Since midcentury, writing on Joseph Smith has not ceased. If anything, the flow has increased. To say that he continues to attract interest is an understatement. Some of these publications add details about his family or the houses he lived in. Others, I must say, make no real contribution beyond pulling together and restating in the author's words what we know about Joseph Smith's activities in a certain situation. Those works that are interpretive, it seems to me, can be grouped roughly into the following categories.

*Attacks.* What is an "attack" depends, of course, on your point of view. Anti-Mormons have continued to do their thing in lectures, pamphlets, radio, and film. For them Joseph Smith was not just a pretender, not sincerely deluded; he was a monster. Other critiques emanating from the anti-Mormon camp have been more substantive, such as the Reverend Wesley P. Walters' effort to demonstrate that there was no religious revival in Palmyra, New York, in 1820, the year of Smith's First Vision.[36] One scholar made an effort to rehabilitate the affidavits from Joseph's neighbors collected by apostate Philastus Hurlbut and published as early as 1834.[37] Polygamy has continued to provide a handle for critics, who repeat the old charges that Smith was immoral, with the added suggestion that he exploited the women of his circle. The discovery of the papyri from which, according to the critics, the Book of Abraham (in the canonized Pearl of Great Price) was in some sense translated led to a flurry of publication. Finally, the Book of Mormon has rightly been recognized as a vulnerable point, for if it could be overturned, Mormons would be deprived of a basic foundation. Here centering my attention on biography, I have not attempted to enter the complex bibliography on the modern scriptures, although admittedly this is an artificial and prudential demarcation.[38] Suffice it to say that critics of the Book of Mormon and the other modern scriptures are challenging the veracity of the Prophet.

*Defenses and appreciations.* Examples of scholars who have consistently emphasized the positive aspects of Joseph Smith's life and have responded to critics are Richard L. Anderson, Milton V. Backman, Jr., and Hugh Nibley. Thoroughly versed in the canons of modern scholarship, familiar with the primary sources, these and other Mormon writers have not been content to leave the field to

147

enemies of the Prophet. When the historicity of Smith's First Vision was called into question on the grounds that no evidence was found of a revival in Palmyra, New York, in the year 1820, Backman wasted no time in scouring the source material and finding quite sufficient indication of revivalistic activity in the "region."[39] When critics continued to exploit affidavits collected by Philastus Hurlbut in 1833 and 1834, Richard L. Anderson challenged the extent to which these "neighbors" were really acquainted with Joseph Smith and suggested a frame-up.[40] Nibley, in particular, has wittily pointed out the inconsistencies in the anti-Smith writings.[41] As long as attacks continue, one supposes, there will be defenders.

Not in the fray in quite the same way, perhaps, are those who continue to produce biographies. Some of these are close to what in another context we call "campaign biographies"—that is, fairly superficial narrative treatments of the life, consistently emphasizing the positive. Others, totally uncritical, repeat the standardized, pasteurized version of Joseph Smith's life and season it with the later reminiscences and folk traditions loved by the faithful. I see no need to be supercilious here, for the fact is that all history is drawn upon by people according to their interest and sense of relevance. What I have called the ritualization of Mormon history[42] is not limited to the simplified understanding of the Prophet, and the process is by no means unique to Mormons.

Deserving of greater credit as biographies, although still in the appreciative camp, are works by Donna Hill and Richard L. Bushman. Hill's *Joseph Smith, the First Mormon*, published by Doubleday in 1977, is perhaps the most satisfactory full biography yet to appear.[43] Although lacking Fawn Brodie's stylistic flair, Hill has done her homework more thoroughly, confronts the major problem areas, and retains our interest as she narrates Joseph's life. Not profound, the book is nevertheless thorough and reflects the expanding body of source material and scholarly studies that had accumulated.

More satisfying for some readers is Richard Bushman's *Joseph Smith and the Beginnings of Mormonism* (1984).[44] A recognized historian, winner of the Bancroft Prize, Bushman is also a devout Mormon. He presents Joseph's life in the traditional mode—that is, as it was experienced and explained by Joseph and those closest to him—but throughout we get Bushman's sensitive, intelligent exposition. Bushman's subject, though, is the *young* Joseph Smith, for he concludes with the year 1830. We might hope for a second and even a third volume to carry the story to 1844, but in the meantime some of the Prophet's most critical, formative years have been elucidated.

*New models of explanation.* Even in the nineteenth century, as we have seen, at least one biographer advanced the suggestion that Joseph Smith was a special kind of spirit medium, thus using a category that was somewhat fashionable in some circles for a few decades. More recently, scholars who do not fit obviously into either the unfriendly or defensive camp have utilized other interpretive models

1. *Political leader.* To the extent that he held public office, as, for example, mayor of Nauvoo, Joseph Smith *was* a political leader. What I am referring to here is treatment of him that places this at the center, not only in the actual decisions of government he was involved but also in his projection of his destiny. Just as he was not merely an ordinary clergymen but was a prophet, so he was not merely an ordinary politician but was head of the kingdom of God on earth. Some biographies have given little attention to this angle of perception; others ignore it entirely.

In 1967 Klaus J. Hansen published *Quest for Empire: The Political Kingdom of God and the Council of Fifty in Mormon History.*[45] After efforts of gathering, of trying to achieve separate economic institutions and political autonomy, the Mormons finally were building their own city in Nauvoo, Illinois. There, in early 1844, Joseph Smith proclaimed, "I calculate to be one of the instruments of setting up the kingdom of Daniel by the word of the Lord, and I intend to lay a foundation that will revolutionize the whole world."[46] With mounting opposition on the outside and on the inside, as summarized previously in chapters 1 and 2, Joseph then proceeded to organize a secret new governing council, the Council of Fifty. Among other things, while anticipating a later take-over in which the Mormon system would dominate, the Fifty participated in the presidential campaign of 1844, promoting, no one knows how seriously, the candidacy of Joseph Smith. At the same time, some of the Fifty were assigned to plan a migration, which of course required a decision as to where the Mormons would go to found their kingdom. Texas, Vancouver Island, Oregon, the Great Basin—all were considered. At one point, according to one witness, Joseph Smith even had himself crowned king.[47]

Brilliantly reinterpreting the history in the light of these political aspirations and using minutes of the Fifty that had been unknown to scholars, Hansen saw Mormonism as anti-pluralistic—as a bone that was simply indigestible by a pluralistic, democratic America. Joseph Smith in this view became not merely the head of a church, nor even just a prophet, but the self-proclaimed monarch of a new empire. One did not have to adopt the old charges of despotism or dictatorship to recognize that his ambitions, however clothed in religious language, were economic and political.

Such was Hansen's thesis. Mormon historian Marvin Hill has given support to the political emphasis by downplaying the religious, scriptural aspect of the Prophet's role and emphasizing his incompatibility with American society.[48] Retracing Mormon history from its beginning through the Ohio, Missouri, and Illinois periods, Hill demonstrates how the movement appeared to outsiders: making extravagant claims, increasing in swarming converts, threatening to overwhelm others economically, almost certain to dominate politically, claiming special privileges and divine approbation. The Mormons must have seemed insufferable, and Joseph Smith symbolized and represented the whole system, if he was not indeed directly responsible for it. Hill's treatment is a valuable one and, although showing little interest in hearing what the Saints had to say in their own defense, is probably perfectly convincing to many.[49]

Going over approximately the same time span is Kenneth H. Winn, whose doctoral dissertation was published in 1989.[50] He examines not only the most provocative statements of the Mormons, or the hot-tempered reactions by their enemies, but the explanations and extenuating circumstances. Like Marvin Hill, he recognizes the millenarian anticipations and the political activities that most of their neighbors found offensive. Interestingly, this non-Mormon historian shows greater sympathy for Joseph Smith. Although not biographies, the books of both Hill and Winn present Joseph Smith as primarily a political leader.

2. *Destroyer of skepticism.* In 1980 the Reverend Robert Hullinger published *Mormonism's Answer to Skepticism: Why Joseph Smith Wrote the Book of Mormon.*[51] Not at all the usual denigration of Joseph Smith, this book goes to considerable effort to understand the context of doubt and infidelity that pervaded America in the early nineteenth century. Growing out of the Enlightenment, criticism of traditional Christianity, sometimes extending to all religion, was widely disseminated in Joseph Smith's America. Thomas Paine's *The Age of Reason*, unoriginal though it may have been, popularized the rejection of miracles and traditional religion. Enter Joseph Smith. What he did was to give his own testimony of modern visions and miracles and, most impressively, to produce the Book of Mormon, which, when read within this context, was a long argument against the modern skeptics.

Hullinger sees Joseph Smith as sincerely motivated, as someone who single-handedly took on the modern anti-religionists, hitting them with arguments and evidence that could be rejected but could not be decisively refuted. To be sure, Hullinger does not accept the historicity of the Book of Mormon, but his careful reading allowed him to see one of its major themes. A believing Mormon, agreeing that the Book of Mormon overcomes doubt and challenges modernist critics, would insist that it was God through the ancient prophets who had provided this answer for our generation.[52]

3. *Magician.* Prompted by some of Mark Hofmann's forgeries, some people in the 1980s began to see Joseph Smith as a practitioner of rural folk magic. The charge that he had been involved in

digging for buried treasure was not new, of course, but now he was portrayed as part of a group who for several years had engaged in this nocturnal activity and practiced strange rites of divination. For a few years, based on a letter mistakenly thought to have been written by Martin Harris, Joseph was thought to ascribe extraordinary powers or meaning to the salamander. Brought into this eerie half-light of prescientific behavior, also, were talismans to which he allegedly ascribed spiritual significance and astrological signs by which he allegedly governed his life at crucial points, even including the conception and birth of his children. At least this was the argument, which was expressed in its most scholarly form by historian D. Michael Quinn.[53]

Quinn did not see the magic as inconsistent with the divine calling of prophet. The explanation that any tinkering with magic was either compatible with or superseded by genuine prophetic achievement was expressed by defenders such as Ronald W. Walker and Richard L. Anderson.[54] Yes, they granted, the Smith family was not highly educated and no doubt did accept some of the popular lore of the early nineteenth century. If Joseph was a magician, he was a magician-prophet, or, more accurately, a magician-turned-prophet, for he outgrew his earlier conception of himself as simply leader of a group of rustic treasure hunters. As Richard Bushman wrote:

> The power of Enlightenment skepticism had far less influence on Joseph Smith, perhaps at first because rationalism had not penetrated Smith family culture very deeply. The Prophet showed no sign of wavering when exposed to the scorn of Palmyra's rationalist editors and to the criticism of [Alexander] Campbell himself. Joseph told of the visits of angels, of direct inspiration, of a voice in the chamber of Father Whitmer, without embarrassment. . . . His world was not created by Enlightenment rationalism with its deathly aversion to superstition. The Prophet brought into modern America elements of a

more ancient culture in which the sacred and the profane intermingled and the Saints enjoyed supernatural gifts and powers as the frequent blessing of an interested God.[55]

For Bushman, in some sense, Joseph Smith's openness to realities and experiences beyond the limits of respectable rationalism was a strength, not a weakness.

Two questions must be confronted here. First, how convincing is the evidence that Joseph Smith was involved in the magical activities? The answer varies according to the time—1820, 1825, 1830—and the particular subject of supposed magic. One reviewer, Stephen Robinson, took Quinn to task for logical fallacies and for failing to establish, for example, even the ownership, much less any specific use, of talismans and magic parchments.[56]

Second, just how much of all this continued to be a part of Joseph's adult life as he brought forth the Book of Mormon, organized a church, received revelations, and led his people for the fourteen years from 1830 to his death in 1844? Most would say that magic entered into the full-blown religion only slightly, if at all. Everything depends on definitions, of course. Some of my university colleagues would dismiss prayer itself as ridiculous mumbo jumbo, some kind of infantile incantation by which naive people think they can influence events.

At any rate, here was a new label. It could even be applied with some respect by those who were using for their comparison such thinkers as Paracelsus. And at a time when "new age" religion even among the educated included mind-altering drugs, astrology, and crystals, it could be high praise to say of Joseph Smith that he was a magus. It could also, of course, be a dismissive form of guilt by association.[57]

4. *Mystic.* I don't know who first suggested that Joseph Smith might be a kind of mystic. I. Woodbridge Riley used the term rather loosely, as previously noted. Paul Edwards, a direct descendant of the Prophet and leader in the Reorganized Church of Jesus Christ of Latter Day Saints, has suggested that the term describes the tendency in the

Smith family, and of course especially in the prophet, to seek and make contact with the divine.[58] They were not ordinary, practical people, so to speak, but were in some sense mystics.

For those already familiar with others of the nineteenth century of whom the same might be said, this usage has the advantage of making the Smith experiences intelligible. In a valuable corrective to the perception that Americans were all hard-nosed, down-to-earth types, Hal Bridges has surveyed several examples of what he called "American mysticism."[59] If what we need is a frame of reference in which to place Joseph Smith, this term offers certain advantages. All too often modern people, approaching the subject without any awareness of the larger picture, are quick to see uniqueness, or craziness, in attitudes that had many parallels. If *mysticism* serves the purpose of breaking down barriers to an understanding of Smith, I suggest, let it be used.

For myself, I find it unhelpful. Bridges' working definition— "Mysticism is selfless, direct, transcendent, unitive experience of God or ultimate reality, and the experient's interpretation of that experience"[60]—would seem to exclude the revelations of Joseph Smith, which were not selfless and not unitive. He never lost his own identity, never merged or melted into the divine. I agree with Max Nolan that Joseph Smith's revelations simply do not fit the definitions of classical mysticism as it was expounded by Plotinus or, closer to the present, St. John of the Cross.[61] There is no real union with the divine in Joseph's experiences, no "flight of the alone to the alone" (Plotinus). Nor were his experiences ineffable except in the sense that they could not be fully communicated, for many of them in fact did convey precise messages, even elaborate teachings and instructions.

For strict secularists, of course, both St. Theresa of Avila and Joseph Smith were off the wall. For them, any genuine connection with God, however we describe it, is quite out of the question. But for those who have become familiar with the literature on mysticism, both Christian and non-Christian, and have some respect for the validity of that experience, perhaps the willingness to accept the possibility of continued interaction between God and humans leaves the door open for the kind of revelations Joseph Smith described.[62]

5. *Psychopath.* In a general sense people in Joseph Smith's lifetime could describe him as "crazy," but it was not until the rise of psychology as a learned discipline that the exact nature of his supposed mental derangement could be discussed with any real specificity.

The first serious psychological interpretation, by I. Woodbridge Riley, has been examined previously. A little later Bernard DeVoto, who had his own hang-ups about Mormonism and who had apparently come across some popularized Freudianism, advanced the theory that Joseph Smith was afflicted with paranoia.[63] Neither epilepsy nor paranoia have credibility. After examining the literature, T. L. Brink has no hesitation in rejecting these claims. "No category disease, neurological or psychiatric," he writes, "can account for the complexity of Smith's behavior, or its social dimension."[64]

A thoughtful effort to understand the psychology of Joseph Smith has come from historian Lawrence Foster.[65] Drawing from anthropologist Anthony F. C. Wallace, Foster says that "far from being unique, Joseph Smith's first vision and related experiences were almost a classic model of such phenomena in all times and cultures." Although Foster does not accept the historicity of the First Vision in the literal sense, he is remarkably willing to concede sincerity and even a kind of validity:

> Even if Joseph's visions reflected his own personal psychology rather than contact with beings from another dimension of reality, the perceived source of a vision by no means determines whether the message itself is not also true in some deeper sense. Joseph Smith was one of the most complex individuals who ever lived; if he interpreted the deeply felt inner truth of his prophetic mission as an objective experience, that interpretation in no way invalidates the truth of the mission itself. Surely if God works through fallible human agency, then it may well be

that he has to operate at times through psychological experiences perceived as literally true. This may be necessary in order to communicate a complex divine message to the limited human agents through whom that message must be transmitted.[66]

More recently, in 1992, Foster advanced a more specific psychological interpretation.[67] Joseph Smith was a manic-depressive. Not a psychiatrist or psychologist, Foster surveyed the literature. Several of the characteristics now associated with manic depression were found in the Mormon prophet's life, especially at the end: he was expansive and grandiose, manically enthusiastic, sexually hyperactive, and of course intermittently depressed. To his credit, Foster was both tentative and careful in his conclusions.

If Joseph Smith was manic-depressive to any degree, even though this may explain some of his characteristic reactions, it did not prevent him from being enormously productive in both ideas and institutional innovations. Non-Mormon Foster may not agree with the religious views, but he knows that validity is independent of the subject's mental or physical condition. He quotes William James: "If there were such a thing as inspiration from a higher realm, it might well be that the neurotic temperament would furnish the chief condition of the requisite receptivity."

A variation is the interpretation of LDS psychiatrist C. Jess Groesbeck, who sees the family dynamics as crucial.[68] Reading through the details of the family history as recalled by Joseph's mother, Lucy Mack Smith, Groesbeck discerns serious tension between the father and the mother. Obsessed with a search for the true church, she sought answers in organized religion. He, on the other hand, was clinically depressed as a result of losing the family's resources in speculation. He had a series of dreams, interpreted by Groesbeck, sometimes on multiple levels, as a reflection of the frustration, the differences between husband and wife, the longing for a solution. For a time, Alvin, the oldest son, played the role of healer and breadwinner. With his tragic death, Hyrum and Joseph had to take over. Joseph's visions and founding of the Church, therefore, served the purpose not only of restoring the true church but also of solving a family problem, bringing father and mother back together.

Groesbeck is careful not to deny the reality of the First Vision, "a remarkable, compensatory collective response from the archetypal level of the psyche in which multiple, significant problems were resolved for Joseph himself, his father, for his mother and other members of his family, for his forefathers, and"—note the jump from the individual and familial to the universal—"finally for many others in his generation."[69]

In the early 1990s two psychiatrists, William D. Morain and Robert Anderson, separately interpreted Joseph Smith largely in terms of his childhood operation.[70] My original reaction is to be unconvinced. As William James wrote of the early Roman Catholic effort to explain Luther's Reformation as the result of his desire to marry a nun, "the effects are infinitely wider than the alleged causes, and for the most part opposite in nature."[71] Dr. Anderson's detailed correlation of the members of the Smith family with those of Lehi's family in the Book of Mormon is similarly deficient.[72]

6. *Genius.* A term quite readily used by many now to describe Joseph Smith is *genius.* We find in Fawn Brodie a kind of reluctant concession to his creativity, the extraordinary quality of his imagination. Historian Jan Shipps has used this term as well, although she has also suggested that Joseph can be fruitfully considered to be a kind of prodigy.[73] Lawrence Foster, while seeing manic depression as the underlying condition, is also not reluctant to concede genius to Smith. The term had been used by William James in describing many religious innovators.

In 1992 Yale literary scholar Harold Bloom devoted a surprising number of pages to Joseph Smith.[74] Using a term made fashionable by Max Weber, Bloom praises Smith's charisma: "Whatever account of charisma is accepted, the Mormon prophet possessed that quality to a degree unsurpassed in American history." But it is not his charismatic leadership that is Bloom's main interest but rather his "imaginative vitality." As a "Jewish Gnostic," Bloom is not express-ing belief in Joseph Smith, but his admiration is unsparing:

> My observation certainly does find enormous validity
> in Smith's imaginative recapture of crucial elements
> in the archaic Jewish religion, elements evaded by
> normative Judaism, and by the Church after it. The
> God of Joseph Smith is a daring revival of the God of
> some of the Kabbalists and Gnostics, prophetic sages
> who, like Smith himself, asserted that they had
> returned to the true religion of Yahweh or Jehovah.[75]

However we might agree or disagree with Bloom's analysis, or his emphasis, he is clearly quite willing to see Joseph Smith as "an authentic religious genius."[76]

What all of these explanatory models have in common is a pro-fessed desire to understand Joseph Smith by putting him into a rec-ognized category but one that avoids the uncomfortable alternatives of true prophet or fraud. Those who have advanced the newer inter-pretations intend to be complimentary, or at least to separate them-selves from those who are simply shouting denunciations. Some of these authors even cling to belief in Joseph Smith's prophetic calling, simply arguing that God, as in biblical times, used someone shaped by secondary influences. Others among the modern writers by no means accept Joseph as a prophet but obviously admire him and do not wish to be among his old-fashioned denouncers. In that sense they see themselves as occupying a middle ground.

As for believing Mormons, most are unfamiliar with these schol-arly reappraisals. To the extent that they might find them convincing, however, they would simply insist on combining models. If Joseph Smith was a political leader, for example, he was for them a prophet, part of whose role, as circumstances developed, was also to provide political leadership. If he challenged the skeptics of his time, he was simply doing what a prophet does, under divine inspiration, in speak-ing to the needs of his generation. If he was a magician or magus, his followers would say, he was one selected by God and who then moved into the larger, vastly more significant role of prophet. If he was a mystic (a term most Latter-day Saints would not find descriptive of their founder), he was one who, far from focusing his primary concern on his own union with the divine, transformed his vocation into that of prophetically mediating between God and human beings. They would not relish a term like psychopath but, with William James, might well accept the idea that God takes a person with a given set of strengths and weakness—personal and familial, psychological and physical— and uses that person as an instrument. The same would be true of Joseph as genius. Of the many who have a high intelligence quotient a few achieve greatness in different areas of life. The significant thing for believing Latter-day Saints would be that God selected this particular genius, if you will, and used him. Cutting through to the heart of the matter, they are usually content to see Joseph Smith as a prophet.

## ENDNOTES

1. Charles Mackay, *History of the Mormons: or, Latter-day Saints, with Memoirs of the Life and Death of Joseph Smith, the "American Mahomet"* (Auburn, NY: Derby and Miller, 1852). On Mackay as a historian, see Leonard J. Arrington, "Charles Mackay and His 'True and Impartial History' of the Mormons," *Utah Historical Quarterly* 36 (Winter 1968): 24–40.

2. Liverpool: Latter-day Saints' Book Depot, 1853. A "corrected" edition was published in Salt Lake City in 1902. RLDS editions were published in 1880, 1908, and 1912.

3. Jan Shipps, "The Prophet, His Mother, and Early Mormonism: Mother Smith's History as a Passageway to Understanding," mimeograph, LDS Church Archives.

4. Edward W. Tullidge, *Life of Joseph, the Prophet* (New York: Privately printed, 1878); (Plano, IL: Board of Publication of the Reorganized Church of Jesus Christ of Latter Day Saints, 1880). On Tullidge as a historian, see Davis Bitton and Leonard J. Arrington, *Mormons and Their Historians* (Salt Lake City: University of Utah Press, 1988).

5. See my "Mormonism's Encounter with Spiritualism," in Davis Bitton, *The Ritualization of Mormon History and Other Essays* (Urbana/Chicago: University of Illinois Press, 1994).

6. Salt Lake City: Juvenile Instructor Office, 1888. A second edition appeared in 1907 and a Tahitian translation in 1925.

7. I. Woodbridge Riley, *The Founder of Mormonism: A Psychological Study of Joseph Smith, Jr.* (New York: Dodd Mead & Co., 1902).

8. I. Woodbridge Riley, *The Founder of Mormonism: A Psychological Study of Joseph Smith, Jr.* (London: William Heinemann, 1903), 63–4.

9. Riley, 31.

10. Riley, 43.

11. Riley, 50.

12. Riley, 61.

13. Riley, 68.

14. Riley, 68.

15. Riley, 73.

16. Riley, 74.

17. Riley, 193.

18. Riley, 194.

19. Riley, 195.

20. Riley, 198.

21. Riley, 208.

22. Riley, 226.

23. Riley, 226.

24. Riley, 232.

25. He had been discussing the revelations of Mohammed, which are pronounced "from the unconscious sphere." Then: "In the case of Joseph Smith (who had prophetic revelations innumerable in addition to the revealed translation of the old plates which resulted in the Book of Mormon), although there may have been a motor element, the inspiration seems to have been predominantly sensorial." The "peep-stones" were "apparently a case of crystal-gazing." James gives no real analysis of the revelations in the Doctrine and Covenants, which one might think would attract the scholar's interest. He does reproduce an interesting letter from "an eminent Mormon" (I am guessing it was Joseph F. Smith), including: "This Church has at its head a prophet, seer, and revelator, who gives to man God's holy will. Revelation is the means through which the will of God is declared directly and in fullness to man. These revelations are got through dreams of sleep or in waking visions of the mind, by voices without visional appearance, or by actual manifestations of the Holy Presence before the eye. We believe that God has come in person and spoken to our prophet and revelator."

26. John Henry Evans, *Joseph Smith: An American Prophet* (New York: Macmillan, 1933).

27. Evans, 427–28.

28. Preston Nibley, *Joseph Smith, the Prophet* (Salt Lake City: Deseret News Press, 1944).

29. New York: Knopf, 1945. A second edition, substantially unchanged but with an afterword, appeared in 1971.

30. In *Mormons and Their Historians*, 111–15.

31. "An Appraisal of the So-Called Brodie Book," *Church News*, 11 May 1946.

32. *No, Ma'am, That's Not History: A Brief Review of Mrs. Brodie's Reluctant Vindication of a Prophet She Seeks to Expose* (Salt Lake City: Bookcraft, 1946). Incorporating the changes of subsequent editions, now in the volume of the *Collected Works of Hugh Nibley* entitled *Tinkling Cymbals and Sounding Brass*, ed. David J. Whitaker (Provo and Salt Lake City, UT: F.A.R.M.S. and Deseret Book, 1991).

33. Hugh Nibley, 34.

34. Louis Midgley, "The Brodie Connection: Thomas Jefferson and Joseph Smith," *Brigham Young University Studies* 20 (Fall 1979): 59–67. On the Nixon biography, see Frank Gannon, "The Good Dog Richard Affair," in R. Emmett Tyrell, Jr., ed., *Orthodoxy: The American Spectator Anniversary Anthology* (New York: Harper & Row, 1987), 442-52. A general evaluation of Brodie is F. L. Stewart, *Exploding the Myth about Joseph Smith, the Mormon Prophet* (New York: House of Stewart Publishing, 1967).

35. Salt Lake City: Deseret News, 1951.

36. Wesley P. Walters, "New Light on Mormon Origins from the Palmyra Revival," *Evangelical Theological Society Bulletin* 10 (1967): 227–41; and *Dialogue: A Journal of Mormon Thought* 4 (Spring 1969): 60–81.

37. Rodger I. Anderson, *Joseph Smith's New York Reputation Reexamined* (Salt Lake City: Signature Books, 1990), critically reviewed by Richard L. Anderson in *Review of Books on the Book of Mormon* 3 (1991): 52–80.

38. The easiest way to keep up with the ongoing research on the Book of Mormon, on both sides, is to follow *Reviews of Books on the Book of Mormon* 1 (1989–).

39. Milton V. Backman, *Joseph Smith's First Vision* (Salt Lake City: Bookcraft, 1971). See also Milton V. Backman, *Eyewitness Accounts of the Restoration* (Salt Lake City: Deseret Book, 1983).

40. See Anderson's review in *Review of Books on the Book of Mormon* 3 (1991): 52-80. See also Richard L. Anderson, *Joseph Smith's New England Heritage* (Salt Lake City: Deseret Book, 1971).

41. In addition to *No Ma'am, That's Not History*, previously cited, see Hugh Nibley, *Censoring the Joseph Smith Story* (Salt Lake City: Deseret Book, 1961); and Hugh Nibley, *The Myth Makers* (Salt Lake City: Deseret Book, 1961).

42. Davis Bitton, *The Ritualization of Mormon History* (Urbana: University of Illinois Press, 1994).

43. Garden City, NY: Doubleday, 1977.

44. Urbana: University of Illinois Press, 1984.

45. East Lansing: Michigan State University Press, 1967.

46. Joseph Smith, *History of The Church of Jesus Christ of Latter-day Saints* 6 vols. (Salt Lake City: Deseret News, 1902–1912), 6:364.

47. Insisting that Joseph's kingship, connected with the temple ceremonies, was decidedly not of this world is Gordon C. Thomasson, "Foolsmate," *Dialogue: A Journal of Mormon Thought* 6 (Autumn-Winter 1971): 148-51.

48. Marvin S. Hill, *Quest for Refuge: The Mormon Flight from American Pluralism* (Salt Lake City: Signature Books, 1989).

49. The most penetrating review, by Gordon D. Pollock, criticizes Hill for a feeble, naive definition of class and an unclear understanding of pluralism. *Journal for the Scientific Study of Religion* 29 (1990): 418–19.

50. Kenneth H. Winn, *Exiles in a Land of Liberty: Mormons in America, 1830–1846* (Chapel Hill/London: University of North Carolina Press, 1989).

51. St. Louis: Clayton Publishing Co., 1980. The work has been republished under a different title: *Joseph Smith's Response to Skepticism* (Salt Lake City: Signature Books, 1992).

52. Richard L. Bushman emphasizes the extent to which Joseph Smith did not use miracles as proof, but he acknowledges that this was sometimes done. Faith and the witness of the Holy Ghost are the important things. "This is our evidence." Bushman, "How Did the Prophet Joseph Smith Respond to Skepticism in His Time?" *Ensign* 20 (February 1990): 61–63.

53. *Early Mormonism and the Magic World View* (Salt Lake City: Signature Books, 1987).

54. Richard L. Anderson, "The Mature Joseph Smith and Treasure Seeking," *Brigham Young University Studies* 24 (Fall 1984): 489–560; Ronald W. Walker, "Joseph Smith: The Palmyra Seer," *Brigham Young University Studies* 24 (Fall 1984): 461–72.

55. Richard L. Bushman, *Joseph Smith and the Beginnings of Mormonism* (Urbana/Chicago: University of Illinois Press, 1984) 184.

56. Review in *Brigham Young University Studies* 27 (Fall 1987): 88–95. See also reviews in the same issue by William A. Wilson and Benson Whittle.

57. Appearing after I had written this chapter was John L. Brooke, *The Refiner's Fire: The Making of Mormon Cosmology, 1644-1844* (Cambridge: Cambridge University Press, 1994), which sees Joseph Smith as one who tapped into the tradition of backwoods magic but also borrowed from something called the "hermetic" tradition, a cover term that includes a great many ingredients, to put it mildly. For my negative review of Brooke's misguided polemic, which predictably was lauded by the secular historical profession and the current anti-Mormons, see *Brigham Young University Studies* 34 (1994–1995): 182–92.

58. Paul M. Edwards, "The Secular Smiths," *Journal of Mormon History* 4 (1977): 3–17.

59. Hal Bridges, *American Mysticism: From William James to Zen* (New York: Harper & Row, 1970).

60. Bridges, 4.

61. Max Nolan, "Joseph Smith and Mysticism," *Journal of Mormon History* 10 (1983): 105–16.

62. I am aware that the great mystics held little regard for visions and voices, although some of them experienced them. Bridges, 7. It is instructive to review the many manifestations, often quite sensory if not sensual, of St. Theresa of Avila and St. Ignatius Loyola—both of whom lived in the sixteenth century—by comparison with the far more linear, verbal, communicative revelations of Joseph Smith.

63. Bernard DeVoto, "The Centennial of Mormonism," *American Mercury* 19 (January 1930): 1–13; "Joseph Smith" in *Dictionary of American Biography* (1935). See Leland A. Fetzer, "Bernard DeVoto and the Mormon Tradition," *Dialogue: A Journal of Mormon Thought* 3–4 (Autumn-Winter 1971): 23–38.

64. T. L. Brink, "Joseph Smith: A Study in Analytical Psychology" (Ph.D. diss., University of Chicago, 1978), 272-73.

65. Lawrence Foster, "First Visions: Personal Observations on Joseph Smith's Religious Experience," *Sunstone* 8 (September-October 1983): 39–43.

66.. Foster, "First Visions," 42.

67.. Lawrence Foster, "The Psychology of Religious Genius: Joseph Smith and the Origins of New Religious Movements," paper presented at the annual meeting of the Mormon History Association, St. George, UT, 16 May 1992.

68. C. Jess Groesbeck, "The Smiths and Their Dreams and Visions," *Sunstone* 12 (March 1988): 22–29.

69. The existence of different versions of the vision "in no way indicates that all of the aspects of the vision were not experienced in the actual event. In no way would it invalidate the vision in its complexity and intricacy as a psychic datum, answering the needs of Joseph Smith in a personal way." Groesbeck, 29.

70. William D. Morain, "The Sword of Laban: Joseph Smith, Jr., and the Unconscious," paper presented at the annual meeting of the Mormon History Association, Ogden, UT, May 1993; Robert Anderson, "The Sword of Laban: The Book of Mormon as Autobiography," paper presented at the annual meeting of the Sunstone Symposium, Salt Lake City, UT, August 1993.

71. William James, *The Varieties of Religious Experience: A Study in Human Nature* (New York/London: Longmans, Green, and Co., 1902), 21n.

72. Dr. C. Jess Groesbeck's perceptive comments on Robert Anderson's paper included the following: "There are too many things in Joseph's life that are not accounted for in the Book of Mormon and, vice versa, the Book of Mormon has too many things in it that do not just relate to Joseph's life."

73. "Joseph Smith [like Benjamin Franklin] was also a 'human multitude,' an extraordinarily talented individual—a genius beyond question." Jan Shipps, "The Prophet Puzzle: Suggestions Leading towards a More Comprehensive Interpretation of Joseph Smith," *Journal of Mormon History* 1 (1974): 19.

74. Harold Bloom, "The Religion-Making Imagination of Joseph Smith," *Yale Review* 80 (1992): 26–43; repeated and expanded upon in Harold Bloom, *The American Religion: The Emergence of the Post-Christian Nation* (New York: Simon & Schuster, 1992). My references here are to the article.

75. Bloom, "The Religion-Making Imagination of Joseph Smith," 29.

76. See "Four LDS Views on Harold Bloom: A Roundtable," *Brigham Young University Studies* 35, no. 1 (1995): 173–204. Introduced by M. Gerald Bradford, the essays are by Eugene England, Truman G. Madsen, Charles Randall Paul, and Richard F. Haglund, Jr. Haglund is especially important in recognizing the fundamental inaccuracy and political motivation of Bloom's interpretation.

# Epilogue

"I feel like shouting hallelujah, all the time, when I think that I ever knew Joseph Smith, the Prophet whom the Lord raised up and ordained, and to whom He gave keys to powers to build up the kingdom of God on earth and sustain it."

—Brigham Young[1]

"The blood of Joe Smith, spilled by murderous hands, will be like the fabled dragon's teeth sown broadcast, that everywhere sprang up armed men."

—Horace Greeley[2]

In the preceding pages we have had occasion to go over quite a number of images of the man Joseph Smith, friendly and unfriendly, past and present. I make no claim to having exhausted the possibilities of this kind of analysis. My *The Martyrdom Remembered: A One-hundred-fifty-year Perspective on the Assassination of Joseph Smith* (Aspen Books, 1994) studies the image of that single momentous event. But those facets of the subject treated in the present book do allow certain conclusions. By no means obvious or unimportant is the fact that people act not according to the way things are but the way they think they are. (I am paraphrasing roughly the French historian Roland Mousnier, who was himself stating a truism.) During his lifetime, different people perceived Joseph Smith differently and behaved accordingly. The same is true of the present.

Closely related is the fact that our perceptions are shaped to a significant degree by our expectations. More basically, if our paradigm of reality—the map of possibilities by which we govern our lives—allows room for God, angels, miracles, prophets, and the like, in the present as in the past, we are in the population that at least potentially might follow Joseph Smith or someone like him. If our paradigm simply rules out such possibilities, we inevitably look for alternative explanations. The truism bears repeating: what we see is to a large degree shaped by preconceptions.[3] Joseph Smith should not have been surprised that many in the materialistic America of the 1830s saw him as a con man, for peddlers of snake oil, or their equivalent, were on every side, and a certain element of the population was cynical and suspicious of all religious claims. The miracle, perhaps, is that he found some people who were still living within, or who could move into, a framework more like ancient Israel than like Tocqueville's America.

Who then *was* Joseph Smith? Like all human beings, he played several roles.[4] Joseph Smith was a *son*, a *brother*, a *husband*, a *father*, a *friend*. How good he was in these capacities may be subject for discussion, but those related to him in these ways were staunchly loyal, holding him in the highest regard.

He was also a *businessman*, for he dealt with money and building projects and retail stores. Some have suggested that here he sometimes proved inadequate, granting credit too readily or getting caught up in speculation. As an *administrator* he can be scrutinized and evaluated by those trained in organizational behavior, a discipline that did not exist in his lifetime. He may have been deficient in his choice of advisors—one thinks especially of John C. Bennett—but he used very effectively the highly loyal Hyrum and had the acuity to give increasing responsibility to the Twelve. The organization itself, starting simply and developing to include bishopric, Twelve, patriarch, Seventy, and such ad hoc committees as the Nauvoo House and Temple committees, was an accomplishment of someone who bravely tackled a multitude of challenges.

As *leader* how did Joseph Smith measure up? Because of the complexity of the concept "leadership," on which an extensive literature now exists, the question is not simple. There are different leadership styles. But of certain things there is little room for doubt. For example, Joseph had charisma; he could capture the attention of a crowd and could communicate effectively his own sincerity. Even through the terrible trials of Ohio, Missouri, and Illinois, he retained a surprisingly large portion of his following. It required more than casual commitment to "hang in there" after being violently expelled from homes several times. And new disciples continued to flock in. Even those who disliked his religion or who regarded him as a tyrant would, I think, have had to concede that he was indeed a leader.

The analysis of different roles, as with all of us, could go on and on. As *singer*, for all I know, he may have been a disaster. As a *foot racer* he probably would not lead at the finish line, for his childhood surgery left him with a slight limp. As a *wrestler* we happen to know that he was a tough competitor, which may say something about his basic physical strength and the determination of his character.

I realize that role theory, as usually understood, is concerned more centrally with social roles.[5] What, then, about Joseph Smith's basic claim to being a *prophet* of God? In a University of Chicago doctoral dissertation, T. L. Brink, after considering the old charge that Joseph Smith was an impostor, concludes: "Psychoanalysis has identified generalized patterns of imposture, and the life and behavior of Joseph Smith clearly do not conform to those patterns."[6]

But does this mean that Joseph Smith was exactly what he claimed to be? Brink's words of summary are carefully chosen:

> Was Joseph Smith a self-deluded enthusiast? To the extent that he was totally committed to his religious vocation, he was an enthusiast. To the extent that he confused psychic reality with physical reality, he was deluded. But to the extent that he formulated a new system of myths, symbols, rituals, and social organization, which his followers found relevant to their needs, he was a true prophet.[7]

Within this scholar's frame of reference, this is a highly positive evaluation.

It is worth dwelling on this particular answer for a moment. What is being said here, if I am understanding correctly, is that to those who accepted Joseph Smith as a prophet he was a prophet. He functioned as a prophet; he gave them direction, communicated the will of God (or what they accepted as such) to them, acted as a "forth-teller" in taking stock of the state of the world and its morals and calling people to a standard, and even told about the future, thus fulfilling the prophetic role of "foreteller." This is a functional definition, not a meaningless concession. Those working within a totally naturalistic set of assumptions might well say that one can go no further in evaluating Jeremiah or Jesus Christ.

The obverse of the medal is not so complimentary. To those who did not accept Joseph Smith in this way he was no prophet at all. To them he was indeed some kind of raving fanatic, a pretender, a megalomaniac. We are left with the different images. Insofar as the theme of this book has been to set forth some of these images, we might well stop here.

For secularists who find any claim to divine calling simply unthinkable, for the perfectly adequate reason that, to them, God does not exist, the question does end here. For them it was never a serious question to begin with. But those who believe in a biblical God capable of revealing himself and intervening in human affairs might still entertain the question. Is it possible that this man of the nineteenth century was in fact an instrument of God, someone who channeled a divine message to the human race?

Most theists, including most Christians, rule out any such possibility without feeling any necessity to examine what Joseph Smith said and did. Others have looked over the facts of his life, however cursorily, and found what they consider incompatibilities with his claim. For example, a true prophet would not practice polygamy, or a true prophet would not fire a revolver at his assassins. The list goes on and on. In such statements there is always an undisclosed syllogism by which one defines in advance the means by which God must reveal himself. Major premise: a true prophet would not do X. Minor premise: Joseph Smith did X. Conclusion:

Joseph Smith was not a true prophet. I cannot refrain from noting that this same type of reasoning sufficed for all who rejected the biblical prophets and indeed the messianic mission of Jesus Christ. Perfectly convincing to those who use it, such logic is indeed airtight, but the conclusion is imbedded in the rigid definition of the major premise.

Presuming that for those who believe in God the question is at least intelligible, one answer is to say that the one who knows who is and who is not a prophet of God, indeed the decisive and only final authority on the subject—is God. Not claiming access to the mind of God, I *as historian* must humbly confess my incompetence to proceed further.

When Joseph Smith said, "No man knows my history . . . ," he was admitting that he had no way of providing such irresistible evidence in his favor that all must accept it. "Just wait and see," he was saying. "You will know later who I am." In this sense, he could easily have applied to himself the following Book of Mormon passage, the words of the prophet Nephi as he takes leave of his readers:

> And if they are not the words of Christ, judge ye—
> for Christ will show unto you, with power and great
> glory, that they are his words, at the last day; and you
> and I shall stand face to face before his bar; and ye
> shall know that I have been commanded of him to
> write these things, notwithstanding my weakness.
> (2 Ne. 33:11)

In essence, the Prophet says, God knows I am his prophet and some day you too will know. In the meantime, if you will sincerely pray to God, if you will put the teachings into your heart and life, confirmation is available. At least this seems to have been the basic process by which people like Brigham Young became undeviating followers and wished to shout hallelujah.

Back in the days before the corruption of our language, before the flattening of our reality into a stark, naturalistic, horizontal plane, there used to be a name for the leap, the signing onto something magnificently demanding and all-encompassing, the living out of something as if it were true, the growing conviction of the reality of things hoped for, things unseen. It used to be called *faith*.

## ENDNOTES

1. *Journal of Discourses*, 26 vols. (Liverpool and London: Latter-day Saints' Book Depot, 1854-1886), 3:51. Sermon of 6 October 1855.

2. *Nauvoo Neighbor*, 24 July 1844.

3. This basic point is spelled out most profoundly by Kant. As it affects our scientific understanding, the most influential work of this generation has been Thomas Kuhn, *The Structure of Scientific Revolutions* (Chicago: University Press, 1970). On a more accessible level, I like E. F. Schumacher's *A Guide for the Perplexed* (New York: Harper & Row, 1977).

4. I have no desire to claim that human beings are *only* the sum of the social roles they play, an oversimplification unfairly attributed to G. H. Mead.

5. J. A. Jackson, ed., *Role* (London, 1972); Erving Goffman, *The Presentation of the Self in Everyday Life* (1956).

6. T. L. Brink, "Joseph Smith: A Study in Analytical Psychology," (Ph.D. diss., University of Chicago, 1978), 281. Notice that Brink is writing twenty years after Phyllis Greenacre, "The Impostor," *Psychoanalytic Quarterly* 27 (1958): 359–82, quoted with approval by Fawn Brodie, *No Man Knows My History: The Life of Joseph Smith, the Mormon Prophet*, 2d ed. (New York: Knopf, 1971), 418–19.

7. Brink, 282.

# Select Bibliography

A "complete" bibliography of Joseph Smith is not so easy to create as some might imagine. Setting aside for the moment the unpublished material in the LDS Church Archives and elsewhere, we discover that almost everything published about the Church in its first fourteen years (and to some extent afterwards) mentions Joseph Smith or relates to him by implication. Every biography of early Mormons, for example, will likely contain references to the Prophet. Anything written on the any of the scriptures he produced—Book of Mormon, Doctrine and Covenants, Pearl of Great Price—relates to him at least indirectly. I do not attempt to list studies relating specifically to the scriptures here. Since 1989 *Review of Books on the Book of Mormon* helps in keeping abreast of many such writings, but for works published earlier the task is much more challenging.

When *BYU Studies* published its index volume in 1992, covering volumes 1 to 31, the subject index under the heading "Smith, Joseph" included more than six columns of entries in small print. From 1943 to 1985 an annual Joseph Smith memorial sermon was delivered at the Institute of Religion, Utah State University. Each year several papers are presented at conventions. This is to say nothing of sermons or less scholarly commentary in magazines for the larger audience or the depressing wasteland of anti-Mormon pamphlets. Although some might smile at the comparison, Joseph Smith, like Shakespeare and Montaigne, Petrarch and Luther, Emerson and Marx, shows every indication of inspiring a continued interest and thus an uninterrupted flow of scholarship year after year after year.

The following works are not necessarily "recommended" titles and are certainly not all equal in value. While I have deliberately omitted some of the sermons on the one side and some of the irresponsible diatribes on the other, the list still includes works that those on either extreme would dismiss as worthless. Of the many sermons, editorials, and newspaper articles mentioning Joseph Smith I have here listed only a few.

An alternative bibliography covering much of the same ground but differing in emphasis is David J. Whittaker, "Joseph Smith in Recent Research: A Selected Bibliography," in David J. Whittaker, ed., *Mormon Americana: A Guide to Sources and Collections in the United States* (Provo, UT: BYU Studies, 1995).

## Published Primary Sources

Arrington, Leonard J., ed. "James Gordon Bennett's 1831 Report on 'The Mormonites.'" *Brigham Young University Studies* 10 (Spring 1970): 353–64.

Burton, Alma P., comp. *Discourses of the Prophet Joseph Smith.* Salt Lake City: Deseret Book, 1977.

Cannon, Brian Q. "John C. Calhoun, Jr., Meets the Prophet Joseph Smith Shortly before the Departure for Carthage." *Brigham Young University Studies* 33 (1993): 772–80.

Cannon, Donald Q. "Reverend George Moore Comments on Nauvoo, the Mormons, and Joseph Smith." *Western Illinois Regional Studies* 5 (1982): 5–16.

_____. *The Wisdom of Joseph Smith.* Orem, UT: Grandin Books, 1983.

Cannon, Donald Q., and Larry E. Dahl. *The Prophet Joseph Smith's King Follett Discourse.* Provo, UT: BYU Religious Studies Center, 1983.

Cook, Lyndon W. *The Revelations of the Prophet Joseph Smith: A Historical and Biographical Commentary of the Doctrine and Covenants.* Provo, UT: Seventy's Mission Bookstore, 1981.

_____, ed. "'A More Virtuous Man Never Existed on the Footstool of the Great Jehovah': George Miller on Joseph Smith." *Brigham Young University Studies* 19 (Spring 1979): 402–7.

Ehat, Andrew F., and Lydon W. Cook, eds. *The Words of Joseph Smith: The Contemporary Accounts of the Nauvoo Discourses of the Prophet Joseph.* Provo and Salt Lake City, UT: BYU Religious Studies Center, and Bookcraft 1980.

Faulring, Scott H., ed. *An American Prophet's Record: The Diaries and Journals of Joseph Smith.* Salt Lake City: Signature Books, 1987.

Heidt, Stephen C., comp. *Un-Canonized Revelations of the Prophet Joseph Smith.* Oquirrh Mountain Publishing Co., [1994?].

Huntress, Keith. *Murder of an American Prophet: Events and Prejudice Surrounding the Killings of Joseph and Hyrum Smith; Carthage, Illinois, June 27, 1844.* San Francisco: Chandler Publishing Co., 1960.

Jessee, Dean C., ed. "Howard Coray's Recollections of Joseph Smith." *Brigham Young University Studies* 17 (Spring 1977): 341–47.

_____, ed. *The Papers of Joseph Smith.* Vols. 1– . Salt Lake City: Deseret Book, 1989– .

_____, ed. *The Personal Writings of Joseph Smith.* Salt Lake City: Deseret Book, 1984.

Jones, Dan. "The Martyrdom of Joseph Smith and His Brother Hyrum." *Brigham Young University Studies* 24 (Winter 1984): 78–109.

Kirkham, Francis W. *A New Witness for Christ in America.* 2 vols. Independence, MO: Zion's Printing and Publishing Co., 1942–1951.

Marquadt, H. Michael, ed. *Joseph Smith's 1832–34 Diary; Also, Joseph Smith's 1832 Account of His Early Life.* Salt Lake City: Modern Microfilm, 1979.

_____, ed. *Joseph Smith's 1835–36 Diary.* Salt Lake City: Modern Microfilm, 1979.

Millet, Robert L., ed. *Joseph Smith: Selected Sermons and Writings.* In Sources of American Spirituality series. New York/Mahwah, NJ: Paulist Press, 1989.

Nelson, Leland R., comp. *The Journal of Joseph: The Personal Diary of a Modern Prophet.* Provo, UT: Council Press, 1979.

Partridge, G. F., ed. "The Death of a Mormon Dictator." *New England Quarterly* 9 (1936): 583–617.

Smith, Joseph. "General Smith's Views of the Powers and Policy of the Government of the United States." *Dialogue: A Journal of Mormon Thought* 3 (Autumn 1968): 28–34.

_____. *History of The Church of Jesus Christ of Latter-day Saints.* 6 vols. Salt Lake City: Deseret News, 1902–1912. Vol. 7. Salt Lake City: Deseret News, 1932. Index volume. Salt Lake City: Deseret Book, 1970.

Smith, Joseph Fielding, comp. *Teachings of the Prophet Joseph Smith.* Salt Lake City: Deseret Book, 1976.

Van Wagoner, Richard S., and Steven C. Walker, eds. "The Joseph/Hyrum Smith Funeral Sermon." *Brigham Young University Studies* 23 (Winter 1983): 3–18.

## Books

Anderson, Mary Audentia. *Ancestry and Posterity of Joseph Smith and Emma Hale.* Independence, MO: Herald House, 1929.

Anderson, Richard Lloyd. *"His Mother's Manuscript": An Intimate View of Joseph Smith.* Provo, UT: Brigham Young University Press, 1976.

_____. *Joseph Smith's New England Heritage.* Salt Lake City: Deseret Book, 1971.

Anderson, Rodger I. *Joseph Smith's New York Reputation Reexamined.* Salt Lake City: Signature Books, 1990. *Review in Review of Books on the Book of Mormon* 3 (1991): 52–81.

Andrus, Hyrum. *Joseph Smith: The Man and the Seer.* Salt Lake City: Deseret Book, 1960.

_____. *Joseph Smith and World Government.* Salt Lake City: Deseret Book, 1958.

Andrus, Hyrum L., and Helen Mae Andrus, comps. *They Knew the Prophet.* Salt Lake City: Bookcraft, 1974.

Backman, Milton V. *Eyewitness Accounts of the Restoration.* Salt Lake City: Deseret Book, 1983.

_____. *Joseph Smith and the Doctrine and Covenants.* Salt Lake City: Deseret Book, 1992.

_____. *Joseph Smith's First Vision: Confirming Evidences and Contemporary Accounts.* 2d ed., rev. and enl. Salt Lake City: Bookcraft, 1980.

_____. *Joseph Smith's First Vision: The First Vision in Its Historical Context.* Salt Lake City: Bookcraft, 1971.

Barrett, Ivan J. *Great Moments in the Life of Joseph Smith.* Provo, UT: Brigham Young University Press, 1963.

_____. *Joseph Smith, the Extraordinary.* Provo, UT: Brigham Young University Press, 1964.

_____. *The Last Seven Days of the Life of Joseph Smith.* Provo, UT: Brigham Young University Press, 1962.

Beardsley, Harry M. *Joseph Smith and His Mormon Empire.* Boston: Houghton Mifflin, 1931.

Bennett, John C. *The History of the Saints: An Expose of Joe Smith and Mormonism.* Boston: Leland & Whiting, 1842.

Berrett, William E., Lowell L. Bennion, and T. Edgar Lyon. *Contributions of Joseph Smith*. Salt Lake City: Deseret Book, 1940.

Bitton, Davis. *The Martyrdom Remembered*. Salt Lake City: Aspen Books, 1994.

Black, Susan Easton, and Charles D. Tate, Jr., eds. *Joseph Smith: The Prophet, the Man*. Provo, UT: BYU Religious Studies Center, 1993.

Blake, Reed. *24 Hours to Martyrdom*. Salt Lake City: Bookcraft, 1973.

Bloom, Harold. *The American Religion: The Emergence of the Post-Christian Nation*. New York: Simon & Schuster, 1992.

Brewster, Hoyt W., Jr. *Martyrs of the Kingdom*. Salt Lake City: Bookcraft, 1990.

Briggs, Kay W. *Brother Joseph: Stories and Lessons from the Life of the Prophet*. Salt Lake City: Bookcraft, 1994.

Brodie, Fawn M. *No Man Knows My History*. New York: Alfred A. Knopf, 1945.

Bushman, Richard L. *Joseph Smith and the Beginnings of Mormonism*. Urbana/Chicago: University of Illinois Press, 1984.

_____. *Joseph Smith and Skepticism*. Provo, UT: Brigham Young University Press, 1974.

Cannon, George Q. *The Latter-day Prophet: History of Joseph Smith Written for Young People*. Salt Lake City: Juvenile Instructor, 1900.

_____. *The Life of Joseph Smith, the Prophet*. Salt Lake City: Juvenile Instructor Office, 1888. Latest reprint Salt Lake City: Deseret Book, 1986.

Carmer, Carl. *The Farm Boy and the Angel*. Garden City, NY: Doubleday, 1970.

Caswall, Henry. *The Prophet of the Nineteenth Century*. London: Rivingtons, 1843.

Chase, Daryl. *Joseph the Prophet: As He Lives in the Hearts of His People*. Salt Lake City: Deseret Book, 1944.

Cheville, Roy A. *Joseph and Emma Smith: Companions for Seventeen and a Half Years, 1827–1844*. Independence, MO: Herald Publishing House, 1977.

Clark, George Edward. *I Cry Joseph: Fifty-four Evidences of the Divine Calling of Joseph Smith*. N.p.: Privately published, 1952.

Conkling, J. Christopher. *A Joseph Smith Chronology*. Salt Lake City: Deseret Book, 1979.

Cook, Lyndon W. *Joseph Smith and the Law of Consecration*. Provo, UT: Grandin Book Company, 1985.

Crowther, Duane S. *The Life of Joseph Smith, 1805–1844*. Bountiful, UT: Horizon Publishers, 1989.

_____. *The Prophecies of Joseph Smith*. Salt Lake City: Bookcraft, 1963.

Curtis, Lindsay R. *The Making of a Prophet*. Salt Lake City: Deseret Book, 1967.

Doxey, Stephen B. *Joseph Smith and the Constitution: A Subjective Analysis*. N.p., 1985.

Draper, Maurice L. *The Founding Prophet: An Administrative Biography of Joseph Smith, Jr*. Independence, MO: Herald Publishing House, 1991.

Durham, G. Homer. *Joseph Smith: Prophet-Statesman*. Salt Lake City: Bookcraft, 1944.

Evans, John Henry. *Joseph Smith: An American Prophet*. New York: Macmillan, 1933. Reprinted, 1943, 1946, 1961, 1966, 1985, 1989.

Fischer, Norma J. *Portrait of a Prophet*. Salt Lake City: Bookcraft, 1960.

Gibbons, Francis M. *Joseph Smith: Martyr, Prophet of God*. Salt Lake City: Deseret Book, 1977.

Gibbons, Ted. *Like a Lamb to the Slaughter*. Orem, UT: Keepsake Paperbacks, 1990.

Gillmor, B. F. *Joseph Smith, the Mormon Prophet: A Study of a Religious Psychopath*. Kansas City: Medical Herald, 1914.

Grant, Carter E. *Important Events during the 38 1/2 Years of the Prophet's Life*. Sandy, UT: Privately published,1960.

Gregg, Thomas. *The Prophet of Palmyra: Mormonism Reviewed and Examined in the Life, Character, and Career of Its Founder*. New York: John B. Alden, 1890.

Hartshorn, Leon R. *Joseph Smith, Prophet of the Restoration*. Salt Lake City: Deseret Book, 1970.

Heinerman, John. *Joseph Smith and Herbal Medicine*. Monrovia, CA: Majority of One Press, 1980.

_____. *Joseph Smith and Natural Foods*. Manti, UT: Mountain Valley Productions, 1976.

Hill, Donna. *Joseph Smith: The First Mormon*. Garden City, NY: Doubleday. 1977.

Hogan, Mervin B. *Joseph Smith and Free Masonry*. Salt Lake City: Author, 1983.

_____. *Joseph Smith, Man and Mason*. Salt Lake City: Author, 1983.

_____. *Joseph Smith, the Frontier Prophet*. Salt Lake City: Author, 1987.

_____. *Joseph Smith's Embracement of Freemasonry*. Salt Lake City: Author, 1988.

_____. *The Two Joseph Smith Masonic Experiences*. Salt Lake City: Author, 1987.

Howard, Marcia. *Joseph Hears God's Call*. Independence, MO: Herald House, 1982.

Howard, Richard P. *Restoration Scriptures: A Study of Their Textual Development*. Independence, MO: Reorganized Church of Jesus Christ of Latter Day Saints, Department of Religious Education, 1969.

Hullinger, Robert N. *Mormon Answer to Skepticism: Why Joseph Smith Wrote the Book of Mormon*. St. Louis: Clayton Publishing House, 1980. Later published as *Joseph Smith's Response to Skepticism*. Salt Lake City: Signature Books, 1992.

Jackson, Ronald Vern. *The Seer, Joseph Smith: His Education from the Most High*. Salt Lake City: Hawkes Publications, 1977.

Johnson, J. Edward. *Joseph Smith*. Berkeley, CA: Gillick Press, 1944.

Jones, Gracia N. *The Priceless Gifts: Celebrating the Holidays with Joseph and Emma Smith*. Murray, UT: Roylance Publishing, 1989.

Lundwall, N. B., ed. *The Fate of the Persecutors of the Prophet Joseph Smith*. Salt Lake City: Bookcraft, 1952.

McCloud, Susan Evans. *Joseph Smith: A Photobiography*. Salt Lake City: Aspen Books, 1992.

McConkie, Mark L. *The Father of the Prophet: Stories and Insights from the Life of Joseph Smith, Sr.* Salt Lake City: Bookcraft, 1993.

McConkie, Joseph Fielding. *His Name Shall Be Joseph: Ancient Prophecies of the Latter-day Seer*. Salt Lake City: Hawkes Publishing Co., 1980.

Madsen, Truman. *Joseph Smith among the Prophets*. Salt Lake City: Deseret Book, 1965. A pamphlet.

_____. *Joseph Smith the Prophet*. Salt Lake City: Bookcraft, 1989.

Matthews, Robert J. *"A Plainer Translation": Joseph Smith's Translation of the Bible: A History and Commentary*. Provo, UT: Brigham Young University Press, 1975.

Millet, Robert L., ed. *"To Be Learned Is Good If . . ."* Salt Lake City: Bookcraft, 1987. Separate chapters listed below under articles.

Morris, Nephi L. *Prophecies of Joseph Smith and Their Fulfillment*. Salt Lake City: Deseret Book, 1920.

Nibley, Hugh. *Eduard Meyer's Comparison of Mohammed and Joseph Smith*. Provo, UT: F.A.R.M.S., [198?].

_____. *Tinkling Cymbals and Sounding Brass: The Art of Telling Tales about Joseph Smith and Brigham Young*. Salt Lake City Provo, UT: Deseret Book and F.A.R.M.S., 1991. Includes *No, Ma'am, That's Not History: A Brief Review of Mrs. Brodie's Reluctant Vindication of a Prophet She Seeks to Expose* (1946); *Censoring the Joseph Smith Story* (1961); and *The Myth Makers* (1961).

Nibley, Preston. *Joseph Smith, the Prophet*. Salt Lake City: Deseret News Press, 1946.

Parry, Edwin F., comp. *Stories about Joseph Smith the Prophet*. Salt Lake City: Deseret News, 1934.

Parry, Jay A. and Steven Songer. *Joseph Smith: The Boy . . . The Prophet*. Salt Lake City: Bookcraft, 1981.

Persuitte, David. *Joseph Smith and the Origins of the Book of Mormon*. Jefferson, NC: McFarland, 1985. Reviewed in RBBM 1 (1990).

Peterson, LaMar. *Hearts Made Glad: The Charges of Intemperance Against Joseph Smith, the Mormon Prophet*. Salt Lake City: Dumac Press, 1975.

Peterson, Mark E. *The Forerunners*. Salt Lake City: Bookcraft, 1979.

Porter, Larry C. and Susan Easton Black, eds. *The Prophet Joseph: Essays on the Life and Mission of Joseph Smith*. Salt Lake City: Deseret Book, 1988. Separate chapters listed below under articles.

Pratt, David N. *Joseph Smith: America's Son of Perdition*. Unity, Maine: Privately printed, 1988.

Proctor, Scot Facer. *Witness of the Light: A Photographic Journey in the Footsteps of the American Prophet Joseph Smith*. Salt Lake City: Deseret Book, 1991.

Quinn, D. Michael. *Early Mormonism and the Magic World View*. Salt Lake City: Signature Books, 1987.

Riley, I. Woodbridge, Ph.D. *The Founder of Mormonism: A Psychological Study of Joseph Smith, Jr.* London: William Heinemann, 1903.

Roberts, B.H. *Joseph Smith, the Prophet-Teacher*. Princeton, NJ: Deseret Club of Princeton University, 1967. 1st ed., 1908.

Sampson, Joe. *Written by the Finger of God: A Testimony of Joseph Smith's Translations: Decoding Ancient Languages*. Wellspring Publishing, 1994?

Smith, Henry A. *The Day They Martyred the Prophet*. Salt Lake City: Bookcraft, 1963.

Stewart, F.L. *Exploding the Myth About Joseph Smith, the Mormon Prophet*. New York: House of Stewart Publications, 1967.

Stewart, John J. *Joseph Smith, Democracy's Unknown Prophet*. Salt Lake City: Mercury Publishing, 1960.

_____. *Joseph Smith: The Mormon Prophet*. Salt Lake City: Mercury Publishing Co., 1966.

Stokes, William Lee. *Joseph Smith and the Creation*. Salt Lake City: Starstone, 1991. Orem, UT: Cedar Fort, 1991.

Tanner, Jerald and Sandra Tanner. *Joseph Smith and Polygamy*. Salt Lake City: Modern Microfilm, 1966.

_____. *Joseph Smith and Money Digging*. Salt Lake City: Modern Microfilm, 1970.

Taves, Ernest H. *Trouble Enough: Joseph Smith and the Book of Mormon*. Buffalo, NY: Prometheus Books, 1984.

Tinney, Thomas Milton. *The Royal Family of the Prophet Joseph Smith, Jr*. Salt Lake City: Green Family Organization, 1973.

Tracy, Shannon M. *In Search of Joseph*. Orem, UT: Kenning House, 1995.

Tullidge, Edward. *Life of Joseph Smith, the Prophet*. New York: privately printed, 1878.

Underwood, Grant. *The Millenarian World of Early Mormonism*. Urbana and Chicago: University of Illinois Press, 1993.

Widtsoe, John A. *Joseph Smith as a Scientist*. Salt Lake City: General Board of the Young Men's Mutual Improvement Association, 1908.

_____. *Joseph Smith: Seeker After Truth, Prophet of God*. Salt Lake City: Deseret News, 1951.

## Articles

Alexander, Thomas G. "'A New and Everlasting Covenant': An Approach to the Theology of Joseph Smith." In *New Views of Mormon History: Essays in Honor of Leonard J. Arrington*, ed. Davis Bitton and Maureen Ursenbach Beecher. Salt Lake City: University of Utah Press, 1987.

_____. "The Place of Joseph Smith in the Development of American Religion: A Historiographical Inquiry." *Journal of Mormon History* 5 (1978): 3–17.

Allaman, John Lee. "Joseph Smith's Visits to Henderson County." *Western Illinois Regional Studies* 8 (Spring 1985): 46–55.

Allen, James B. "Emergence of a Fundamental: The Expanding Role of Joseph Smith's First Vision in Mormon Religious Thought." *Journal of Mormon History* 7 (1980): 43–61.

_____. "The Significance of Joseph Smith's First Vision in Mormon Thought," *Dialogue: A Journal of Mormon Thought* 1 (Autumn 1966): 29–45.

Anderson, A. Gary. "The Mack Family and Marlow, New Hampshire." In *Regional Studies in Latter-day Saint Church History: New England*, ed. Donald Q. Cannon (Provo, UT: BYU Department of Church History and Doctrine, 1988), 43–52.

Anderson, Richard Lloyd. "Circumstantial Confirmation of the First Vision through Reminiscences." *Brigham Young University Studies* 9, 3 (1969): 373–404.

_____. "The Credibility of the Book of Mormon Translators." In Noel B. Reynolds, ed., *Book of Mormon Authorship: New Light on Ancient Origins* (Provo, UT; Religious Studies Center, Brigham Young University, 1982), 213–37.

_____. "Joseph Smith and the Millenarian Time Table." *Brigham Young University Studies* 3, 3 (1961): 55–66.

_____. "Joseph Smith's Final Self-Appraisal." In *The Prophet Joseph: Essays on the Life and Mission of Joseph Smith* (Salt Lake City: Deseret Book, 1988), 320–32.

_____. "Joseph Smith's New York Reputation Reappraised." *Brigham Young University Studies* 10, 3 (1970): 283–314.

_____. "Joseph Smith's Prophecies of Martyrdom." *Sidney B. Sperry Symposium* (Provo, UT: Religious Instruction, 1980), 1–14.

_____. "The Mature Joseph Smith and Treasure Searching." *Brigham Young University Studies* 24, 4 (1984): 489–560.

_____. "The Reliability of the Early History of Lucy and Joseph Smith." *Dialogue: A Journal of Mormon Thought* 4, 2 (Summer 1969): 12–28.

_____. "The Religious Dimension of Emma's Letters to Joseph." In *Joseph Smith: The Prophet, The Man* (Provo, UT: Religious Studies Center, Brigham Young University, 1993), 117–25.

_____. Review of Rodger I. Anderson, *Joseph Smith's New York Reputation Re-examined*. In *Review of Books on the Book of Mormon* 3 (1991): 52–80.

Anderson, Robert D. "Toward an Introduction to a Psychobiography of Joseph Smith." *Dialogue: A Journal of Mormon Thought* 27, 3 (Fall 1994): 249–72.

Andrus, Hyrum L. "Joseph Smith and the Law of Consecration." *Seminar on the Prophet Joseph Smith*. Provo, UT: Adult Education and Extension Services, 1962.

_____. "Joseph Smith and the West." *Brigham Young University Studies* 2, 2 (1960): 129–47.

Arrington, Leonard J. "Joseph Smith." In *The Presidents of the Church*, ed. Leonard J. Arrington. (Salt Lake City: Deseret Book, 1986) 3–42.

_____. "The Looseness of Zion: Joseph Smith and the Lighter View." *Task Papers in LDS History*, No. 7 (Salt Lake City: Historical Department of the Church, 1976).

_____. "Joseph Smith, Builder of Ideal Communities." In *The Prophet Joseph: Essays on the Life and Mission of Joseph Smith* (Salt Lake City: Deseret Book, 1988), 115–37.

Bachman, Danel W. "Joseph Smith, a True Martyr." In *Joseph Smith: The Prophet, The Man* (Provo, UT: Religious Studies Center, Brigham Young University, 1993), 317–32.

Backman, Milton V., Jr. "Awakenings in the Burned-Over District: New Light on the Historical Setting of the First Vision." *Brigham Young University Studies* 9 (Spring 1969): 301–20.

_____. "Defender of the First Vision." In *Regional Studies in Latter-day Saint Church History: New York*, eds. Larry C. Porter, Milton V. Backman, Jr., and Susan Easton Black (Provo, UT: BYU Department of Church History and Doctrine, 1992), 33–48.

_____. "Establish a House of Prayer, a House of God: The Kirtland Temple." In *The Prophet Joseph: Essays on the Life and Mission of Joseph Smith* (Salt Lake City: Deseret Book, 1988), 208–25.

_____. "Joseph Smith and the Restitution of All Things." In *Joseph Smith: The Prophet, The Man* (Provo, UT: Religious Studies Center, Brigham Young University, 1993), 89–99.

_____. "Joseph Smith's First Vision: Cornerstone of a Latter-day Faith." In *"To Be Learned Is Good If . . ."* (Salt Lake City: Bookcraft, 1987).

_____. "Lo, Here! Lo, There! Early in the Spring of 1820." In *The Prophet Joseph: Essays on the Life and Mission of Joseph Smith* (Salt Lake City: Deseret Book, 1988), 19–35.

Barlow, Philip L. "Before Mormonism: Joseph Smith's Use of the Bible, 1820–1829." *Journal of the American Academy of Religion* 57 (Winter 1989): 739–71.

_____. "Joseph Smith's Revision of the Bible: Fraudulent, Pathologic, or Prophetic?" *Harvard Theological Review* 83 (1990): 1–30.

Barrett, Ivan S. "Joseph Smith's Personality." *Seminar on the Prophet Joseph Smith.* Provo, UT: Adult Education and Extension Services, 1962.

Baugh, Alexander L. "Joseph Smith's Athletic Nature." In *Joseph Smith: The Prophet, The Man* (Provo, UT: Religious Studies Center, Brigham Young University, 1993), 137–50.

Benson, Alvin K. "Joseph Smith on Modern Science." In *Joseph Smith: The Prophet, The Man* (Provo, UT: Religious Studies Center, Brigham Young University, 1993), 151–67.

Bentley, Joseph I. "Legal Trials of Joseph Smith." *Encyclopedia of Mormonism.* 4 vols. (New York: Macmillan, 1992), 3: 1346–348.

Bergera, Gary James. "Joseph Smith and the Hazards of Charismatic Leadership." *John Whitmer Historical Association Journal* 6 (1986): 33–42.

Bernauer, Barbara Hands. "Still 'Side by Side': The Final trial of Joseph and Hyrum Smith." *John Whitmer Historical Association Journal* 11 (1991): 17–33.

Berrett, LaMar C. "An Impressive Letter from the Pen of Joseph Smith." *Brigham Young University Studies* 11 (Summer 1971): 517–23.

_____. "Joseph, a Family Man." In *The Prophet Joseph: Essays on the Life and Mission of Joseph Smith* (Salt Lake City: Deseret Book, 1988), 36–48.

Bitton, Davis. "Joseph Smith in the Mormon Folk Memory." *Restoration Studies* 1 (1980): 75–94.

_____. "The Martyrdom of Joseph Smith in Early Mormon Writings." *John Whitmer Historical Association Journal* 1 (1981): 29–39.

Black, Susan Easton. "Hiram, Ohio: Tribulation." In *The Prophet Joseph: Essays on the Life and Mission of Joseph Smith* (Salt Lake City: Deseret Book, 1988), 161–74.

_____. "Isaac Hale: Antagonist of Joseph Smith." In *Regional Studies in Later-day Saint Church History: New York*, eds. Larry C. Porter, Milton V. Backman, Jr., and Susan Easton Black (Provo, UT: BYU Department of Church History and Doctrine, 1990), 93–111.

_____. "Joseph's Experience in Hiram, Ohio: A Time of Contrasts." In *Regional Studies in Latter-day Saint History: Ohio*, ed. Milton V. Backman, Jr. (Provo, UT: BYU Department of Church History and Doctrine, 1990), 27–44.

Bloom, Harold. "The Religion-Making Imagination of Joseph Smith," *The Yale Review* 80 (April 1992): 26–43.

Booth, Howard J. "An Image of Joseph Smith, Jr.: A Personality Study." *Courage: A Journal of History, Thought and Action* 1 (September 1970): 4–14.

Bringhurst, Newell G. "Joseph Smith, the Mormons, and Antebellum Reform—A Closer Look." *John Whitmer Historical Association Journal* 14 (1994): 73–91.

Brink, T.L. "Joseph Smith: The Verdict of Depth Psychology." *Journal of Mormon History* 3 (1976): 73–83.

Buerger, David John. "Salvation in the Theology of Joseph Smith." In *Line Upon Line*, ed. Gary James Bergera (Salt Lake City: Signature Books, 1989), 159–69.

Bushman, Richard L. "The First Vision Story Revisited." *Dialogue: A Journal of Mormon Thought* 4 (Spring 1969): 82–93.

_____. "Joseph Smith's Family Background." In *The Prophet Joseph: Essays on the Life and Mission of Joseph Smith* (Salt Lake City: Deseret Book, 1988), 1–18.

_____. "Joseph Smith in the Current Age." In *Joseph Smith: The Prophet, The Man* (Provo, UT: Religious Studies Center, Brigham Young University, 1993), 33–48.

_____. "Treasure-seeking Then and Now." *Sunstone* 11 (September 1987): 5–6.

Bushman, Richard L. and Dean C. Jessee. "The Prophet." *Encyclopedia of Mormonism.* 4 vols. (New York: Macmillan, 1992), 3: 1331–339.

Cannon, Donald Q. "The Founding of Nauvoo." In *The Prophet Joseph: Essays on the Life and Mission of Joseph Smith* (Salt Lake City: Deseret Book, 1988), 246–60.

_____. "Joseph Smith and the University of Nauvoo." In *Joseph Smith: The Prophet, The Man* (Provo, UT: Religious Studies Center, Brigham Young University, 1993), 285–300.

_____. "The King Follett Discourse: Joseph Smith's Greatest Sermon in Historical Perspective." *Brigham Young University Studies* 18 (Winter 1978): 179–92.

Cannon, M. Hamlin, ed. "Bankruptcy Proceedings against Joseph mith in Illinois." *Pacific Historical Review* 14 (December 1945): 425–33.

Clark, James. "Joseph Smith and the Lebolo Egyptian Papyri." *Brigham Young University Studies* 8 (Winter 1968): 195–203.

Collins, William P. "Thoughts on the Mormon Scriptures: An Outsider's View of the Inspiration of Joseph Smith." *Dialogue: A Journal of Mormon Thought* 15, 3 (Autumn 1982): 49–59.

Crawley, Peter. "A Comment on Joseph Smith's Account of His First Vision and the 1820 Revival." *Dialogue: A Journal of Mormon Thought* 6,1 (Spring 1971): 106–09.

Dahl, Larry E. "The Theological Significance of the First Vision." In Robert L. Millet and Kent P. Jackson, eds., *Studies in Scripture, Vol. 2: The Pearl of Great Price.* (Salt Lake City: Randall Book, 1985.)

Dillenberger, John. "Grace and Works in Martin Luther and Joseph Smith." In Truman G. Madsen, ed., *Reflections on Mormonism: Judaeo-Christian Parallels* (Provo, UT: Brigham Young University, Religious Studies Center, 1978), 175–86. Also in *Sunstone* 3 (May-June 1978): 18–21.

Durham, Reed C., Jr. "Joseph Smith's Own Story of a Serious Childhood Illness." *Brigham Young University Studies* 10,4 (1970): 480–82.

Edwards, Paul M. "The Secular Smiths." *Journal of Mormon History* 4 (1977): 3–17.

Ehat, Andrew F. "It Seems Like Heaven Began on Earth: Joseph Smith and the Constitution of the Kingdom of God." *Brigham Young University Studies* 20,3 (1980): 253–80.

Ellsworth, Paul D. "Mobocracy and the Rule of Law: American Press Reaction to the Murder of Joseph Smith." *Brigham Young University Studies* 20,1 (1979): 71–82.

Enders, Donald L. "The Joseph Smith, Sr., Family: Farmers of the Genesee." In *Joseph Smith: The Prophet, The Man* (Provo, UT: Religious Studies Center, Brigham Young University, 1993), 213–25.

Esplin Ronald K. "Discipleship: Brigham Young and Joseph Smith." In *Joseph Smith: The Prophet, The Man* (Provo, UT: Religious Studies Center, Brigham Young University, 1993), 241–69.

_____. "Joseph, Brigham and the Twelve: A Succession of Continuity." *Brigham Young University Studies* 21 (Summer 1981): 301–41.

_____. "Joseph Smith's Mission and Timetable: `God Will Protect Me Until My Work is Done.'" In *The Prophet Joseph: Essays on the Life and Mission of Joseph Smith* (Salt Lake City: Deseret Book, 1988), 280–319.

_____. "A Place Prepared: Joseph, Brigham and the Quest for Promised Refuge in the West." *Journal of Mormon History* 9 (1982): 85–111.

Foster, Lawrence. "First Visions: Personal Observations on Joseph Smith's Religious Experience." *Sunstone* 8,5 (September-October 1983): 39–43.

Garr, Arnold K. "Joseph Smith: Man of Forgiveness." In *Joseph Smith: The Prophet, The Man* (Provo, UT: Religious Studies Center, Brigham Young University, 1993), 127–36.

Garrard, LaMar A. "Traditions of Honesty and Integrity in the Smith Family." In *"To Be Learned Is Good If . . ."* (Salt Lake City: Bookcraft, 1987).

Garvey, Keven. "The Prophet from Palmyra: Joseph Smith and the Rise of Mormonism." In David A. Halperin, ed., *Psychoanalytical Perspectives on Religion, Sect, and Cult.* (Boston: John Wright, 1983).

Gayler, George R. "Attempts by the State of Missouri to Extradite Joseph Smith, 1841–1843." *Missouri Historical Review* 58 (1963): 21–36.

_____. "Governor Ford and the Death of Joseph and Hyrum Smith." *Journal of the Illinois State Historical Society* 50 (1957): 391–411.

Godfrey, Kenneth W. "Joseph Smith and the Masons." *Journal of the Illinois State Historical Society* 64 (1971): 79–90.

_____. "A New Look at the Alleged Little Known Discourse of Joseph Smith." *Brigham Young University Studies* 9 (Autumn 1968): 49–53.

_____. "Non-Mormon Views of the Martyrdom: A Look at Some Early Published Accounts." *John Whitmer Historical Association Journal* 17 (1987): 12–20.

_____. "Remembering the Deaths of Joseph and Hyrum Smith." In *Joseph Smith: The Prophet, The Man* (Provo, UT: Religious Studies Center, Brigham Young University, 1993), 301–15.

_____. "The Road to Carthage Led West." *Brigham Young University Studies* 8 (Winter 1968): 204–5.

Goodyear, Imogene. "Joseph Smith and Polygamy: An Alternative View." *John Whitmer Historical Association Journal* 4 (1984): 16–21.

Green, Arnold H. "The Muhammed-Joseph Smith Comparison: Subjective Metaphor or a Sociology of Prophethood." In Spencer J. Palmer, ed., *Mormons and Muslims* (Provo, UT: Religious Studies Center, Brigham Young University, 1983).

Green, Arnold H. and Lawrence P. Goldrup. "Joseph Smith, an American Muhammed? An Essay on the Perils of Historical Analogy." *Dialogue: A Journal of Mormon Thought* 6, 1 (Spring 1971): 46–58.

Groesbeck, C. Jess. "The Smiths and Their Dreams and Visions," *Sunstone* 12, 2 (March 1988): 22–29.

Hale, Van. "The Doctrinal Impact of the King Follett Discourse." *Brigham Young University Studies* 18 (Winter 1978): 209–25.

_____. "The King Follett Discourse: Textual History and Criticism." *Sunstone* 8, 5 (September-October 1983): 5–12.

Hansen, Klaus. "Joseph Smith and the Political Kingdom of God." *The American West* 5 (1968): 20–24, 63.

Hartley, William G. "Close Friends as Witnesses: Joseph Smith and the Joseph Knight Families." In *Joseph Smith: The Prophet, The Man* (Provo, UT: Religious Studies Center, Brigham Young University, 1993), 271–83.

_____. "'Upon You My Fellow Servants': Restoration of the Priesthood." In *The Prophet Joseph: Essays on the Life and Mission of Joseph Smith* (Salt Lake City: Deseret Book, 1988), 49–72.

Hess, John W. "Recollections of the Prophet Joseph Smith." *Juvenile Instructor* 27 (15 May 1892): 302–4; 27 (1 August 1892): 470–72.

Hickman, Martin B. "The Political Legacy of Joseph Smith." *Dialogue: A Journal of Mormon Thought* 3 (Autumn 1968): 22–27.

Hicks, Michael. "Joseph Smith, W.W. Phelps, and the Poetic Paraphrase of 'The Vision'." *Journal of Mormon History* 20, 2 (Fall 1994): 63–84.

Hill, Marvin S. "Brodie Revisited: A Reappraisal." *Dialogue: A Journal of Mormon Thought* 7 (Winter 1972): 72–85.

_____. "The First Vision Controversy: A Critique and Reconciliation." *Dialogue: A Journal of Mormon Thought* 15, 2 (Summer 1982): 31–46.

_____. "Joseph Smith and the 1826 Trial: New Evidence and New Difficulties." *Brigham Young University Studies* 12 (Winter 1972): 223–33.

_____. "Joseph Smith the Man: Some Reflections on a Subject of Controversy." *Brigham Young University Studies* 21, 1 (1981): 175–86.

_____. "Money-Digging Folklore and the Beginnings of Mormonism: An Interpretive Suggestion." *Brigham Young University Studies* 24, 4 (1984): 473–88.

_____. "On the First Vision and Its Import in the Shaping of Early Mormonism." *Dialogue: A Journal of Mormon Thought* 12, 1 (Spring 1979): 90–99.

_____. "The 'Prophet Puzzle' Assembled; or, How to Treat Our Historical Diplopia Toward Joseph Smith." *Journal of Mormon History* 3 (1976): 101–5.

_____. "Secular or Sectarian History? A Critique of *No Man Knows My History*." *Church History* 43 (March 1974): 78–96.

Hogan, Mervin B. "Henry Clay, Joseph Smith, and the Presidency." *The Royal Arch Mason* (Winter 1986): 229–34.

_____. "Joseph Smith: A Modern Enigma." *The Royal Arch Mason* (Spring 1967): 3–11, 30.

Howard, Richard P. "An Analysis of Six Contemporary Accounts Touching Joseph Smith's First Vision." *Restoration Studies* 1 (1980): 95–117.

_____. "Joseph Smith's First Vision: The RLDS Tradition." *Journal of Mormon History* 7 (1980): 23–29.

Hullinger, Robert N. "Joseph Smith, Defender of Faith." *Concordia Theological Monthly* 42 (February 1971): 72–87.

Huntress, Keith. "Governor Thomas Ford and the Murderers of Joseph Smith." *Dialogue: A Journal of Mormon Thought* 4 (Summer 1969): 41–52.

Jessee, Dean C. "The Early Accounts of Joseph Smith's First Vision." *Brigham Young University Studies* 9, 3 (1969): 275–94.

_____. "Joseph Smith and the Beginnings of Mormon Record Keeping." In *The Prophet Joseph: Essays on the Life and Mission of Joseph Smith* (Salt Lake City: Deseret Book, 1988), 138–60.

_____. "Joseph Smith's 19 July 1840 Discourse." *Brigham Young University Studies* 19, 3 (1979): 390–94.

_____. "Lucy Mack Smith's 1829 Letter to Mary Smith Pierce." *Brigham Young University Studies* 11 (Fall 1982): 455–65.

_____. "Priceless Words and Fallible Memories: Joseph Smith as Seen in the Effort to Preserve His Discourses." *Brigham Young University Studies* 31 (Spring 1991): 19–40.

_____. "The Reliability of Joseph Smith's History." *Journal of Mormon History* 3 (1976): 23–46.

————. "Sources for the Study of Joseph Smith." In *Mormon Americana: A Guide to Sources and Collections in the United States*. Provo, UT: BYU Studies, 1995.

————. "Return to Carthage: Writing the History of Joseph Smith's Martyrdom." *Journal of Mormon History* 8 (1981): 3–19.

————. "The Writing of Joseph Smith's History." *Brigham Young University Studies* 11 (Summer 1971): 439–73.

————. "Writings of Joseph Smith." *Encyclopedia of Mormonism* (New York: Macmillan, 1992) 3: 1343–346.

Johnson Clark V. "Let Far West Be Holy and Consecrated." In *The Prophet Joseph: Essays on the Life and Mission of Joseph Smith* (Salt Lake City: Deseret Book, 1988), 226–45.

Jolley, Clifton Holt. "The Martyrdom of Joseph Smith: An Archetypal Study." *Utah Historical Quarterly* 44 (Fall 1976): 329–50.

King, Arthur Henry. "Joseph Smith As a Writer." In *The Abundance of the Heart* (1986), 197–205.

Lambert, Neal E. and Richard H. Cracroft. "Literary Form and Historical Understanding: Joseph Smith's First Vision." *Journal of Mormon History* 7 (1980): 33–42.

Larsen, David R. "The Case Against the Alleged Psychotic Joe Smith; or One Hallucinating José, Imaginary or Real?" *Journal of the Association of Mormon Counselors and Psychotherapists* 10 (January 1984): 10–11, 23.

Larson, Stan. "The King Follett Discourse: A Newly Amalgamated Text." *Brigham Young University Studies* 18 (Winter 1978): 193–208.

Launius, Roger D. "Joseph Smith's Encounter with Spiritualism." *Restoration Trails Forum* 9 (November 1983): 3, 8.

Ludlow, Daniel H. "A Tribute to Joseph Smith, Jr." In *The Prophet Joseph: Essays on the Life and Mission of Joseph Smith*. (Salt Lake City: Deseret Book, 1988), 333–48.

Lyon, T. Edgar. "Joseph Smith: The Wentworth Letter and Religious America of 1842." *Joseph Smith Memorial Sermons* (Logan, UT: LDS Institute of Religion) 2 (1966): 116–27.

McCollum, Adele Brannon. "The First Vision: Re-Visioning Historical Experience." In Neal A. Lambert, ed., *Literature of Belief*. (Provo, UT: Brigham Young University, Religious Studies Center, 1981), 177–96.

McConkie, Bruce R. "Joseph Smith: A Revealer of Christ." *Speeches of the Year*. Provo, UT: Brigham Young University, 1978.

————. "This Generation Shall Have My Word Through You." *Sperry Symposium*. Provo, UT: Brigham Young University, 1979. In *Hearken, O Ye People: Discourses on the Doctrine and Covenants* (Sandy, UT: Randall Book 1984), 79–92. Edited version in *Ensign* 10 (June 1980): 54–59.

Madsen, Ann N. and Susan Easton Black. "Joseph and Joseph: He Shall Be Like Unto Me (2 Nephi 3:15)." In *The Old Testament and the Latter-day Saints*. (Salt Lake City: Randall Books, 1986), 125–40.

Madsen, Gordon A. "Joseph Smith's 1826 Trial: The Legal Setting." *Brigham Young University Studies* 30, 2 (1990): 91–108.

Madsen, Truman G. "Joseph Smith and the Problem of Ethics." In *Perspectives in Mormon Ethics: Personal, Social, Legal, and Medical*, ed. Donna G.Hill (Salt Lake City: Publishers Press, 1983), 29–48. Reprinted from *Seminar on the Prophet Joseph Smith* (Provo, UT: Adult Education and Extension Services, 1962), 43–62.

_____. "Joseph Smith and the Sources of Love." *Dialogue: A Journal of Mormon Thought* 1, 1 (Spring 1966): 122–34.

_____. "Teachings of Joseph Smith." *Encyclopedia of Mormonism* 4 vols. (New York: Macmillan, 1992), 3:1339–343.

Matthews, Robert J. "Joseph Smith—Translator." In *Joseph Smith: The Prophet, The Man.* (Provo, UT: Religious Studies Center, Brigham Young University, 1993), 77–87.

_____. "The Prophet Translates the Bible by the Spirit of Revelation." In *The Prophet Joseph: Essays on the Life and Mission of Joseph Smith* (Salt Lake City: Deseret Book, 1988), 175–191.

Melville, J. Keith. "Joseph Smith, the Constitution, and Individual Liberties." *Brigham Young University Studies* 28, 2 (1988): 65–74.

Merrill, Byron R. "Joseph Smith and the Lamanites." In *Joseph Smith: The Prophet, The Man.* (Provo, UT: Religious Studies Center, Brigham Young University, 1993), 187–202.

Midgley, Louis. "The Brodie Connection: Thomas Jefferson and Joseph Smith." *Brigham Young University Studies* 20, 1 (Fall 1979): 59–67.

Millet, Robert L. "Joseph Smith and Modern Mormonism: Orthodoxy, Neoorthodoxy, Tension, and Tradition." *Brigham Young University Studies* 29, 3 (1989): 49–68.

_____. "Joseph Smith Among the Prophets." In *Joseph Smith: The Prophet, The Man.* (Provo, UT: Religious Studies Center, Brigham Young University, 1993), 15–31.

_____. "Joseph Smith, the Book of Mormon, and the Nature of God." In *"To Be Learned Is Good If . . .".* (Salt Lake City: Bookcraft, 1987).

_____. "Joseph Smith's Translation of the Bible: Impact on Mormon Theology." *Religious Studies and Theology* 7 (January 1987): 43–53.

_____. "Joseph Smith's Translation of the Bible and the Synoptic Problem." *John Whitmer Historical Association Journal* 5 (1985): 41–46.

Moench, Melodie. "Joseph Smith: Prophet, Priest, and King." *Task Papers in LDS History*, No. 25 (Salt Lake City: Historical Department of the Church, 1978).

Murdoch, Norman H. "Joseph Smith, the Book of Mormon, and Mormonism: A Review Essay." *New York History* 67 (1986): 224–30.

Nibley, Hugh. "Their Portrait of a Prophet." In *Nibley on the Timely and the Timeless*. Provo, Utah: Religious Studies Center, Brigham Young University, 1978.

Nibley, Preston. "Joseph Smith and the Three Witnesses." In *1961 Seminar on the Prophet Joseph Smith*, comp. Truman G. Madsen. (Provo, UT: Brigham Young University, 1961), 16–24.

Nolan, Max. "Joseph Smith and Mysticism." *Journal of Mormon History* 10 (1983): 105–116.

Oaks, Dallin H., et al. "Joseph Smith and Legal Process: In the Wake of the Steamboat *Nauvoo*." *Brigham Young University Studies* 19, 2 (1979): 167–98.

Olsen, Steven L. "Joseph Smith and the Structure of Mormon Identity." *Dialogue* 14 (Autumn 1981): 89–100.

_____. "Joseph Smith's Concept of the City of Zion." In *Joseph Smith: The Prophet, The Man*. (Provo, UT: Religious Studies Center, Brigham Young University, 1993), 203–11.

Owens, Lance S. "Joseph Smith and the Kabbalah: The Occult Connection." *Dialogue: A Journal of Mormon Thought* 27, 3 (Fall 1994): 117–94.

Parry, Keith. "Joseph Smith and the Clash of Sacred Cultures." *Dialogue: A Journal of Mormon Thought* 18 (Winter 1985): 65–80.

Partridge, Elinore H. "Characteristics of Joseph Smith's Style and Notes on the Authorship of the Lectures on Faith." *Task Papers in LDS History*, No. 14 (Salt Lake City: Historical Department of the Church, 1976).

Paul, Robert. "Joseph Smith and the Manchester (New York) Library." *Brigham Young University Studies* 22, 3 (1982): 333–56.

_____. "Joseph Smith and the Plurality of Worlds Idea." *Dialogue: A Journal of Mormon Thought* 19, 2 (Summer 1986): 12–36.

Perkins, Keith W. "The Prophet Joseph Smith in 'the Ohio': The Schoolmaster." In *The Prophet Joseph: Essays on the Life and Mission of Joseph Smith* (Salt Lake City: Deseret Book, 1988), 90–114.

Petersen, Roger K. "Joseph Smith: Prophet-Poet." In *Sidney B. Sperry Symposium*. (Provo, UT: BYU College of Religious Instruction, 1980), 265–79.

Peterson, Paul H. "Understanding Joseph: A Review of Published Documentary Sources." In *Joseph Smith: The Prophet, The Man* (Provo, UT: Religious Studies Center, Brigham Young University, 1993), 101–16.

Poll, Richard D. "Joseph Smith and the Presidency." *Dialogue: A Journal of Mormon Thought* 3, 3 (Autumn 1968): 17–21.

Porter, Larry C. "'The Field Is White Already to Harvest': Earliest Missionary Labors and the Book of Mormon." In *The Prophet Joseph: Essays on the Life and Mission of Joseph Smith*. (Salt Lake City: Deseret Book, 1988), 73–89.

Poulson, Richard C. "Fate and the Persecutors of Joseph Smith: Transmutations of an American Myth." *Dialogue: A Journal of Mormon Thought* 11, 4 (Winter 1978): 63–70.

Proper, David R. "Joseph Smith and Salem." *Essex Institute Historical Collections* 100 (April 1964): 88–97.

Quinn, D. Michael. "The Mormon Succession Crisis of 1844." *Brigham Young University Studies* 16 (Winter 1976): 187–233.

Raisanen, Heikki. "Joseph Smith und die Bibel: die Leistung des Mormonischen Propheten in neuer Beleuchtung." *Theologische Literaturzeitung* 109 (February 1984): 81–92.

Ricks, Stephen D. and Daniel C. Peterson. "Joseph Smith and 'Magic': Methodological Reflections on the Use of a Term." In *"To Be Learned Is Good If . . ."* (Salt Lake City: Bookcraft, 1987).

Riddle, Chauncey C. "As a Prophet Thinketh in His Heart, So Is He: The Mind of Joseph Smith." In *The Prophet Joseph: Essays on the Life and Mission of Joseph Smith* (Salt Lake City: Deseret Book, 1988), 262–79.

Romig, Ronald E. and Lachlan Mackay. "What Did Joseph [Smith] Look Like?" *Saints Herald* 141:12 (December 1994): 8–10, 12.

Searle, Howard C. "Authorship of the History of Joseph Smith: A Review Essay." *Brigham Young University Studies* 21 (Winter 1981): 101–22.

Shipps, Jan. "The Prophet Puzzle: Suggestions Leading Toward a More Comprehensive Interpretation of Joseph Smith." *Journal of Mormon History* 1 (1974): 3–20.

Smith, Brian L. "Joseph Smith: Gifted Learner, Master Teacher, Prophetic Seer." In *Joseph Smith: The Prophet, The Man.* (Provo, UT: Religious Studies Center, Brigham Young University, 1993), 169–86.

Snow, Edgar C., Jr. "One Face of the Hero: In Search of the Mythological Joseph Smith." *Dialogue: A Journal of Mormon Thought* 27,3 (Fall 1994): 233–47.

Sondrup, Steven P. "The Articles of Faith: Language of Confession in Mormon Belief." In Neal A. Lambert, ed., *Literature of Belief* (Provo, UT: Religious Studies Center, Brigham Young University, 1981), 197–215.

Stott, Graham St. John. "Just War, Holy War, and Joseph Smith, Jr." In *Restoration Studies* 4 (1988): 134–41.

Taylor, Alan. "Rediscovering the Context of Joseph Smith's Treasure Seeking." *Dialogue: A Journal of Mormon Thought* 19 (1986): 18–28.

Tickemyer, Garland E. "Joseph Smith and Process Theology." *Dialogue: A Journal of Mormon Thought* 17 (Autumn 1984): 75–85.

Turner, Rodney. "Joseph Smith and the Apocalypse of John." *The New Testament and the Latter-day Saints.* Orem, UT: Randall Book Co., 1987, 319–45.

Van Orden, Bruce A. "The Compassion of Joseph Smith." In *"To Be Learned Is Good If . . .".* Salt Lake City: Bookcraft, 1987.

_____. "Zion's Camp: A Refiner's Fire." In *The Prophet Joseph: Essays on the Life and Mission of Joseph Smith.* Salt Lake City: Deseret Book, 1988, 192–207.

Van Wagoner, Richard and Steven C. Walker. "Joseph Smith: The Gift of Seeing." *Dialogue: A Journal of Mormon Thought* 15,2 (Summer 1982): 48–68.

Vernon, Glenn N. "Joseph Smith and the Challenge of Change." *Seminar on the Prophet Joseph Smith.* Provo, UT: Adult Education and Extension Services, 1962.

Vlahos, Clare D. "Joseph Smith, Jr.'s Conception of Revelation." In *Restoration Studies* 2 (1983): 63–74.

Vogel, Dan and Brent Lee Metcalfe. "Joseph Smith's Scriptural Cosmology." In *The Word of God: Essays on Mormon Scripture,* ed. Dan Vogel. Salt Lake City: Signature Books, 1990, 187–219.

Vogel, Dan. "The Locations of Joseph Smith's Early Treasure Quests." *Dialogue: A Journal of Mormon Thought* 27,3 (Fall 1994): 197–231.

Voros, J. Frederic, Jr. "Was the Book of Mormon Buried with King Follett? The Essential Unity of Joseph's Message" *Sunstone* 11, 1 (March 1987): 15–18.

Walker, Ronald W. "Joseph Smith: The Palmyra Seer." *Brigham Young University Studies* 24, 4 (1984): 461–72.

_____. "The Persisting Idea of American Treasure Hunting." *Brigham Young University Studies* 24, 4 (1984): 429–59.

Walters, Wesley P. "From Occult to Cult with Joseph Smith." *Journal of Pastoral Theology* 1 (Summer 1977): 121–31.

_____. "Joseph Smith's Bainbridge, N.Y., Court Trials." *Westminster Theological Journal* 36 (Winter 1974): 123–44.

_____. "Joseph Smith's First Vision Story Revisited." *Journal of Pastoral Practice* 4 (1980): 92–109.

_____. "New Light on Mormon Origins From the Palmyra Revival." *Evangelical Theological Society Bulletin* 10 (1967): 227–41. Also published in *Dialogue: A Journal of Mormon Thought* 4 (Spring 1969): 60–81.

Williams, Peter W. "New World Revelation: Joseph Smith and the Rise of Mormonism." In *America's Religions: Traditions and Cultures* New York: Macmillan, 1990, 219–25.

Winder, Lorie. "In Search of the Real Joseph Smith." *Sunstone* 5 (Nov./Dec. 1980): 30–34.

Wirthlin, Leroy S. "Joseph Smith's Boyhood Operation: An 1813 Surgical Success." *Brigham Young University Studies* 21, 2 (1981): 131–54.

_____. "Nathan Smith (1762–1828), Surgical Consultant to Joseph Smith." *Brigham Young University Studies* 17, 3 (1977): 319–37.

Zucker, Louis C. "Joseph Smith as a Student of Hebrew." *Dialogue: A Journal of Mormon Thought* 3, 2 (Summer 1968): 41–55.

## Sermons and Church Magazines

Allen, James B. "Eight Contemporary Accounts of Joseph Smith's First Vision—What Do We Learn from Them?" *Improvement Era* 73 (April 1970): 4–13.

_____. "Was Joseph Smith a Serious Candidate for President of the United States?" *Ensign* 3 (September 1973): 21–22.

Anderson, Lavina Fielding. "139-Year-Old Portraits of Joseph and Emma Smith." *Ensign* 11 (March 1981): 62–64.

Anderson, Richard Lloyd. "The Alvin Smith Story: Fact and Fiction." *Ensign* 17 (August 1987): 58–72.

_____. "By the Gift and Power of God." *Ensign* 7 (September 1977): 79–85.

_____. "Confirming Records of Moroni's Coming." *Improvement Era* 73 (September 1970): 4–8.

_____. "Heritage of a Prophet." *Ensign* 1 (February 1971): 15–19.

_____. "Joseph Smith's Brothers: Nauvoo and After." *Ensign* 9 (September 1979): 30–33.

_____. "Joseph Smith's Home Environment." *Ensign* 1 (July 1971): 57–59.

_____. "Parallel Prophets: Paul and Joseph Smith." *Ensign* 15 (April 1985): 12–17.

_____. "The Personality of the Prophet." *New Era* 17 (December 1987): 14–19.

_____. "The Trustworthiness of Young Joseph Smith." *Improvement Era* 73 (October 1970): 82–89.

Arrington, Leonard J. "The Human Qualities of Joseph Smith, the Prophet." *Ensign* 1 (January 1971): 35–38.

_____. "Joseph Smith and the Lighter View." *New Era* 6 (August 1976): 8–13.

Backman, Milton V., Jr. "Confirming Witnesses of the First Vision." *Ensign* 16 (January 1986): 32–37.

_____. "Did Brigham Young Confirm or Expound on Joseph Smith's First Vision?" *Ensign* 22 (April 1992): 59–60.

_____. "Joseph Smith, Popularizer or Restorer?" *Improvement Era* 70 (March-April 1967): 58–61, 76–83.

_____. "Joseph Smith's Recitals of the First Vision." *Ensign* 15 (January 1985): 8–17.

Baker, LeGrand L. "On to Carthage to Die." *Improvement Era* 72 (June 1969): 10–15.

Ball, Isaac B. "The Poetic Qualities in the Writings of Joseph Smith." *Improvement Era* 38 (December 1935): 734–35.

Ballard, M. Russell. "The Family of Joseph Smith." *Ensign* 21 (November 1991): 5–7.

Berrett, William E. "Joseph Smith: Five Qualities of Leadership." *New Era* 7 (June 1977): 40–43.

Black, Susan Easton. "I Am Not Any Longer To Be Alone." *Ensign* 19 (January 1989): 50–56.

Bushman, Richard L. "The Character of Joseph Smith: Insights from His Holographs." *Ensign* 7 (April 1977): 11–13.

_____. "How Did the Prophet Joseph Smith Respond to Skepticism in His Time?" *Ensign* 20 (February 1990): 61–63.

Cannon, Donald Q., Larry E. Dahl and John W. Welch. "The Restoration of Major Doctrines Through Joseph Smith." *Ensign* 19 (January 1989): 26–33; 19 (February 1989): 6–13

Cummings, B.F. "The Prophet's Last Letters." *Improvement Era* 18 (March 1915): 388–93.

Done, Willard. "Joseph Smith as a Man." *Improvement Era* 9 (December 1905): 114–22.

Durham, G. Homer. "Joseph Smith and the Political World." *Improvement Era* 55 (October 1952): 712–13, 746–51.

_____. "Joseph Smith's Statecraft." *Improvement Era* 45 (December 1942): 782–83, 823–26.

Esplin, Ronald K. "God Will Protect Me Until My Work Is Done." *Ensign* 19 (August 1989): 16–21.

Evans, John Henry. "Genius or Seer?" *Improvement Era* 9 (December 1905): 170–78.

Gates, Susa Young. "What Joseph Smith Did for the Womanhood of the Church." *Improvement Era* 9 (December 1905): 179–83. Reprinted in *Improvement Era* 73 (November 1970): 43–46.

Gibbons, Francis M. "The Savior and Joseph Smith—Alike Yet Unlike." *Ensign* 21 (May 1991): 32–33.

Grant, Carter E. "The Joseph Smith Home." *Improvement Era* 62 (December 1959): 898–99, 976–80.

Green, Doyle L. "Are These Portraits of the Prophet Joseph Smith?" *Improvement Era* (December 1966).

Hart, Charles H. "Joseph the Prophet." *Improvement Era* 23 (April 1920): 491–95.

Hartley, William G. "Joseph Smith and Nauvoo's Youth." *Ensign* 9 (September 1979): 26–29.

Hatch, Ephraim. "What Did Joseph Smith Look Like?" *Ensign* 11 (March 1981): 65–73.

Hinckley, Gordon B. "Praise To The Man." *Ensign* 13 (August 1983): 2–6.

Horton, George A., Jr. "Ancient Gifts for a New Dispensation: The Prophet Joseph Smith Restored Major Documents Recorded by Earlier Prophets." *Ensign* 23 (January 1993): 11–13.

_____. "Prophecies in the Bible About Joseph Smith." *Ensign* 19 (January 1989): 20–25.

Howard, Richard P. "Christmas Day, 1832: Joseph Smith Responds to the Nullification Crisis." *Saints' Herald* 116 (May 1969): 54.

_____. "'Try the Spirits' Wrote Joseph, Jr., in 1842." *Saints' Herald* 131 (September 1984): 24.

Jackson, Kent P. "Moroni's Message to Joseph Smith." *Ensign* 20 (August 1990): 13–16.

Jessee, Dean C. "Joseph Smith, Jr.—In His Own Words." *Ensign* 14 (December 1984): 22–31; 15 (January 1985): 18–24.

_____. "Joseph Smith's Reputation Among Historians." *Ensign* 9 (September 1979): 56–61.

_____. "The Spirituality of Joseph Smith." *Ensign* 8 (September 1978): 14–20.

_____ and William G. Hartley. "Joseph Smith's Missionary Journal." *New Era* 4 (February 1974): 34–36.

"Joseph Smith, The Prophet." *Young Woman's Journal* 17 (December 1906): 537–48.

Josephson, Marba C. "What Did the Prophet Joseph Smith Look Like?" *Improvement Era* 56 (May 1953): 311–15, 371–75.

Kimball, Spencer W. "The Pattern of Martyrdom." *Improvement Era* (May 1946): 286, 316–18.

King, Arthur Henry. "A Man Who Speaks to Our Time from Eternity." *Ensign* 19 (March 1989): 12–16.

Knight, Hal. "Joseph Smith as a City Planner." *Improvement Era* 72 (December 1969): 11, 14.

Knowles, Duane C. "Foes Became His Friends." *Ensign* 23 (January 1993): 27–30.

McConkie, Bruce R. "This Generation Shall Have My Word Through You." *Ensign* 10 (June 1980): 54–59.

Madsen, Truman G. "Joseph Smith and the Depth of Discipleship." CES. Ninth Annual Religious Education Symposium. 43–47.

_____. "Joseph Smith's Reputation Among Theologians." *Ensign* 9 (September 1979): 61–63.

Matthews, Robert J. "Joseph Smith's Inspired Translation of the Bible." *Ensign* 2 (December 1972): 61–63.

_____. Joseph Smith's Efforts to Publish His Bible Translation." *Ensign* 13 (January 1983): 57–64.

_____. "Plain and Precious Things Restored." *Ensign* 12 (July 1982): 14–20.

Maxwell, Neal A. "A Choice Seer." *Ensign* 16 (August 1986): 6–15.

_____. "Joseph, the Seer." *Ensign* 13 (November 1983): 54–56.

_____. "My Servant Joseph." *Ensign* 22 (May 1992): 37–39.

Millet, Robert L. "Joseph Smith and the New Testament." *Ensign* 16 (December 1986): 28–34.

Osmond, Alfred. "Joseph Smith as Educator." *Improvement Era* 17 (January-February 1914): 259–62, 360–65.

Parry, Edwin F. "Joseph Smith's Last Prophecy." *Improvement Era* 24 (July 1921): 797–99.

Perkins, Keith. "Thou Art Still Chosen." *Ensign* 23 (January 1993): 14–19.

Porter, Larry C. "Christmas With the Prophet Joseph." *Ensign* 8 (December 1978): 9–11.

_____. "How Did the U.S. Press React When Joseph and Hyrum Were Murdered?" *Ensign* 14 (April 1984): 22–23.

Reeder, William H., Jr. "Proclamation of the Twelve Apostles on the Death of Joseph Smith." *Improvement Era* 52 (March 1949): 149, 176–77.

Roberts, B.H. "Joseph Smith the Modern American Prophet." *Improvement Era* 23 (April 1920): 526–32.

_____. "The Probability of Joseph Smith's Story." *Improvement Era* 7 (March-April 1904): 321–31, 417–32.

Skidmore, Rex A. "Joseph Smith: A Leader and Lover of Recreation." *Improvement Era* 43 (December 1940): 716–17, 762–63.

Smith, Calvin N. "Joseph Smith as a Public Speaker." *Improvement Era* 69 (April 1966): 277–79, 308–12.

Stewart, D. Michael. "What Do We Know About the Purported Statement of Joseph Smith that the Constitution Would Hang by a Thread and that the Elders Would Save It?" *Ensign* 6 (June 1976): 64–65.

Taylor, J. Lewis. "Joseph Smith the Prophet: A Self-Portrait." *Ensign* 3 (June 1973): 40–44.

Top, Brent L. "'I Was With My Family': Joseph Smith—Devoted Husband, Father, Son, and Brother." *Ensign* 21 (August 1991): 22–27.

Wadsworth, Richard. "Does the Book of Mormon Prophesy of Joseph Smith?" *Ensign* 19 (April 1989): 52–53.

Widtsoe, John A. "Did Joseph Smith Introduce Plural Marriage?" *Improvement Era* 49 (November 1946): 721, 766–77.

_____. "How Can Joseph Smith Be Explained?" *Improvement Era* 49 (October 1946): 641, 670–71.

_____. "Was Joseph Smith Honest in Business?" *Improvement Era* 49 (September 1946): 577, 604–07.

_____. "What Manner of Boy and Youth Was Joseph Smith?" *Improvement Era* 49 (August 1946): 513, 542–43.

_____. "What Was the Vocabulary of Joseph Smith?" *Improvement Era* 54 (June 1951): 399, 476–77.

_____. "What Were the Sources of Joseph Smith's Greatness?" *Ensign* 17 (December 1987): 26–27.

_____. "Why Did Joseph Smith Become a Mason?" *Improvement Era* 53 (September 1950): 694–95.

Wirthlin, LeRoy S. "Joseph Smith's Surgeon." *Ensign* 8 (March 1978): 58–60.

Woodford, Robert J. "How the Revelations in the Doctrine and Covenants Were Received and Compiled." *Ensign* 15 (January 1985): 26–33.

Young, S. Dilworth. "What Joseph Smith Teaches Us of Jesus Christ." *Ensign* 3 (December 1973): 41–44.

## Unpublished Theses and Dissertations

Andrus, Helen Mae H. "A Study of Joseph Smith's Teachings and Practices as They Influence Welfare in the LDS Church." Master's thesis, Brigham Young University, 1952.

Andrus, Hyrum L. "Joseph Smith: Social Philosopher, Theorist, Prophet." DSS (Doctor of Social Science) dissertation, Syracuse University, 1955.

Brink, T.L. "Joseph Smith: A Study in Analytical Psychology." Ph.D. dissertation, University of Chicago, 1978.

Cheesman, Paul R. "An Analysis of the Accounts Relating to Joseph Smith's Early Visions." M.A. thesis, Brigham Young University, 1965.

Ehat, Andrew F. "Joseph Smith's Introduction of Temple Ordinances and the 1844 Mormon Succession Question." M.A. thesis, Brigham Young University, 1983.

Goshay, Thomas Gerard. "An Examination of the Biblical Scholarship of Joseph Smith, the Mormon Prophet." B.D. thesis, Talbot Theological Seminary, 1962.

Gottfredson, Montchesney Riddle. "The Relationship of the Extant Eschatalogically-Oriented Work of Joseph Smith to That of Selected Twentieth-Century New Testament Scholars." Ph.D. dissertation, Brigham Young University, 1967.

Graham, Bruce L. "The Presidential Campaign of Joseph Smith, Jr., 1844." Master's thesis, Lamar University, 1976.

Guthrie, Gary Dean. "Joseph Smith as an Administrator." Master's thesis, Brigham Young University, 1969.

Hansen, Warren David. "Re-Establishing Community: An Analysis of Joseph Smith's Social Thought in the Context of Philosophical Tradition." Ph.D. dissertation, Rutgers University, 1980.

Harris, James Roy. "A Comparison of the Educational Thought of Joseph Smith with That of Certain Contemporary Educators." Ed.D. dissertation, Brigham Young University, 1965.

Jones, Edward T. "The Theology of Thomas Dick and Its Possible Relationship to That of Joseph Smith." Master's thesis, Brigham Young University, 1969.

Launius, Roger D. "Zion's Camp and the Redemption of Jackson County, Missouri." Master's thesis, Louisiana State University, 1978.

McBrien, Dean D. "The Influence of the Frontier on Joseph Smith." Ph.D. dissertation, George Washington University, 1929.

McCarl, William B. "The Visual Image of Joseph Smith." Master's thesis, Brigham Young University, 1962.

McConkie, Joseph Fielding. "A Historical Explanation of the Views of The Church of Jesus Christ of Latter-day Saints and the Reorganized Church of Jesus Christ of Latter Day Saints on Four Distinctive Aspects of the Doctrine of Deity Taught by the Prophet Joseph Smith." Master's thesis, Brigham Young University, 1968.

McLaws, Monte B. "Joseph Smith, 1838–1839." Master's thesis, Arizona State University, 1963.

Norton, Walter A. "Joseph Smith as a Jacksonian Man of Letters: His Literary Development As Evidenced in His Newspaper Writings." Master's thesis, Brigham Young University, 1976.

Olive, Cherel Jane Ellsworth. "Mazeway Reformation and Revitalization Movements: The Wallace Model as Applied to the Development of Mormonism." Master's thesis, University of Nevada, Las Vegas, 1977.

Petersen, Roger Kent. "Joseph Smith, Prophet-Poet: A Literary Analysis of Writings Commonly Associated with His Name." Ph.D. dissertation, Brigham Young University, 1981.

Peterson, Elmer. "The Character of Joseph Smith: A Study Based on His Own Literary Production." Master's thesis, Brigham Young University, 1938.

Porter, Larry C. "A Study of the Origins of The Church of Jesus Christ of Latter-day Saints in the States of New York and Pennsylvania." Ph.D. dissertation, Brigham Young University, 1971.

Robertson, Raymond Dale. "Joseph Smith in Historical Perspective." Master's thesis, Ball State University, 1972.

Searle, Howard C. "Early Mormon Historiography: Writing the History of the Mormons, 1830–1858." Ph.D. dissertation, University of California, Los Angeles, 1979.

Smith, Calvin N. "A Critical Analysis of the Public Speaking of Joseph Smith." Ph.D. dissertation, Purdue University, 1965.

Takayama, Machiko. "Poetic Language in Nineteenth Century Mormonism: A Study of Semiotic Phenomenology in Communication and Culture." Ph.D. dissertation, Southern Illinois University, 1990.

Thompson, Edward George. "A Study of the Political Involvements in the Career of Joseph Smith." Master's thesis, Brigham Young University, 1966.

Tickemyer, Garland E. "The Philosophy of Joseph Smith and Its Educational Implications." Ph.D. dissertation, University of Texas, 1963.

Ward, Lane Dennis. "The Teaching Methods of Joseph Smith." Ed.D. dissertation, Brigham Young University, 1979.

_____. "The World and Joseph Smith." Master's thesis, Brigham Young University, 1980.

Whipple, Walter L. "An Analysis of Textual Changes in `The Book of Abraham' and in the `Writings of Joseph Smith, the Prophet,' in the Pearl of Great Price." Master's thesis, Brigham Young University, 1959.

Whitney, Clarissa I. "A Critical Analysis of the Forensic and Religious Speaking of Joseph Smith." Master's thesis, California State College, Fullerton, 1967.


## Unpublished Papers

Anderson, Robert D. "The Autobiography of Joseph Smith in Third Nephi." Sunstone Symposium, 1994.

_____. "The Sword of Laban: The Book of Mormon as Autobiography." Sunstone Symposium, August 1993. Tape in possession of author, including comment by C. Jess Groesbeck.

Bushman, Richard L. "The Visionary World of Joseph Smith." Mormon History Association, June 1995.

Compton, Todd. "Polygamy, Polygyny, Polyandry: An Overview of Joseph Smith's Plural Wives." Sunstone Symposium, August 1995.

Crabb, A. Richard. "Why Did Joseph Smith Let Nauvoo Die?" Mormon History Association, May 1989.

England, Eugene. "Joseph Smith and the Dilemmas of American Romanticism." Mormon History Association, May 1980.

Foster, Lawrence. "The Psychology of Religious Genius: Joseph Smith and the Origins of New Religious Movements." Mormon History Association, St. George, Utah, May 16, 1992.

Geary, Edward A. "Joseph Smith, Jr., Henry James, Sr., and the Emerson Generation." Mormon History Association, May 1980.

Godfrey, Kenneth. "Joseph Smith, Son, Husband, Father: The Roots for a Family-Centered Society." Mormon History Association, May 1980.

_____. "Joseph Smith, The Hill Cumorah, and Book of Mormon Geography: A Historical Study, 1823–1844." Mormon History Association, May 1989.

_____. "Return to Carthage: The Martyrdom of Joseph and Hyrum Smith Revisited." Mormon History Association, May 1989.

Griggs, C. Wilfred. "Joseph Smith and Apocalypticism in history." Mormon History Association, May 1980.

Groesbeck, C. Jess. "Joseph Smith and his Nauvoo Dreams: A Step in His Individuation." Mormon History Association, June 1990.

_____. "Joseph Smith and His Path of Individuation." Sunstone Symposium, 1991.

_____. "Joseph Smith and the Archetype of Eternal Marriage." Sunstone Symposium, August 1995.

_____. "Joseph Smith and the Book of Mormon—The Archetypal Connection (A Basis for Faith in a New World)." Sunstone Symposium, 1994.

Groesbeck, C. Jess, M.D., Sharon Groesbeck and David Groesbeck. "Joseph Smith and the Shaman's Vision: A Psychoanalytic Exploration in Mormonism." Copy in possession of author.

Hamilton, Marshall. "People vs. the Prophet: Joseph Smith and the Criminal Process in Nauvoo." Mormon History Association, June 1990.

Jessee, Dean C. "The Writings of Joseph Smith." Mormon History Association, June 1995.

Jorgensen, Lynne Watkins. "The 'Mantle of the Prophet': A Collective Spiritual Experience." Mormon History Association, June 1995.

_____. "The Mantle of the Prophet Joseph Passes to Brother Brigham and the Twelve Apostles: A Collective Spiritual Witness." Sunstone Symposium, August 1995.

Madsen, Gordon A. "The Lawrence Estate Revisited: Joseph Smith and Illinois Law Regarding Guardianships." Nauvoo Symposium, 1989.

Marsh, W. Jeffrey. "Chosen Vessels Unto Me: The Apostle Paul and the Prophet Joseph Smith." Sidney B. Sperry Symposium, October 1994.

Morain, William D. "The Sword of Laban: Joseph Smith, Jr. and the Unconscious." Mormon History Association, May 1993.

Olsen, Steven L. "The Joseph Smith Story: Structure and Ideology." Mormon History Association, May 1980.

Owens, Lance. "The Gnostic Joseph: Early Mormonism as a Classical Heresy." Sunstone Symposium, August 1992.

_____. "The Prophet's Bride: Joseph Smith, Sacred Sexuality, and the Occult Tradition." Mormon History Association, May 1994.

_____. "A Similarity of Priesthood: Joseph Smith and the Hermetic Tradition." Sunstone Symposium, 1994.

Parkin, Warren S. "Redefining Martyrdom: The One Hundred-Fiftieth Anniversary of the Murder of Joseph Smith." Sunstone Symposium, 1994.

Pollock, Gordon D. "The Prophet before the Bar: The Richmond Court Transcript." Mormon History Association, May 1988.

Porter, Larry C. "Joseph Smith: Prophet, Teacher, Theologian." Nauvoo Symposium, 1989.

Shipps, Jan. "The Prophet, His Mother, and Early Mormonism: Mother Smith's History as a Passageway to Understanding." Mormon History Association, May 1978.

Simmons, Larry. "Tibet's Diamond Vehicle, John the Revelator's Clear Precious Stone, and Joseph Smith's Secret Treasure." Sunstone Symposium, August 1984.

Vogel, Dan. "Joseph Smith's Treasure Seeking Revisited: An Appraisal of Some Recent Interpretations." Mormon History Association, May 1993.

Walker, Ronald W. "Beyond Magic: Telling the Unknown Story of Joseph Smith." Mormon History Association, May 1986.

Walton, Michael. "Joseph Smith and Science: The Methodist Connection." Sunstone Symposium, Friday, August 1984.

# Index

# About the Author

Davis Bitton holds a B.A. from Brigham Young University and an M.A. and Ph.D. from Princeton. He is a professor emeritus of history at the University of Utah and has published numerous articles and ten books, including *The Mormon Experience: A History of the Latter-day Saints* with Leonard J. Arrington and, in 1994, *The Ritualization of Mormon History* and *The Historical Dictionary of Mormonism*. He is a charter member and past president of the Mormon History Association. He and his wife, JoAn, currently live in Salt Lake City.

*The Martyrdom Remembered,* another unique work on the Prophet Joseph Smith by Davis Bitton.

In *The Martyrdom Remembered* LDS historian Davis Bitton brings together one hundred and fifty years of personal and public reactions to and recollections of the death of the Prophet Joseph Smith. Beginning with the diaries and letters of the Saints at Nauvoo and abroad, we hear a story of a people stunned with astonishment and grief at the news from Carthage. Bitton chronicles the works of early Mormon poets, who began publishing their laments four days after the event, as well as reactions of the press across the nation, which ranged from outrage against the murders to presumptious headlines proclaiming "Thus Ends Mormonism." Bitton closes with a look at how the martyrdom continues to be portrayed in our own century in histories, novels, poetry, and art.

This insightful, limited edition work is a must for anyone interested in the life and death of the Prophet Joseph Smith. In it we find that what most believers remember was "a man who lived great and died great in they eyes of God and his people." Their recollections of Joseph's death combine to become a stirring testimony to the work of a prophet of God.